Take and Read

TAKE and READ

Reflecting Theologically on Books

PAUL G. DOERKSEN

Foreword by Denny Smith

WIPF & STOCK · Eugene, Oregon

TAKE AND READ
Reflecting Theologically on Books

Copyright © 2016 Paul G. Doerksen. All rights reserved. Except for brief quotations in critical publications or reviews, no part of this book may be reproduced in any manner without prior written permission from the publisher. Write: Permissions, Wipf and Stock Publishers, 199 W. 8th Ave., Suite 3, Eugene, OR 97401.

Wipf & Stock
An Imprint of Wipf and Stock Publishers
199 W. 8th Ave., Suite 3
Eugene, OR 97401

www.wipfandstock.com

PAPERBACK ISBN: 978-1-4982-0150-6
HARDCOVER ISBN: 978-1-4982-8570-4
EBOOK ISBN: 978-1-4982-0151-3

Manufactured in the U.S.A.   09/22/16

To Cecely, Hannah, and Greta

Contents

Foreword by Denny Smith | ix
Introduction | xi

1. In the Ruins of the Church | 1
2. What about Hitler? | 7
3. The Mystery of the Child | 12
4. God Laughs and Plays | 17
5. Living the Sabbath | 25
6. The Omnivore's Dilemma | 30
7. Jayber Crow | 38
8. The Year of Living Biblically | 45
9. Atheist Delusions | 52
10. Original Sin | 61
11. Acedia and Me | 69
12. Shop Class as Soulcraft | 77
13. Following Jesus in a Culture of Fear | 86
14. Confessions | 94
15. Just War as Christian Discipleship | 103
16. Love Wins | 109
17. Working with Words | 117
18. The Undoing of Death | 125
19. Migrations of the Holy | 134
20. The Cross and the Lynching Tree | 140
21. Spirit and Trauma | 146
22. Ravished by Beauty | 152
23. Scripture, Culture, and Agriculture | 158

24 *Christianity after Religion* | 165
25 *Dementia* | 174
26 *When I Was a Child I Read Books* | 180
27 *David and Goliath* | 187
28 *My Bright Abyss* | 195
29 *The Good Funeral* | 201

Sermons
30 And Grace, Too . . . | 211
31 Called to Working with (the) Word(s) in the Light of Faith | 219
32 Simultaneously Satisfying and Insatiable: The Desire for God | 225
33 The Gospel as Prisoner *and* Liberator of Culture | 234
34 Why I Am (Still) a Christian | 240

Bibliography | 249

Foreword

This collection of essays, to which a couple of sermons have been added, originated within a literature program that was begun in 1993 by Dr. Gordon Matties of Canadian Mennonite University. Over the years, two or three dozen participants have met four times per year, each time having read an assigned book of significant moral value. The program had some features of a typical reading group, including informal conversation, coffee, and dessert, but the group meetings exhibited the distinct characteristic of being centered about an exceedingly thoughtful essay delivered in response to each book. During the last eleven years these essays have been the works of Dr. Paul Doerksen, convenor of the group, and it is from this body of essays that the contents of this book are drawn.

Not long after Paul began to lead the reading program, he named the group "Take and Read" in response to St. Augustine's famous conversion experience. Many will recall the story of Augustine, who, while crying in self-examination, heard a child singing the Latin words *tolle lege*, "take up and read." Augustine, believing the song to be a message from God, located a Bible and opened it to Romans 13:13–14:

> Not in riots and drunken parties, not in eroticism and indecencies, not in strife and rivalry, but put on the Lord Jesus Christ and make not provision for the flesh in its lusts.[1]

This was the point of Augustine's conversion to Christianity. He experienced a fundamental change in his life—from a life of uncontrolled passions to Christian sainthood—by way of taking up a book and reading. So, considering that this collection of essays arises from a group of people taking and reading substantial literature, it is fitting that the essays might be termed *tolle lege* essays.

---

1. Augustine, *Confessions*, 153.

The essays have served as the primary stimulus for most attendees to participate in the Take and Read program. They have provided the main insights into each book, and they have inspired deep moral reflection within, and among, participants. It is not abusing the St. Augustine metaphor to suggest that the *tolle lege* essays have been richly enlightening to participants and that they have stimulated reflection that has led to meaningful conversions in participants' moral perspectives.

The *tolle lege* essays arise from a mind with great intellectual reach. That is to say: the rich concepts forming the essays—whether aligned with the ideas of the book being studied or, on occasion, running opposite to the theme of the book—reach deeply into the topic being addressed. Importantly, these essays also reach widely across scholarly disciplines, bringing to bear ideas that greatly expand upon the main topics of the books being studied. Conversations among participants have frequently included references to the privilege of being directed deeply into a subject and being transported widely across related ideas as they hear the essays. Take and Read participants have been granted intellectual access beyond their reach.

The request, from within the group, for publication of *tolle lege* essays was bipartite: first, the request was inspired by the intellectual reach of the essays; and second, it arose from a realization that the richness of these essays cannot be unpacked within a single exposure to an orally delivered essay. These essays are to be read and reread.

This volume of essays, itself a petition for further volumes, engages a wide range of topics and a wide range of literary styles, along with personal moral and intellectual struggles. Each subject in these essays is addressed from a Christian perspective that directly informs a Christian audience and, indirectly, serves to stimulate and to inspire conscientious moral reflection by people of all beliefs.

I commend these *tolle lege* essays to those who seek a rich understanding of a particular book that is the subject of one of these essays. More significantly, I commend this collection of essays to anyone—Christian or other—seeking intellectual stimulation and seeking to gain understanding in regard to moral life.

Tolle lege; take and read.

Denny Smith

Introduction

Since 2004, I have led a theological book discussion group, now titled Take and Read, in Winnipeg, Manitoba. Over the years that the group has met, I have always been interested in who has been interested in reading these books. The group has included farmers and physicians, teachers, poets, novelists, scientists, people involved in business, finance, relief work, and many other walks of life, ranging in age from twenty-something to eighty. Some have participated for one year, others sign up every year, still others come and go. However, the old adage that no one learns more than the teacher holds especially true for me in my experience of Take and Read. My reading of certain books has been challenged in some cases, supported in others, and sometimes ignored. I have received suggestions for what other books might be considered for the group, and what other sources I should consult to enhance my understanding of issues raised by the books under discussion. In sum, I have learned an enormous amount from participating in this group and want to express gratitude to each person who has participated over the years.

Leading this discussion group has been and continues to be exhilarating and intimidating. I confess I viscerally feel the weight of choosing good books in this setting, given that a couple dozen people will buy and read these books. I don't really have a system for choosing them; rather, I'm always looking for books that will provide the impetus for upbuilding discourse, constructive conversation, edifying interaction. My intent in preparing reflections on each book is to read them theologically. To take this approach does not mean that I am limited to choosing only "Christian" books (whatever that might mean), but it does mean that I reflect on them as a Christian.

My prepared reflections for our Take and Read gatherings are never meant to draw conclusions about the books themselves, or about the topics addressed by the authors. This of course does not preclude comparisons to other related thought, presenting my opinions or even strong judgments, but I am keenly aware that in this context I am not writing reviews for an academic journal—in fact, these reflections were not originally written with a view to publication. Therefore, many of these essays have what may feel like a decidedly inconclusive or even unfinished quality to them (or so it seems to me). Insofar as that is the case, they have that quality precisely because they were intended to open discussion with and among the participants who had also read the book at hand and had important things to say about the issues it raised. It is not an overstatement to say that these essays formed the preliminaries of each of our evenings together, while much or most of the constructive learning and discussion took place in the process of reading and then in the discussions of group members with each other, which of course cannot be captured on the page. Put another way, these essays represent only a very partial snapshot of what actually happens ahead of and during Take and Read gatherings.

I have not included all of the reflections I've written for Take and Read meetings. Each essay simply bears the title of the book being discussed. The brief italicized paragraph at the beginning of each essay is material I used to describe and promote the book to potential group participants. I have also included a handful of sermons at the end of the book, a kind of writing that is closely related to the other essays included here, in that sermons are written to be presented orally, often include reflections on books of various kinds, and are offered in the hope that people who hear and/or read them might be edified in some way.

I wish to acknowledge Professor Gordon Matties, now my colleague at Canadian Mennonite University (CMU), who began a theological book discussion group entitled Interchange in 1993. I participated for a number of years in this activity, reading books chosen for a group of interested people, joining them four times during the academic year to hear Gordon talk about each book in turn, and also to eat desserts and discuss these books with fellow participants. Interchange attracted a fairly disparate group of people who nonetheless had in common an abiding interest in reading, thinking, and working at theological material with a view to shaping our lives in increasingly faithful ways. I was not able to join the group every year and missed a number of consecutive years when our family moved to another province for my graduate studies. In 2004, I was asked to lead Interchange as Gordon pursued his continuing interest in film and faith. Things began rather modestly, but after several years the renamed group (I changed the name to Take and Read) seemed to find its feet. The group continues to meet, retaining the basic practices that have marked it since its inception. I also want to acknowledge the support of Canadian Mennonite University, where the group now meets (and where I teach), and Mennonite Brethren Collegiate Institute, which provided meeting space and administrative support for a number of years. I'm also grateful to the people who have been responsible for the provision of the desserts over these years.

As always, I'm grateful to my wife, Julie, for her interest and enthusiasm. And it is with great love and affection, however incompletely expressed (by me) in our lives together, that I dedicate this book to our three daughters, Cecely, Hannah, and Greta—I love you, sweet girls.

1

In the Ruins of the Church

Russell R. Reno. *In the Ruins of the Church: Sustaining Faith in an Age of Diminished Christianity*. Grand Rapids: Brazos Press, 2002.

If you find the church frustrating, then Reno's book will (at first glance) confirm that frustration, since he agrees that the church can be seen as a failure, as hypocritical and faithless, and something from which we may want to distance ourselves. In fact, this "aloof ecclesiology" is something we come by honestly in our current situation, where ironic distance is often celebrated. The church is in ruins, no doubt of that, says Reno, but his counsel is that to be in the church in these days is precisely to embrace that broken way of life, and "to dwell within the ruins of the church." Reno is specific about the failures of his particular church (Episcopalian), but his message is worth considering by each of us within our particular church tradition.

Reno's vision is worth considering, as the paragraph above notes, not least because of a powerful cruciform theological vision: "We should not seek any other city, however redolent with spiritual power and life it might seem. For in the ruins of Jerusalem, in the pierced, dead, and ruined body of our Lord Jesus Christ, in which we now dwell far more literally than any of us might have imagined, the Lord brings us to see, as only eyes cleansed by tears of repentance can, the omnipotence of his cruciform love."[1]

---

1. Reno, *In the Ruins of the Church*, 147. Subsequent references to the text will be included in the body of the essay.

It was impossible for me to read this book with scholarly detachment or ironic distance. I've been influenced enough by Stanley Hauerwas and by my Anabaptist forebears that a defense of staying *with* the church ("dancing with the one that brung ya") is a welcome resource. I have spent a lot of time thinking about what might constitute a theological warrant for leaving the church or for moving from one to another, but Reno's book puts the lie to many of the lines of thinking I have entertained from time to time. Without glossing over the problems of the church, Reno argues for a concrete Christianity that entails going to a real church that actually exists, and practicing authentic spiritual disciplines such as prayer and reading the Bible. His thesis is basic but challenging: loyalty to Christ requires us to dwell within the ruins of the church, to draw near to Christ in his body, the church.

In his introduction, Reno rejects the desire he sees all around for "'liberating distance,'" something he sees especially evident in the work of J.N. Darby, whom we have to thank for dispensationalism. Darby typifies the modern ecclesial project of recognizing a problem and arguing for separation as a way to holiness, a move that can be seen in both liberal and conservative thought. We all indulge in a "distancing habit that keeps at bay the demands of suffering intimacy with the concrete and particular forms of the apostolic witness" (26). By way of challenging such habits, Reno introduces us to the work of Nehemiah as the way to redoubled intimacy, a way wherein "we must dwell as closely as possible to the ruined forms of modern Christianity" (27). The three parts of Reno's book then articulate his vision, which is generated by his reading of Nehemiah.

First, Reno addresses the question of why distance and separation have become the watchwords of our postmodern age. He identifies a move from Promethean (focus on pride—technology, fire) to Petronian (focus on sloth and cowardice) humanism. This latter form embraces satire, cynicism, and irony. Nothing is really destroyed, but neither is it resolved. Instead, we get to an ironic detachment from all of it, a postmodern horror of obedience to anything. What we need, says Reno, is to nurture an ambition that has the courage of obedience, which is necessary to reshape our identity, but people resist the inner spiritual demand that would involve personal change (44–46).

Further, Reno suggests that we do not want what Christianity teaches; the problem really isn't scientific method, historical consciousness, and the like, it's a matter of moral rebellion, as seen so clearly in the way Augustine delivers his account in the *Confessions*, where he describes so eloquently his own prideful self-sufficiency, horror of dependence and fear of difference. The Gospel is relevant, all right, but we just don't like what it has to say.

One of the current attempts to address the problem of this ironic distance is the Radical Orthodoxy movement, led by John Milbank, Graham Ward, and Catherine Pickstock. Reno describes this work as a postmodern movement that rejects distance in favor of a recovered classical vision, while using all the jargon and tools of postmodern thought. Radical Orthodoxy puts forward an Augustinian vision, as opposed to a Nietzschean vision of original violence—this is a participatory framework, a comprehensive framework in which the whole world is fit for absorption into a theological framework. It's very exciting, but in the end, Reno judges the movement to be too modern, because it uses what he calls a "'speculative grasp,'" which is a general tendency to substitute the creative production of theological theory for the redemptive power of Christ. That is, the Radical Orthodoxy movement transfers loyalty from a concrete Christianity to an ideal, which while it may be Christ-formed is not incarnate.

Reno's work in the second section of the book focuses more tightly on the ruinous situation of the Episcopalian church, of which he is a part. He identifies considerable dysfunction in the living out of the theological vocation of the church, particularly in the posture wherein the visible life of the church is detached from scripture, in the handling of the Creed, which is no longer seen as ruling out any belief or liturgical practice, in the work of the episcopate, as bishops have become personal prophets and leaders of warring theological factions, in the practice of baptism and the Eucharist, which status has become ambiguous. Because of all this, the vision of the Episcopalians has become obscured, where what is needed is to submit to these sources in their premodern forms. Therefore, Reno calls for a retrospective, receptive, and reiterative disposition instead of a drive for liturgical change that he considers to be misguided. He suspects that people believe that the more thoroughly the liturgy can be revised, the more can the images of God and teachings on morality be changed. In the present climate of opinion, he finds three disturbing trends: a) an intense desire to strike an affirmative pose, i.e. therapeutic tolerance; b) a distrust of the particular, because supposedly that puts God in a box; and c) the widespread notion that change is inevitable. These attitudes are debilitating for the common life of the church.

Reno marshals further evidence for his assertion that the Episcopal Church is in ruins from the debate concerning sexuality, and especially homosexuality. The issues around homosexuality are decidedly *not* theological, he argues, but primarily based on class loyalties combined with an interest in freedom in general, resulting in constant revisionary pressure, especially on traditional teachings about sexuality. What we want is to secure recognition and affirmation of our practices chosen on grounds other than theological understanding.

The third section of Reno's book evokes what a Nehemian dwelling in the ruins of Jerusalem means for church life.[2] Reno begins this exhortative section with discussion of postliberal ecclesial spirituality, used here to refer to the many efforts to find life in *concreta Christiana*. Spirituality can be defined as the x that closes the gap between first-order language and the practices that constitute the visible forms of the Christian life. Modern spirituality embraces some x that levers us into first-order language and practice, carrying in its wake the danger that we will move to a religion of that x itself.

Currently, at least in the Episcopalian church, the plausibility of apostolic Christianity has collapsed. Those very things that are first-order language and practice—reading the Bible, baptism, and so on—have become the barriers to Christianity. Evangelicals turn to the Bible, but cannot sustain community; Anglo-Catholics turn to the sacraments, which endorse loyalty to a church that does not exist.

At this juncture of the book, Reno turns to his constructive task, beginning with the reading of scripture. Reno finds the way Origen read scripture to be instructive, especially the fact that Origen found barriers to understanding within the scriptures themselves. Instead of ignoring these barriers, we must submit to them and allow them to teach us. Reno suggests that we must follow that same lead in reading his book, submitting to stumbling blocks such as the ones he has uncovered, striving to see the church in ruins but refusing to look away, because the scattered stones we see constitute the very material of rebuilding, as was the case for Nehemiah. Reno also highlights the importance of the Daily Office, which he describes as an engine of intimacy that shapes us in the way of discipleship, in the narrow way of the cross. We are to pray as those who came before us. Just as the Daily Office is an engine of intimacy, so too is the task of interpreting scripture not primarily technical but spiritual. History does not necessarily distance us from the word of God but provides opportunity to intensify our reading and draw near to God,[3] a dimension of reading that Reno displays in his treatment of John's first epistle, in which we draw near to the cruciform ruins of the church.

---

2. Bergen, Review of *In the Ruins of the Church*, 270–71.

3. Reno suggests two exegetical techniques—figural reading and intensive reading. In figural reading, an event or a person has a recognizable shape that he calls a "figure" and gives the example of the deliverance of Israel from the Egyptians. The association of this event allows the reader to bridge historical distance (174–76). Intensive reading focuses on the surplus of meaning that is available in signs or episodes of scripture.

In reflecting on Reno's book, I find several theological points especially rich. First, his emphasis on the cruciform love of Jesus, which here is no soft liberal notion of 'why can't we all just get along,' or a pale promotion of 'tolerance,' but rather a rich suggestion that the love of Jesus, which sustains us and shapes our lives, and which calls us to suffer divine things, is itself in the shape of the cross. I believe this emphasis to be timely, and basically correct in its orientation. Further, Reno's sustained critical analysis of the liberal side of church life as opposed to a trashing of fundamentalism is also welcome.[4]

I'm not quite sure what to make of Reno's suggestions that we need to be premodern or primitive in our approach to scripture. The concern he raises addressing the church's pursuit of putative relevance as we often understand that term (i.e., as something that necessarily involves PowerPoint and a worship team, and discusses the 'other') is convincing. The crux of the problem is decidedly not irrelevance; rather, it's that we don't like what Christianity has to say. This seems exactly right, but it remains unclear to me how or if a premodern approach to scripture can be achieved. Reno's own readings of scripture resist classification as primitive or premodern as well. Perhaps he means that we need to take a certain kind of stance toward scripture that evokes a premodern attitude, a propensity toward obedience rather than ironic distance.

I confess that I find that the three sections of the book are successively less interesting. The first section's critique of the temptations of distance is incisive and convicting, the second section tends toward cranky in places, while the third feels considerably less developed than the previous sections. In addition, the practices Reno puts forward tend to be oriented to the individual rather than to corporate church structures,[5] rendering his overall argument a bit truncated.

Charles Bellinger, in his review of Reno's book, puts forward a series of probing questions that are worth considering here. For example, Bellinger asks what kinds of events might overwhelm the vision of building in the ruins that Reno presents. What if the Nicene Creed were removed, or something like that? At what point would Reno finally leave the ruins of the Episcopalian church and turn to Rome or the Orthodox church?[6]

Of course, these kinds of questions take on a certain poignancy given Reno's reception into the Roman Catholic Church not long after the publication of this book. As these things go, I chose the book after Reno left

---

4. Bellinger, Review of *In the Ruins of the Church*, 181.
5. Bergen, Review of *In the Ruins of the Church*, 271.
6. Bellinger, Review of *In the Ruins of the Church*, 182.

the Episcopalian Church but prior to the actual public discussion of his action.[7] His account of the move thus has become part of the discussion of the book—whatever disclaimers Reno may have offered and whatever encouragement given to the reader to live and build in the ruins of the church, nonetheless it seems that the inner logic of the book led Reno almost inexorably to Rome. This may help to explain why his description of the ruins remains much more compelling than his argument to stay there.

---

7. See Reno, "Out of the Ruins," for his account of these matters.

2

What about Hitler?

Robert Brimlow. *What about Hitler? Wrestling with Jesus's Call to Nonviolence in an Evil World.* Grand Rapids: Brazos Press, 2006.

Any discussion considering Christian pacifism somehow brings up "the Hitler question." Robert Brimlow is a Catholic philosopher who espouses pacifism, and in taking seriously the question so often posed uses meditations, personal anecdotes, as well as thoughtful and accessible discussion of some of the issues surrounding pacifism and the existence of evil. And he does answer the question—in the space of a single page—although you may not like his "answer."

Brimlow's book places on the table the question of Hitler; namely, if one wants to act as a pacifist, a peaceful disciple of Jesus, what should one do about people like Hitler? As someone espousing pacifism, Brimlow has often had to deal with that question. I too can attest to something of the experience that he describes. Inevitably some version of such a question is raised if you claim that you are a pacifist. In the classroom setting, I am often also faced with a related query, something along the lines of, "What would you do if someone was beating up your wife or three daughters?" This is a deadly serious question that deserves an answer, but instead of turning to a Mennonite author, who might be expected to toe the traditional party line (although it's no longer clear that this is the accepted position among Mennonites), I want to consider the work of a Catholic philosopher who is at least a bit subversive in his circles, since the Catholic church traditionally espouses the Just War Tradition.

The basic structure of Brimlow's book is interesting; in addition to philosophical, theological and (somewhat thin) exegetical work, he offers a series of meditations, perhaps better described as reflections on biblical passages and personal experience. The book therefore is rigorous, accessible, and useable, thus fitting nicely into the Brazos Press series entitled The Christian Practice of Everyday Life. Brimlow repeats this invocation at the beginning of each chapter:

> *Bless my mind to illuminate me with your wisdom;*
> *Bless my lips to allow me to speak your word;*
> *And bless my heart that I might live your gospel.*

The substance of the book might be rightly understood as being half a page long, while the rest of the book is just footnotes on that half page. Further, what he has to say is, by his own admission, absurd. That is, "what the call to discipleship means in the concrete is unrealistic, implausible, and absurd."[1] However, "Christian peacemaking makes sense and ceases to be absurd only when it is embedded in a life of faithfulness and the practices that arise from our faithfulness" (13).

Brimlow makes his central argument in a chapter entitled "The Christian Response," which, as noted above, takes up a mere half a page. It is worth quoting here:

> At this juncture it is time for me to respond to the Hitler question: how should Christians respond to the kind of evil Hitler represents if just war theory and supreme emergencies are precluded, and if we live with different meanings of success?
>
> We must live faithfully; we must be humble in our faith and truthful in what we say and do; we must repay evil with good; and we must be peacemakers. This may also mean as a result that the evildoers will kill us. Then, we shall also die.
>
> That's it. There is nothing else—or rather, everything else is only a footnote to this. We are called to live the kingdom as he proclaimed it and be his disciples, come what may. We are, in his words, flowers flourishing and growing wild today, and tomorrow destined for the furnace. We are God's people, living by faith.
>
> The gospel is clear and simple, and I know what the response to the Hitler question must be. And I desperately want to avoid

---

1. Brimlow, *What about Hitler?*, 11. Subsequent references to the book will be included in the body of the essay.

this conclusion. When my time comes, I may well trot out every nuanced argument I can develop, or seek a way out in St. Thomas Aquinas or Paul Ramsey. This would serve me and my fear, my hypocrisy, and my faithlessness very well. But I would not be telling the truth or living as I ought and as I am called to live. (151)

It is easy to react to this cryptic argument negatively, as was the case when I used some of the material from this book in an adult education class in my church. I handed out a copy of this page to the group one Sunday and then began the next class by asking if this argument was an adequate response to "the Hitler question." The most memorable reaction from the class was also cryptic and firm: "That is no answer."

Of course, Brimlow's book also contains nearly two hundred additional pages of his so-called 'footnotes' to his argument. I think it makes sense to go both backward and forward from his "Christian Response" in order to see first how that argument is generated, and then to see his subsequent elaboration of that argument. The six chapters that precede the statement of his argument might be described as going round and round in ever-tightening circles, trying to be more and more concrete and specific until he gets to the point where he can dramatically assert his substantive argument.

Brimlow begins with two chapters in which he explores the foundations of the Just War Tradition (JWT) and its development in contemporary thought. The first of these chapters is, of course, an extended discussion of Augustine and his introduction of the JWT, primarily seen as a *change* in Christian thought and practice. To provide just one example of the early church's embrace of peace and rejection of violence, Brimlow draws on the writings of an earlier church father, Tertullian, who resists the Augustinian split between action and internal disposition for Christians, which according to Brimlow is a mistake that plagues the Christian church to the present day. Brimlow describes Augustine as "a saint, a father of the church, a good theologian, and a wonderful philosopher. He is also wrong" (30). The development of the JWT in our time comes under the same judgment, being founded on criteria that are simply "insufficient to outlaw even the most immoral of wars and even may well be used to justify them. It justifies the killing of innocents and other heinous acts—even if foreseen—as long as the intention of the actor is pure" (56).

Following the broad strokes of the first two chapters, Brimlow turns to take on more specific issues as he wends his way toward his central position. He addresses the argument of the so-called good war, which asserts that even if many wars would not be considered just, surely World War II must count as a "good war," especially because it is understood as having been a "supreme emergency." Hitler constitutes a "supreme emergency," we often say, which opens the door to do things that we would not ordinarily do. This leads to what Brimlow calls the "Hitler Test," or Hitlerization, especially as put forward in the work of Michael Walzer. That is, if someone or something appears to be as evil or threatening as Hitler was, then normative standards and rights may be suspended in the face of such an emergency. Brimlow refuses such reasoning, claiming that he simply does not know what to do with the kind of thinking that argues it may be necessary to violate rights in order to preserve their inviolability (70).

Brimlow also finds that the JWT is incapable of helping us navigate the difficulties of addressing terrorism, in questions such as, Should terrorism be understood as criminal activity or war? Rather, the JWT leaves us in the untenable situation whereby, in conjunction with the notion of "supreme emergencies," we have a basis to sanction killing and destruction, a line of argument that Brimlow insists is the same logic employed by terrorism. As he puts it, "To accept one as right and proper is to accept the other, and this means we have no moral basis to object to what Al Qaeda and other terrorist organizations are doing" (98).

A further dimension of this complex set of issues addressed by Brimlow is that of the possible necessity of sin in certain dire circumstances. The heart of this discussion is the involvement of Dietrich Bonhoeffer in a plot to assassinate Hitler, an involvement Brimlow thinks was wrong; he resists any notion that being faithful to Jesus Christ might require a disciple to sin.

The question that bedevils pacifists, and one that Brimlow knows he has to address, is that of responsibility: Is pacifism effective at assuming responsibility in this world? The answer put forward by Brimlow is unconditionally negative: Absolutely not! Working with the concepts of success, failure, and hypocrisy, Brimlow tries to change the way the conversation conventionally runs. That is, the standards of evaluation that we normally use to answer the question of responsibility are themselves less than Christian; rather, they are primarily instrumental. In fact, Jesus himself was a bit of a failure, if the standard of success and failure is largely instrumental. But it is precisely that standard of evaluation that ought *not* to be applied to Jesus's ministry. As Brimlow puts it, "Being a church and being disciples is not like driving a Plymouth to Dallas. While the world should look upon Jesus's life and ministry as failures and what calls us to be as foolish, futile, and contrary to our nature, the Word teaches the church a new meaning of *success* and calls us to follow him" (146).[2]

2. One might think here of other examples of the embrace of unconventional

Brimlow has now reached the point in his argument where he is able to articulate the answer to the Hitler question. Thus he offers us his half-page thesis, which he then expands in the space of his two final chapters of elaboration, which really amount to a meditation on our fear of death and our willingness (or not) to be schooled in the everyday practices of discipleship. "We need to grow stronger in faith, and we also need to become peacemakers in all aspects of our lives, especially the mundane. In short, we need to live the way the gospel teaches us on a daily basis" (180). And further, "through our everyday and common practices we must form ourselves into the kind of people who behave as peacemakers, who live lives of disciples not only in our hearts and souls but also through the expression of our actions. It is only when violence in all aspects of our lives—especially those that seem trivial—becomes incomprehensible that peacemaking and love will show themselves to us as being the 'natural' responses to evil. Through daily acts of mercy we need to habituate ourselves to be the people of God" (185).

Brimlow's brief thesis pushes us to confront the possibility that an answer to the Hitler question is found in thinking and acting like Christians; not in living by the calculus of the wider world. If we are to be a peaceful church, we have to begin to recognize that what we are *not* trying to do is to say that we are peaceful and therefore we can be pacifist. Rather, we confess that Jesus is Lord, we repent of our sins and seek to follow Jesus. This does not make things any easier, but it does make things different—it's a precarious peace.[3]

---

understandings of success, as displayed in the movie *To End All Wars,* or in the remarkable account of faithfulness in the face of Nazi evil in Haillie, *Lest Innocent Blood Be Shed.*

3. To borrow a phrase from my colleague Chris Huebner, in his book *A Precarious Peace.*

3

The Mystery of the Child

Martin Marty. *The Mystery of the Child*. Grand Rapids: Eerdmans Publishing, 2007.

Many of us know that children are sometimes hard to understand, whether we are parents, teachers, childcare professionals, grandparents, and so on. But our attempts at understanding and explanation sometimes reduce children to biological factors or some such thing, and thus we often treat children as though they are objects of adult control. But what happens if we see a child as "a mystery who invokes wonder and elicits creative responses that affect the care provided him or her?" This book treats children as though they matter, and as though God matters.

In Robert Brimlow's *What about Hitler?* we grappled with questions of whether it really is the case that we have to recalibrate our conceptions of success and failure. And now we turn our attention to another mystery—the mystery of the child. I begin with the confession that my children are completely mysterious to me,[1] as are many of my students. And so I chose the book for discussion hoping that I would gain some clarity. Actually, my confession is two-fold: first, that I chose this book for selfish reasons, and second, that I do not comment on the book or topic from a position of expertise in parenting. In reading *What about Hitler?*, I bring some back-

---

1. When I wrote this for presentation, our daughters were all pre-teens.

ground to that book's subject because I study and teach ethics, but here I offer my experience as a parent, which does not qualify me as an expert but has served to make me ever less confident to say anything to anybody. In some fields, the more one participates and engages, the more competence is gained, but in parenting, it sometimes feels as though the opposite happens, no doubt due in part because I have my own existential issues, trying to come to grips with my place in this world and with my faith. So even as I try to keep up with my navel-gazing issues, my kids are changing before my eyes at a pace that is mind-boggling; my wife and I never catch up with one stage or another long enough to figure out if it is just a stage, or if something more serious is happening. Of course at the same time, there are absolutely transcendent moments where we cannot imagine anything sweeter than the place we find ourselves in. So I often feel as though I am in a Charles Dickens novel, experiencing the best of times and the worst of times.

Given all of this, Marty had me at the title: *The Mystery of the Child*. Children *are* mysterious, so it comes as no surprise that the literature is awash with all manner of analysis about how children are to be understood, what they are for, the economics of having and raising them, and so on. Martin Marty is not interested so much in family size, household economics, or similar kinds of issues. Rather, the burden of the book is to have us consider the child not as a problem but as a mystery, a move that will literally make all the difference and one that needs to be made not only by parents. To see children as a mystery carries all kinds of implications for the provision of care broadly understood (by seniors, parents, imaginative people, professionals), and Marty wants all of these groups to pay attention as he consults and converses with people who approach the child with what he calls a "special seriousness."[2]

While all of this must be framed by a sense of mystery, that sense ought always to be chastened by a clear-eyed recognition of finitude (the child is not immortal), contingency (things may happen that we cannot foresee, predict, or control), and transience (the child cannot be frozen in time). Yet Marty wants us to experience the mystery of the child instead of confronting the child as a problem, because if a child is a problem, then the care of that child becomes a matter of control, which constitutes one of the key temptations that we must be confront as being wrong-headed.

This discussion concerning the temptation to control, to which Marty returns many times, is one of the most guilt-inducing dimensions of the book for me. Marty draws on Jerome Miller's notion of the Closed Home,

---

2. Marty, *Mystery of the Child*, 10. Subsequent references to the book will be included in the body of the essay.

which describes the process whereby we confront the Other, become insecure, and therefore try to control that Other. When that Other is a child, this temptation is especially intense, because it just seems as though we should be able to control a child. Indeed, Miller pushes this argument further, asserting that the temptation to control is especially powerful for men, since our culture deeply associates control with masculinity. The "will to control," with its attendant echoes of Nietzsche's will to power, is profoundly phallocentric (35).

It will be useful to pause a little longer to consider the theological significance of the temptation to control. First, it is in this context that Marty takes on the guru of the family in evangelical circles, namely James Dobson. In Marty's view, Dobson is a clear example of this desire to control children. After all, Dobson's big book, *Dare to Discipline*, shows by its very title a significant difference from Marty's book. According to Dobson, a child is something to be disciplined, a strong will that needs to be broken (47, 48). This seems to Marty like an embrace of the child as a problem and not as a mystery. Further, this way of seeing children is transferred to the rest of society, and so Dobson tries to exert significant control over that society, telling people how to vote, what to read, what to watch, and where to shop.

A related theological dimension of this bent toward control, the will to control, suggests in some way a lack of faith in God, it seems to me. I have often run across this very issue in my work in political theology, which considers questions of church and state, violence, and the nature of responsibility in this world, among other things. That is, there are those who advocate for a certain kind of activism as being central to Christian action in this world. As John Howard Yoder puts it, the Christian world is full of people who think that it is possible to grab the handles of history and make history turn out right; not only is it possible, it is what is required of Christians if we are to be faithful—or so goes the argument. Yoder demurs, suggesting that this attempt at grasping is in fact a sign of a lack of faith in God, and shows evidence that the person's eschatology is thin and weak.[3] We are trying to do what is God's work to do, to make things turn out this way or that. I have often thought of children when reading this kind of theology: is it possible that my feeble attempts to control my children and/or my students bring to view a lack of a trust in God? Perhaps this would explain why I try so much harder to control my kids than I do my students; that is, because I think there's more at stake since they are *my* kids. Marty offers a significant gift to the reader in bringing forward this powerful set of concepts. Children are not problems to be solved, but mysteries to be experienced.

---

3. Yoder, *Politics of Jesus*, 237–42.

After all, Jesus said that the little children should come to him, and that unless we become like little children we shall not enter the kingdom. However, the question is what part of being like a child is Jesus bringing to the attention of his listeners—the sweetness? the selfishness? the seemingly inherent violence? What? Marty argues that what Jesus highlights are the two dimensions of receptivity and responsiveness. In conversation with Catholic theologian Karl Rahner, Marty encourages us to transcend biological childishness and immaturity to embrace these two characteristics as marks of the Christian (241, 242). So, to those caregivers who want to experience the mystery of the child and resist the temptation to see the child as a problem and thus something to be controlled, Marty begins to become more and more concrete. For example, we should cultivate wonder, the use of art, play, and stories, and seek to foster delight. He even enters the age-old nature versus nurture fray, choosing to speak of the child as self and circumstance without forcing a choice between the two as part of experiencing the mystery. Further, children need not be understood as either innocent or originally sinful: they do bad things, they do good things, but they are receptive above all.

There's much more to the book, of course, but rather than continue in this expositional mode, let me make a few critical and constructive comments. First, I find the basic structure of the book to be very powerful, compelling. To shape our care of children in terms of experiencing mystery instead of solving a problem is full of rich possibilities, it seems to me. This approach helps to find a way through the notoriously faddish and guilt-ridden worlds of childrearing manuals and educational trends. That is, Marty helps shape responses to statements such as "Children are nothing but . . . ," "What children need is . . . ," or "*The* way to approach raising children . . . ," "*The* way to teach students . . . ," "*The* way to evaluate students . . ." To make statements like these is to reduce children (or students) to something less than what they are. Marty's work helps me see that no thing and no one is only one thing, requiring, by logical extension, only one approach.

I also have some reservations about the book. Sometimes Marty is too keen to make sure everyone is on board with him, and so he often pauses to say that while he may be a Christian, sharing that faith is not necessary in order to agree with him. In this zeal for inclusivity and broad appeal, his Christian framework is reduced. For example, I would like to see more serious appropriation of the theology of incarnation, the Word made Flesh, that real and deep mystery that Christians seek to live with and understand. It is this mystery and not just "God as Mystery" that is central in this discussion of children, and yet it gets very little attention. After all, as theologian Amy Laura Hall puts it, "We mislaid a basic Protestant affirmation, that is, the child on whom our hope ultimately depends has already been born."[4] Jesus appears in this book, but as the one who utters the words that form the foundation of Marty's argument, Jesus does not figure prominently enough. In addition, biblical references to children are more diverse than can be summarized by the declaration by Jesus in Matthew. For example, the apostle Paul suggests that while it used to be the case that when I was a child I thought as a child, and saw as a child, but now that I am a man I have done away with childish things. This is an important passage, as is the passage that encourages us to move on from child's diet to take stronger meat and drink. More specific discussion of these kinds of biblical teachings would be welcome here. And finally, Marty does mention the role of community in caring for children, but is not specific about the role of the church in this discussion.

---

4. Quoted by Leslie Leyland Fields, "The Case for Kids."

4

God Laughs and Plays

David James Duncan. *God Laughs and Plays: Churchless Sermons in Response to the Preachments of the Fundamentalist Right*. Great Barrington, MA: Triad Institute, 2006.

David James Duncan wants to warn us about the putative dangers of fundamentalism, especially the Christian kind. Duncan's award-winning book stands out within this kind of literature—it's funny, creative, insightful, and moving. What else would you expect from a former fundamentalist, conservationist, fly fisherman, and author of two of my favorite novels? But is this collection of stories, recollections, conversations, and cosmological reflections—"churchless sermons"—reliable as a constructive guide for people who want to avoid the rumored pitfalls of fundamentalism?

Before we take up Duncan's book, we should talk a bit about fundamentalism more broadly, not just his specific target. Christian fundamentalism in North America is closely tied to the broader category of Christians described as evangelicals, not so much a reference to a denomination as it is an approach to the Christian faith, or an emphasis on a specific set of beliefs. Perhaps most well-known among definitions of evangelicalism is David Bebbington's: key ingredients include a) conversionism, an emphasis on the "new birth" as a life-changing religious experience; b) biblicism, a reliance on the Bible as ultimate religious authority; c) activism, a concern for sharing the faith; and d) crucicentrism, a focus on Christ's redeeming work on the cross. So using these criteria, one can conceivably identify evangelicals right across denominational lines.[1]

Christian fundamentalism is a subset of evangelicalism and grew out of it, especially in the early part of the twentieth century. "Fundamentalism was a loose, diverse, and changing federation of co-belligerents united by their fierce opposition to modernist attempts to bring Christianity into line with modern thought." Put another way, "it was a movement among American 'evangelical' Christians, people professing complete confidence in the Bible and preoccupied with the message of God's salvation of sinners through the death of Jesus Christ."[2] A series of books published in the early twentieth century gave this movement its name—The Fundamentals: A Testimony to the Truth. The tenets of the Christian faith emphasized included a) the inerrancy of the Bible, b) the virgin birth of Jesus, c) the deity of Jesus, d) the doctrine of substitutionary atonement through God's grace and human faith, e) the bodily resurrection of Jesus, and f) miracles of scripture. These tenets were all considered indispensable and interdependent.[3]

It is this expression of Christianity, a fundamentalism that is militant, sometimes harsh, that has in essence set up certain litmus tests to determine the faithfulness of Christians. This seems entirely too narrow to some people and serves as a target for those who embrace fundamentalism and then leave it because they come to different understandings of the faith. David James Duncan, who has a certain fundamentalist pedigree of his own, is worried about fundamentalism, especially the American instantiation of that movement. Duncan grew up within a Seventh Day Adventist family, an experience on which he draws for some of the hilarious detail in his novel *The Brothers K* (1992), and also refers to several times in *God Laughs and Plays*.[4] Because of those influences and because of the state of conservative religion in the United States, it turns out that he himself has become an evangelist, as he is forced to admit in the preface to the book; he's engaged in a self-proclaimed "compassion rebellion" against fundamentalism, in "compassion as dissent" (xv, xvii).

Duncan believes that he has to take on the roles of dissenter and antifundamentalist evangelist because of the inherent danger of fundamentalism. Apparently he does a good job of dissenting; after all, he's been the co-recipient of the Intellectual Freedom Award given by the American

---

1. Bebbington, *Evangelicalism in Modern Britain*, 2–17.
2. Marsden, *Fundamentalism and American Culture*, 3–4.
3. Dann, *Leaving Fundamentalism*, 6.
4. Duncan, *God Laughs and Plays*, 89–90, 172. Subsequent references to the book will be included in the body of this essay.

Library Association. In Duncan's view, the danger is that fundamentalism is a toxic mix of the neoconservative politics of George Bush and nationalism that has gone to seed and thus has become an unthinking patriotism upheld by jingoism, blind obedience, pandering to the rich, and ignoring the poor. It's a politics that is underwritten by religion and a religion underwritten by right-wing politics, all of which results directly in the kinds of practices and policies that have the tragic end of raping the earth, under the guise of religion and dominion over the earth (108). Duncan is convinced that in the expression of such fundamentalism, love is impossible (173) and life is unlivable in any kind of coherent, consistent way (98). Much of this is set out most clearly in the preface, but the argument is sustained throughout the essays.

Duncan responds to fundamentalism, this unloving threat to life itself, in a number of ways. First, as he says himself, the most developed response to all of this is his fiction, particularly *The Brothers K* and *The River Why* (1983). In these novels, in different yet related ways, he *shows* but does not so much tell what he understands to be the weaknesses and the dangerousness of fundamentalist expressions of the faith. Second, as I have mentioned above, Duncan thinks that rebelling and dissenting through compassion is a way to respond. According to him, the fact that compassion comes to be seen by the powers that be as dissent is itself the greatest accusation against the neoconservative expression of American fundamentalism. Duncan's work here, which sometimes brings Wendell Berry to mind, is exemplary in that Duncan brings to view the utter importance of description as moral writing. That is, describing correctly what is going on is at least as important morally as is some program that might be put forward by this agency or that organization. Often we move quickly to what we think are solutions, without proper regard for analysis of the thing we're trying to fix. Duncan's chapter "When Compassion Becomes Dissent" is a fine example of such moral description.

The third of Duncan's responses to fundamentalism has to do with the relationship of spirit and letter; he claims to embrace the first and resist the second, and does so by invoking his understanding of Jesus's words and example.

> Religious laws, in all the major traditions, have both a letter and a spirit. As I understand the words and example of Jesus, the spirit of a law is all-important, whereas the letter, while useful in conjunction with spirit, becomes lifeless and deadly without it. In accordance with this distinction, a yearning to worship on wilderness ridges or beside rivers, rather than in churches,

could legitimately be called evangelical. Jesus Himself began his mission after forty days and nights in wilderness. According to the same letter-vs.-spirit distinction, the law-heavy literalism of many so-called evangelicals is not evangelical at all: "evangel" means "the gospels"; the essence of the gospels is Jesus; and literalism is (literally!) not something that Jesus personified or taught. (xvi)[5]

Fourth, Duncan links his religious stance to the apophatic tradition. This is the topic of his second chapter, wherein he defines "apophatic" as "an unsaying" (17). The tradition to which he is appealing is one that is longstanding, and includes the notion that God is simply so "other" than humanity that to talk about God in positive terms (He is like this, or like that) is simply to warp things out of shape to the point of incoherence. Apophaticism is pursuing knowledge of God through negation; that is, all we can say about God is what he is not. Duncan finds in this tradition a way of unsaying the word "God" that is parallel to unsaying all kinds of other words for other deities, leaving me to puzzle over whether apophatic theology really has the effect of showing that all deities we dare not speak about are then in essence the same deity; he seems to think so. But his point extends further than that, as he is also concerned that definition is limitation. "The greater a person's confidence in their definition of God, the more sure I feel that their worship of 'Him' has become the worship of their own definition" (19). Apophaticism for Duncan cuts the nerve of such misplaced confidence, especially of the sort that abounds in fundamentalism.

Fifth, Duncan's response to fundamentalism also includes a rejection of structure, institution, and dogma. His definition of church, for example, is "where two or *less* are gathered in His name" (114). He claims early in the book (5) that for the previous thirty-five years, he has had no "experiences as a church-goer," suggesting that any connections he may have with God are entirely unmediated by the church, although they are mediated or inspired by things like a trout stream—he has lived a life rich in rivers, poor in church services, and deep in gratitude (6). So while Duncan dares to suggest that fundamentalists need the rest of us, even there it is not the church they need so much as different opinions to challenge their own.

Duncan has little patience for the kinds of things the church wants us to do from time to time, such as confess our beliefs or humbly agree with a creed. However, let it not be said that he has no room for statements of his own belief. For example, he shares a series of confessional statements early

---

5. Duncan does not distinguish between evangelicalism and fundamentalism in any substantial way in this book.

in the book, confessing "I believe—based on the gospels, and on the words of the excommunicated Meister Eckhart, and the non-Christian Simone Weil; I believe, based on the beautiful Beguine saints burned at the stake by Christians" (15). While this is no Apostles' or Nicene Creed, Duncan cannot be accused of unbelief; in fact, he's even doctrinaire about matters ranging from how a fly reel should be set up to what he thinks the Catholic and Protestant churches ought to believe, along with many other topics about which he is "dogmatic" (174–75). This is his own version of dogmatism, which does not embrace the institutional church, church services, creedal statements, or confessions. Those kinds of dogmatics are part of the fundamentalist problem, according to Duncan.

One more dimension of his response to fundamentalism deserves attention, namely, the sources that he uses (in addition to nature). The cover of the book itself is graced with stylistically rendered names of various gods, underscored by a picture of water, and the book is published by the Triad Institute, an ecological institute. Duncan really likes Jesus, and many of his reflections on Jesus are moving and insightful. One gets the strong sense that the basic thrust of many of Duncan's arguments is in fact shaped by the life and teachings of Jesus. On some kind of intuitive level, Duncan realizes that many of the things done in the name of Christianity just do not fit with the Gospel accounts of Jesus, with the biblical interpretations of Jesus.

But the Gospels are not his only source—he loves to briefly mention a list of sources and suggest that at bottom these figures, whether god or someone else, basically agree on many of the points he's trying to make. He asserts that the "world's major faiths are not identical, but they are alike enough in ultimate aim that those striving to love, emulate, and honor Jesus, Mohammed, Rama, Shakyamuni, and Abraham have, in many times and places, proven themselves able to live side by side in peace" (xvii). The list of religious figures that Duncan "reveres" (6) is long, and he also includes within lists of things in which he really places his faith items such as Toyota pickups, Walla Walla red wines, and Roland keyboards. In sum, one of Duncan's responses to Christian fundamentalism is an embrace of pluralism.

Duncan also displays a very mystical bent, seen primarily in his drawing on the work of Meister Eckhart; indeed the title of the book is borrowed from Eckhart's work. Eckhart, a German mystic (1260–1327) who has been described as laying the foundation for both German philosophy and mysticism, wrote during the time when church scholarship was dominated by what we know as scholasticism. Theology had been moved from the monasteries and churches into new institutions called universities. In addition, Eckhart was writing around the time of a massive medieval famine, the Black Plague, and just before the outbreak of the gruesome and extended

Hundred Years' War. In other words, Europe was in total chaos and the church was struggling, creating a great thirst for things such as stability and for connection to God—hence the popularity of mystical writing. Eckhart was a member of the Dominican order of monks, also known as the Order of Preachers; a mendicant order, mostly urban, and particularly dedicated to the vow of poverty. This was the context for Meister Eckhart, whose work resulted in serious trouble with the institutional church. Right around the time of his death his writings were subjected to serious scrutiny, and he was suspected of pantheism, the belief that God is in everything. Although he is not considered a full-blown heretic, some of his writings are considered heretical while others are simply deemed suspect. This mystic who "finds God in all things" serves Duncan as a muse, an inspiration, and a source for responding to fundamentalism.

I count myself a big fan of Duncan's fiction. Artists, poets, and novelists see things that some of the rest of us do not see quite as clearly, which is why we read fiction in search of truth. Duncan's fiction is the kind that does not slap you upside the head in the way some so-called Christian fiction does, whereby the novel becomes a poorly disguised medium for apologetics or sermonic conversations, with pedantry replacing art. Duncan's showing of religion, religious people, and so on in his fiction is very compelling.

Further, as I hinted above, I like his treatment of Jesus. I think I can see a deep admiration, even a deep desire on Duncan's part to understand Jesus, to emulate or even imitate him, and to refuse easy readings of the Gospels, especially those kinds of readings that would allow him to use Jesus to underwrite some kind of lifestyle that he wanted to live on other grounds, even before reading the Gospels. Jesus serves as a looming presence, but in many ways what Duncan embraces is highly selective. That is, the age-old Christian question of the divine nature of Jesus and the concomitant questions and understandings of salvation are given pretty short shrift. In this way Duncan comes across as a typical early twentieth-century liberal, willing to allow that Jesus is a great guy, worthy to be followed, radical even, but stopping a bit short of an orthodox understanding of Jesus the Messiah.

Duncan's work provides a compelling case for reducing size, most eloquently developed in the seventh chapter, titled "No Great Things . . . ," where he draws extensively on the life and work of Mother Teresa, drawing attention to her assertion that "we can do no great things—only small things with great love" (117). He gives a variety of examples and reasons why he is so enthralled with this notion, with this way of being in the world, partly because it gives him a way to stay sane. It is possible to live here on this earth and be faithful, and be deeply involved on a human scale. Thus he uses the wonderful phrase "politics that is no politics" (118) to describe what he gleans from Mother Teresa and others. We are tempted to think that projects and solutions on a grand scale will address the seemingly intractable problems of the world. So we buy and read books like Stephen Lewis's *Race against Time* (2005), and can easily feel overwhelmed. However in that book, the problems brought to view by Lewis often have to do with his frustrations with organizations such as the United Nations, but then any proposed solutions are also dependent on these same kinds of institutions. This same approach unfolded before our eyes with the economic crisis in the United States in 2008, wherein the government tried to bail out the very system that had led to the crisis in the first place. Duncan suggests that large-scale solutions to large-scale problems may well be part of the spreading of despair, while "Small-Things-with-Great-Love Stories" may save us from succumbing to darkness (128).

More critically, I fear that Duncan's portrayal of fundamentalism often drifts very near to caricature. The targets he sets up are too easy, not nearly nuanced enough; they ignore the positive dimensions that have been part of a movement that includes admittedly nasty sides. It is easy enough to see the militancy, the narrowness, the parochialism, the violence, the arrogance, and so on. And yet it is also easy to ignore the seriousness with which the Bible is taken, the dedication to seeking God, the willingness to speak out about issues that need to remain live issues, and even the warm spirituality that has sometimes marked the movement. It is not a monolith, and when Duncan describes it and responds to it, I feel that he sometimes descends into a self-righteous smugness that is off-putting. For example, Duncan is very critical about the loud public praying that marks the movement but then cannot stop himself from pointing out that he does not sin in this way, very publicly declaring that *he* goes into his closet to pray (112). He just cannot hide the fact that he thinks he has things much more right than the fundamentalists have.

Duncan also seems to be putting himself forward in some category that allows him to be considered a Christian writer and speaker while not embracing orthodox Christian doctrine or institutional Christianity.[6] And it is precisely here that I am most ambivalent about Duncan: I like much what he has to say about fundamentalism, especially the sort he sees in the United States; I agree with at least some of his analysis of the way we need to be in this world; and yet I find myself wondering if are not more reliable guides for my life, for my own constructive responses to those whose expressions of faith seem to be in error.

6. Duncan's letter to his Christian minister friend, found in chapter 13, puts forward a predictable argument against some of her more orthodox beliefs, and here his views are perhaps most clear.

This leads me to my final observation: I think Duncan should go to church; he needs to stop warping the Bible's message about the importance of the body of Christ. His bringing to view the deep interpenetration of God and his world is a message we undoubtedly need, and often people who do this run into just the kinds of criticisms I am raising. We continue to be tempted by views of the gospel that take us out of the created world, and find it difficult to take the Incarnation of Jesus and its attendant implications seriously enough. Fair enough, but fishing and everything that it stands for in Duncan's work falls short. God lives and moves in the city, in subdivisions, and in other places. Where people are involved in the practices of the church—baptism, communion, fellowship, prayer, preaching, good works—there is the incarnate presence of God, which I find to be a truncated dimension of Duncan's work. He is never closer to the truth than when he claims that fundamentalists need the rest of us, but in the end his view of the church, a view that he ironically shares to some extent with fundamentalists, is just too limited. Part of the problem with fundamentalists is that the Bible becomes something that is immediately accessible to the reader—it has a plain sense, a literal sense, supposedly unclouded by theory, liberal notions, or whatever else. If the Bible is indeed accessible in this direct way, then of course the practices of the church become secondary to the individual understanding of the believer. Duncan too thinks he can do without the church, that he can access the deity without the particular practices of the body of Christ.

5

Living the Sabbath

Norman Wirzba. *Living the Sabbath: Discovering the Rhythms of Rest and Delight*. Grand Rapids: Brazos Press, 2006.

Norman Wirzba is an American Christian philosopher who thinks and writes about issues of religion and ecology. In Living the Sabbath: Discovering the Rhythms of Rest and Delight *(part of The Christian Practice of Everyday Life series), Wirzba explores the Sabbath, not just as a day but as a practice that seeks to engage the world in ways that embrace both hard, serious work as well as rest and delight. He then tries to work out ways of practicing the Sabbath in contexts such as the home, the economy, and education.*

How much are our lives shaped by the Sabbath? According to Norman Wirzba, some of the questions we would need to answer to determine this include: a) Where does your food come from? b) How many television sets do you have in your home? c) Do you live in the suburbs? d) does your house have front porch—if not, why not? e) Is your garage attached to the house? f) Do you make your meals from scratch? g) Do you have a big garden? h) Do you have a dishwasher? If so, do you use it? i) Do you shop in big box stores? j) Do you support the radical restriction of computers in the classroom, especially among the young? k) Do you drink bottled water? l) Do you carefully shape your time (not space) around the concept of *menuha*?[1]

According to Wirzba, these kinds of issues are at the heart of living the Sabbath— and true to the title of the series in which this book appears (The Christian *Practice* of Everyday Life), he tries to make his discussion of the Sabbath one that has concrete application and the possibility of instantiation in the lives of regular people. We all want to find ways of putting into practice that which we know, and as one of the blurbs on the back cover suggests, we have all at least begun to live the Sabbath, since we have made time to read this book.

When I think of the Sabbath, my mind is immediately drawn back to my first degree, pursued in the small Saskatchewan town of Caronport. At Briercrest Bible College, Sundays were kind of like a Sabbath, or at the least the school rules were meant to make them so. We were required to attend church, which at Briercrest consisted of the student body and staff families, making it feel quite a bit like a student body assembly. After church and a cafeteria lunch, the campus seemed to draw in on itself, as we were not allowed to play sports or do much of anything (officially at least). After supper we were required to attend another service. All in all, the Sabbath, such as it was, seemed to be an interminable combination of formal services, meals, and restless inactivity.

But I've also sometimes thought of 1998–99 as a Sabbath of sorts for Julie, me, and our very young family at the time. I had a deferred salary leave from my employer, Cecely and Hannah were pre-school age, and halfway through the year Greta was born. We moved to Waterloo, where I studied in pursuit of a master's degree in theology. The factor that made this time seem Sabbath-like was that while I was studying, there was a lot of time for us to explore the area where we were living and to make new friends. Further, neither Julie or I was working at a job that year—I was being paid my deferred salary, and Julie was collecting maternity leave benefits. A full year with two incomes but no jobs—that's what I am tempted to call a Sabbath.

However, Wirzba is at pains to make sure that we do *not* make the mistake of understanding the Sabbath as just a break from life. Put negatively, practicing the Sabbath is a critique of modern industrial life, but put positively, it is at its heart a participation in God's creation, just as the seventh day of creation was exactly that—a day of creation, not a day of pointless inactivity. As Wendell Berry frames the issue: "Will we choose

---

1. Wirzba, *Living the Sabbath*, 33. Wirzba uses the term *menuha* as a conceptual word that embraces notions of rest, tranquility, serenity, the peace of God, the lifting up and celebrating of everything—the climax of creation. Subsequent references to the book will be included in the body of the essay.

to participate by working in accordance with the world's originating principles, in recognition of its inherent goodness and its maker's approval of it, in gratitude for our membership in it, or will we participate by destroying it in accordance with our always tottering, never resting self-justifications and selfish desires?" (12).

Wirzba is keen to help the reader think through what he calls "the inner logic" of the Sabbath, and he thinks we should be able to live the Sabbath without any cultural sanction of complete rest for one day a week. There is no call for lobbying local businesses and governments to close everything down for a day. After all, living the Sabbath has to do with participating regularly in the delight of God's creation, just the kind of delight that marked God's own response to a creation wonderfully made (14, 15). We are to cultivate a "Sabbath bearing," to see the Sabbath as a training ground. These and other kinds of things are necessary because we have become impatient people, which is for Wirzba a theological issue, one that is most fully on display in our relationship to food (this move from some issue or another to a discussion of food is repeated time after time by Wirzba, a point I want to return to below).

Wirzba is admirably conversant with scripture, and so he grounds his contextualization of the Sabbath firmly in the Bible, proceeding through a fine discussion of the Old and New Testament contexts. He develops a number of concepts from his reading of the Old Testament. For example, the Sabbath makes us open to seeing the world the way God has made it; following the Sabbath teaches us to live out of control; the Sabbath helps us to take notice of what is *actually* going on around us; and our keeping of the Sabbath implies that there must be a Sabbath for everyone, not just those of us who are privileged but for our employees too. That is, the Sabbath has an element of justice as well.

The New Testament, while it moves from Sabbath to Sunday in some way, does not supersede what has been given to us in the Hebrew Scriptures. Indeed, we are encouraged to see Sunday as an intensification of the Sabbath, and precisely because of the coming of the Messiah. Sabbath is like a little Easter, a glimpse of creation set right: "creaturely life is most authentic or at its best when it shares in Christ's own life, when it moves in a trajectory that lines up with his" (43).

This biblical material leads Wirzba to the central notion of delight, which I find challenging. The practice of delight is the proper response to what is a gift of God, and is based on the pattern of God taking delight in his creation. All things are part of God's creation; he delights in them and we participate in that delight, if and when we can finally get over ourselves. This kind of delight is not a passive experience, nor is it equal to personal pleasure. Rather, true delight forms the indispensable context for genuine knowledge or understanding of others (59). Then, in a chapter that is written in a more diagnostic mode, Wirzba insists that we have lost this sense of delight and have replaced it with artificiality, lack of connection, commodification of everything, and general malaise.

In the second section of the book, Wirzba turns his attention to living the Sabbath in a practical context. Authentic work is one of the primary means we have to share in God's own continuing work of building and maintaining creation (103). Wirzba identifies the possibility that work can be a number of things, including distraction or escape. However, work understood in a Sabbath framework has to do with reception, namely receiving by participating in the sustaining work of Christ. This is not work understood as career, but work that lines up with God's own work.

Wirzba then tries to apply the principles of the Sabbath to questions of home, economics, environmentalism, and worship. I want to focus on just one of these chapters, namely, "Sabbath Education," as a sample of his setting of the Sabbath in a practical context. Education has become primarily a matter of credentialing, says Wirzba, the preparation for a "career of money," the process of coming to grips with an economy that is based on the seven deadly sins but now positively understood. However, if our understanding of education is based on a Sabbath framework, on discovering the rhythms of rest and delight, on perceiving and engaging the world the way God does, then education becomes a different matter entirely. That is, education now becomes a practice of engaging in the formation of desire, transforming our understandings so that we become attuned to God's intentions rather than just our own. This is a faithful and honest attunement to the world, recognizing our sinfulness, learning the craft of living, and understanding education as an apprenticeship in reality. To see education as apprenticeship flies in the face of the rootlessness that Wirzba diagnoses in our educational attempts. Currently, we produce communicators without regard for the content of the message being communicated, we produce managers without regard for what is being managed, but we do precious little in our education systems that teaches us the basic competencies of life such as growing and preparing food, raising a family, judging quality, maintaining a home, practicing hospitality, or making a toy (134). What is required is an education into wholeness, which requires "serious teaching——the sort that entails many face-to-face hours between student and teacher" (135). Part of serious teaching is to teach our students to embrace the world, the practice of a "hermeneutics of delight" rather than a hermeneutic of suspicion. In partial response to the question of how we might begin to move toward a hermeneutic of delight, Wirzba asserts that we should *greatly restrict* the use of computer technologies in our classrooms, especially among the young (137). While it's possible to learn whatever we need about computers in a relatively short period of time, to spend lots of time on them is expensive and harmful, contributing to problematic developments such as a loss of wonder in the ordinary processes of natural life, the fostering of surface relationships on the computer while ignoring real relationships, the belief that the world is available to us on demand, suggesting to us that we can control whatever we want—all of which creates a manipulative and arrogant disposition within us (138). We need to see education as the transformation of vision (140).

It should be clear by now that I like Wirzba's book, especially the language of lining up our lives with something that is already going on, this language of participation and his notion of delight. I find constructive his analysis of our deep-seated desire for control of every aspect of life, and how that dysfunctional desire needs to be challenged and shaped according to Sabbath sensibilities. His understanding of the Sabbath as having an "inner logic" makes it so much more than a day with rules without reducing it to some notion of us being free to do whatever we like. The Sabbath is real, and we need it as part of what it means to be a faithful Christian.

As impressive and convincing as Wirzba's book is, I also have some cautions. For example, the book contains a whiff of axe-grinding, specifically having to do with issues of ecology and our distorted notions about food. He makes the move to apply Sabbath principles to issues of food early and often. This is actually a two-edged sword. Part of the power of the book is Wirzba's ability to resist circumscribing the Sabbath into a single day, seeing it instead as a way of life, and so he continually pushes us to "live the Sabbath." But it feels as though he has some favorite topics (primarily food) that will surface no matter what theological concept he is ostensibly dealing with.

Further, I am not always convinced by Wirzba's move of translating principles into action, something which he does in his chapter on economics and to a lesser extent in his chapter on environmentalism. To distill principles from a discussion and then apply them always carries with it the danger of reductionism (reducing narratives to principles and then principles to actions). Specifically, the danger in this book, in my view, is that the Sabbath is framed as a set of principles which are then distilled in the practical actions Wirzba discusses, all of which seems to make it possible to practice the Sabbath while dismissing the habit of setting aside a Sabbath day. Put another way, does his presentation of the Sabbath as principles and practices drain away the possibilities of what an actual Sabbath day might bring forward?

6

The Omnivore's Dilemma

Michael Pollan. *The Omnivore's Dilemma: A Natural History of Four Meals.*
New York: Penguin Books, 2007.

> *"Food ethics" is one of the critical dimensions of fidelity to God's world that is the focus of vigorous (but not always rigorous) discussions as people try to find ways of eating, sharing, growing, and distributing food. Michael Pollan is an important voice in this conversation. Here in* The Omnivore's Dilemma: A Natural History of Four Meals, *Pollan traces the backdrop to four different kinds of meals, and in so doing brings to view many of the critical issues confronting the North American scene, which he diagnoses as undergoing "a national eating disorder."*

This book is considered Pollan's breakthrough book, and for obvious reasons, I think. It is well-written, accessible, personal, and it deals with a central societal issue in a timely fashion. What we all face is the omnivore's dilemma, which comes to us as a question in its most basic form: "What should we have for dinner?" Put as an assertion, here's the dilemma: "The blessing of the omnivore is that he can eat a great many different things in nature. The curse of the omnivore is that when it comes to figuring out which of those things is safe to eat, he's pretty much on his own."[1] But of course the book is not just about food, it's about politics. Mark Danner's blurb high-

---

1. Pollan, *Omnivore's Dilemma*, 287. Subsequent references to the book will be included in the body of this essay.

lights "the profound truth half-hidden at the heart of this beautiful book: that the reality of our politics is to be found not in what Americans do in the voting booth every four years but in what we do in the supermarket every day. Embodied in this irresistible, picaresque journey through America's food world is a profound treatise on the hidden politics of our everyday life." As Pollan himself says early in the book, eating is an agricultural act, an ecological act, and a political act, since how and what we eat determines to a great extent the use we make of the world and what is to become of it (11). I applaud Pollan's ability to move people to see that politics is not only that which happens in the conventional halls of political power, and Pollan does this very well. We should also be quick to notice that eating as political can't be reduced to principles but has to actually involve real food. This is not some move toward a notion of "inner disposition," the cultivation only of an attitude toward food. Pollan is calling for us to eat, make no mistake, but to eat in ways that include an ever-deepening knowledge that actually shapes what we eat, how we eat, and where we get what we eat, and there's a lot at stake in all of this. If we get this wrong, we could end up with ruinous practices that have personal, national, international, and global effects, according to Pollan. He writes as a naturalist, a materialist who looks to the evolutionary process to help him understand how things are the way they are. He draws on anthropology, ecology, personal experience, and first-rate journalistic skills to get at these matters. Part of the burden of this discussion is to understand him as best we can, embrace what we can, resist what we ought to, and try to do these things from within a Christian theological framework and practices.

To get at the various dimensions of the omnivore's dilemma, Pollan takes the reader on three journeys that include four meals. First is the "industrial" meal, fast food eaten while driving in a car and consuming copious amounts of petroleum resources, least of these being the gas he is using to drive the car. Incorporated within the car are a number of design features such as cup holders that presume owners of cars want to have meals while they hurtle down the highway from one duty to another. This is his "industrial journey."

The second journey is "organic," but here Pollan has to pursue two different meals, since the concept of "organic" itself has become so difficult to capture. He eats a lovely meal at the end of his "industrial organic" journey and another the end of a "grass-fed" journey, which introduces us to a devout Christian whose faith gets surprisingly short shrift in Pollan's understanding of it. It is clear to me that this is really the most impressive journey and meal of all to Pollan.

The third journey is "personal," wherein he hunts and gathers almost all of the ingredients for what he hopes is the perfect meal, although this journey is anything but easy. He has to confront the ethics of hunting, of killing animals in direct and close confrontation with the formidable work of Peter Singer, the notorious (and mainstream) ethicist from Princeton University.[2]

In his treatment of what he labels as the "industrial chain," Pollan seeks to bring to view a matrix of powers that combine in what is to him a very problematic situation. That is, nature, technology, and capitalism are brought together in such a way that nature is remade, in a sense. Technology's power is used to remake nature in the image of capitalism. People learn first to dry, cure, or pickle food; they learn to can it; but then they learn to process it, this last step being where an almost infinite number of possibilities are introduced, along with a concomitant number of problems, if Pollan is to be believed. At the heart of this industrial chain is corn, which really is not food any more, since it has been turned into a commodity, a monoculture, an intellectual property, and a process of turning fossil fuels to food in ways that force changes onto society. These changes take the evolutionary process and try to make it work within the logic of capitalism. The American system has created a "plague of cheap corn," wherein farmers grow huge amounts of corn at costs that have to be subsidized, even though the yields continue to increase. This increased production provides profit, not for the grower but for the large companies (such as Cargill). So much corn is produced that it becomes the basis of feeding livestock in massive feedlots where cattle are grown quickly and kept healthy only through enormous quantities of chemical drugs. In addition, corn is broken down into so many products that are useable in a variety of forms that a closer look at much of what we buy reveals that corn is ubiquitous. This long and complicated discussion of corn, fertilizer, feedlot cattle, evolution, capitalism, and the creation of a *supply*-driven business shows that food has been liberated from nature, to use Pollan's dramatic turn of phrase. When people eat this kind of food, we see that a monoculture of corn, along with all that it entails, has contributed to a national eating disorder, a "republic of fat." Coupled with the way this food is eaten—often in the form of fast food or at least in highly processed

---

2. Notorious for his rigorously logical but not always easy to accept views about animals, but also for his views on abortion, euthanasia, and so on. For example, Singer advocates the logical possibility of infanticide and euthanasia, positions which are difficult for many people to accept. His views and practices surrounding euthanasia became particularly poignant when confronted with his own mother's dementia. Singer acted inconsistently with his own views and had his mother taken care of at great personal expense.

form, and not together as a family—he notes that a fast food meal is a case of "eating alone together," as often is the case at home when each family member microwaves something personal. As Natan Margalit summarizes, "Pollan's research into the industrial food system is fascinating and scary. We are introduced to the incredible monoculture of corn, not only in Iowa fields, but in the entire supermarket. He shows how, behind the mask of seemingly endless variety in the aisles, practically everything has been either fed on, or manufactured from, corn. And behind all that corn is oil. Between fertilizers, running equipment and transportation, Pollan conservatively estimates 50 gallons of oil are used per acre of industrial corn."[3] Suffice it to say that Pollan does not approve of the industrial eater.

As noted above, Pollan's pastoral journey takes two paths, but it is important to notice the shift of focus from corn to grass, which he claims is parallel to the shift from industrial to organic.[4] Almost immediately, his organic journey hits a snag, since the definition and understanding of concepts such as "organic," "sustainable," and "natural" are highly contestable. He shops at Whole Foods, where he likes to shop because of the literary conceits of the package descriptions, a genre he calls "Supermarket Pastoral." This poetic language evokes small-scale farms, country kitchens, happy animals, and humane killing practices, collectively describing a counterculture. But upon closer examination, what Pollan finds is considerably ambiguous and distressing to him. His industrial organic meal is drenched in fossil fuel, so much so that "the organic food industry finds itself in a most unexpected, uncomfortable, and yes, unsustainable position: floating on a sinking sea of petroleum" (184). After all, you can actually buy "microwaveable organic TV dinners," four words Pollan never expected to see conjoined! Says Pollan, "To the extent that the organic movement was conceived as a critique of industrial values, surely there comes a point when the process of industrialization will cost organic its soul (to use a term still uttered by organic types without irony), when Supermarket Pastoral becomes more fiction than fact: another lie told by marketers" (139). While the organic empire comes out of a countercultural mindset, Pollan is afraid that nature's logic has been co-opted by the logic of capitalism.

The second meal on Pollan's pastoral journey comes after spending a week working at Polyface Farm, run by Joel Salatin, a postindustrial, Christian, libertarian, environmentalist grass farmer who is trying hard to resist the logic of the industrial and capitalism and work with the logic of biology.

---

3. Margalit, Review of *The Omnivore's Dilemma*.

4. Pollan offers an extremely useful comparison chart between industrial and organic (130–31).

Salatin does not really trust the government to protect its citizens and their property, much less to do the morally right thing (205). But this contrarian stance is nonetheless at its best a positive endeavor, an attempt to heal the land. Salatin runs what seems to be a very interesting but complicated hundred-acre farm that produces an astonishing amount of food (222). Salatin resists easy categorization. He is not some kind of retreat-from-the-world character; he's not a proponent of some romantic notion of the "simple life." Instead, if anything he is the Martin Luther of food, says Pollan (260, 261). It is actually Salatin who brings up this possible analogy—he does not intend to overthrow anything as such, in this case the industrial system. Instead, he wants to "empower individuals with the right philosophy and the right information to opt out en masse" (260). However, the point Salatin makes is that it was the printing press that allowed Protestants to break off and form their own communities; now it's the Internet, splintering us into tribes that want to go their own way. Pollan adds his own interpretation of the Reformation when he claims that "the goal wasn't to blow up the church, but simply step around it. Protestantism also comes in many denominations, as I suspect will the future of food" (260). Pollan may know his food issues, but his Reformation history is a bit suspect, and Salatin too does the Reformation a disservice by equating what happened there to the technological development of the printing press and its parallel to the Internet. Nonetheless, here we have another small hint at the theological and spiritual realities that Pollan simply cannot and will not make part of the discussion, a point to which I will return below.

The journey that seems in some ways to be the most fanciful of the three journeys and four meals is Pollan's personal journey. And yet here some of his insights are also the most poignant. He hunts a wild pig, shoots it himself, forages for mushrooms and various other things, and, with a lot of help from a lot of people, creates the "perfect meal" (398). As Pollan tries to find traction for how to go about his business of hunting and gathering, his meditations are quite striking to me as I look for what, if anything, might echo my own faith or could perhaps coincide in some way with the way I understand life, food, and this world. A number of dimensions of his discussion in this section of the book strike a chord. For example, he refers to the organization of the calendar, which does not necessarily take its cue from the strictly secular work world. Here the calendar is seen as something that follows what is given, namely the seasons, and food is intimately connected with what is produced in season. This has certain connections with the Sabbath—the ordering of life around something that is given, that compels us to resist attempts to force our designs on nature.

As he moves toward a section wherein the diagnosis of America's eating disorder occupies his mind, Pollan analyzes national cuisines. Some countries have traditional cuisines that seem at first blush to be a surefire way to die young, but produce instead significant measures of health envied by America. Not only are there certain foods, but also ways of eating food that seem to be part of what it means to have a tradition to guide us, to help us make our way through the omnivore's dilemma. So, one might eat soft cheese, bread, and drink wine, but do so slowly, never have second helpings, and eat more often. The point does not even seem to be the content of these foods as much as it is that many cultures have an accumulated, embodied practice that is referred to as wisdom. After all, if "nature won't draw a line around human appetite, then human culture must step in, as indeed it has done, bringing the omnivore's eating habits under the government of all the various taboos" (298). This leads to a brief mention of Aristotle's notion of virtues that are necessary to govern human appetite; such virtues are needed so that our appetite for food can be channeled and socialized for the good of society (298). Pollan offers fine insights here, asking what I think is exactly the right question, namely, why Americans fall under the spell of every single diet fad, food craze, and so on. The short answer is that there is no such thing as a stable American cuisine. Again, capitalism may be a significant part of the problem, whereby we are such individualist consumers that we become targets of food companies looking to secure a percentage of the market share, and so these companies market new ways of selling convenience, fitting meals in a single container that is meant to fit into a car holder designed exactly for this very purpose. After all, if we would stop acting like this, then the march of commercialization might be halted. Simply eating dinner together as a family, where what is eaten is actually food, where that food is actually prepared through cooking and baking and not just by warming, where the family members all eat the same meal at the same time—who knew that such a ritual could be a powerful act of resistance, nay, outright rebellion, against the logic of capitalism? Imagine how much more successful that resistance might be if the aforementioned meal is *not* accompanied by the watching of television.

Another fascinating dimension of this personal journey of Pollan's is his wonderful discussion of the ethics of eating animals in conversation with Peter Singer. What makes it even more interesting is that these two thinkers are really on the same side of things in many ways, and so we see one naturalist trying to resist another naturalist's arguments. Pollan holds off eating meat until he can figure things out, and eventually he does so enough to carry on with his "perfect meal," where he finds himself searching for words of grace (407) while he and his friends participate in eating the body of the world, an ending to the book that sounds suspiciously like a kind of secular Eucharist.

Some further reflections on Pollan's book: I find his treatment of Christian faith less than satisfactory. I do not mean that he has to have a personal Christian faith. Rather, when he does mention religious matters, he has a bit of a tin ear. An example is his understanding of the term "dust to dust," where Pollan asserts that the psalmist who described life as transit from "dust to dust" would have been more accurate to say "humus to humus" (147). The psalmist's point really is not to describe a biological process as much as acknowledge the reality of our earthly life, which finds its existence from beginning to end in relationship with the reality of Creator God. Pollan takes note of Salatin's family grace, which he describes as having a "tone of easy familiarity," offered to a Lord who apparently was present and keenly interested (203). When Salatin talks about his dad's work as an example of someone who seeks to live out his Christian faith, Pollan notes this but does not ever really attempt to understand the significance of this faith to the way Salatin thinks about life, food, farming, and government.

And yet there are a number of places where the book simply cries out for a theological analysis. For example, Pollan asserts that global capitalism assumes an act of faith that includes a robust eschatology (256). Pollan's view is that we believe that by doing certain things here and now, we will achieve a greater happiness in the future. What is this but a secular eschatology, one that specifically flies in the face of a robust Christian eschatology which believes in a future that is ultimately in the hands of God, but calls forth certain ways of life and faith in the here and now that recognize God's future? What Pollan offers us is not something that necessarily fits within a theological framework, but *is* a theological framework of its own. Or so says Laura Shapiro in a fascinating article in *Slate*, entitled "The Holy Church of Food." She claims that Pollan's work doesn't reflect his politics so much as his religion, "the holy, catholic, and apostolic church of food, where only martyrs and lost souls have to shop at Safeway." His role in this religion admittedly is not tactics and logistics; he's more of a theologian who thinks and writes and persuades. He identifies sin and sinners, and how to be born again—he even participates in what Shapiro calls a faith-based dinner party—the "perfect meal." I would add that this stands in nicely for the Marriage Supper of the Lamb that Christians hope to share when Christ is again all in all. Yes, Pollan is a believer with a membership into the Holy Church of Food.[5]

---

5. Shapiro, "Holy Church of Food."

But perhaps there is another way of seeing these matters that is still related to faith. David Cooper, in the *Times Literary Supplement*, argues that absorbed as we are in how to treat other people in our cities and creatures in faraway rainforests, "little space remains . . . for moral attention to our relationships to farmland, domesticated animals, and much else that straddles the natural/artefactual divide. It is Michael Pollan's achievement, in his several writings, that . . . [h]e widens this space. And I doubt that there is a book which succeeds more than *The Omnivore's Dilemma*—with its richness of information, eloquence of address, and integrity of moral purpose—in rendering visible, and presenting for a 'different' style of ethical reflection, that 'profound engagement' with our world which eating represents."[6]

If Cooper is right, then what Pollan may do for religious believers is help us to open up space that we need to think through these matters from within our faith. Natan Margalit does some of this in a 2006 article: "By showing us what a food chain can mean, and what it has come to mean in the reality of industrial food, Pollan has opened up a new direction that has profound implications for anyone claiming to follow a religious or ethical dietary practice, including kashrut and eco-kashrut, halal, stewardship of creation, concern for the suffering of all sentient beings, and others."[7]

To hint at a robust Christian treatment of some of these matters, Robert Song addresses the complex issues of hunger, food, and genetically modified foods within the framework of the Eucharist, the Lord's Supper. The entire book in which his essay appears is structured by the various elements of the liturgy, and Song tries here to show that the Christian sharing of the Lord's table is precisely the place where we can learn to live as Christians. The Eucharist proclaims that hunger and poverty are not the last word; the messianic feast is a vision of divine abundance that sweeps aside our assumptions of scarcity. At this meal we are taught about generosity and hospitality and we are given to think about practices of fasting, charity, and so on.[8] What would happen if we were to use Pollan's "opening up of space" to practice the truths we learn about eating as we partake in the Lord's Supper?

---

6. Cooper, "Anxiety of Eating."
7. Margalit, Review of *The Omnivore's Dilemma*.
8. Song, "Sharing Communion."

7

Jayber Crow

Wendell Berry. *Jayber Crow*. Washington: Counterpoint, 2000.

Wendell Berry is a farmer-poet who left the big city in order to embrace the much more complex life on a farm in the hills of Kentucky. While farming there, he has also published an impressive body of work, including moral essays, short stories, poetry, and novels. His novel Jayber Crow, *which follows the life of a small-town barber is really an examination of the nature of fidelity—to the land, to a community, to individuals, and ultimately to God and the world. This isn't "just a story" but rather constitutes a serious theological reflection on some of the issues about which we are reading, mapped onto a so-called ordinary life. Berry signals how serious the book is when he threatens that "persons attempting to explain, interpret, explicate, analyze, deconstruct, or otherwise 'understand' it will be exiled to a desert island in the company only of other explainers."*

Wendell Berry is a great American writer, a man of letters, as they say, recipient of a Guggenheim Fellowship, the Lannan Foundation Award for nonfiction, an honorary doctorate, and many awards for his poetry. Perhaps most fundamentally, Berry, along with his wife, Tanya, is a Kentucky farmer.

The primary setting of *Jayber Crow* is fictional Port William, Kentucky, which has been in the making since the late 1950s, when Berry first began writing stories about its membership.[1] Here in *Jayber Crow*, we want to do what we can to understand the book, but we do have to heed Berry's warning at the beginning of the book, which he includes as a "Notice." Berry writes, "Persons attempting to find a 'text' in this book will be prosecuted; persons attempting to find a 'subtext' in it will be banished; persons attempting to explain, interpret, explicate, analyze, deconstruct, or otherwise 'understand' it will be exiled to a desert island in the company only of other explainers."[2] Giving heed to this warning, I will not look for theory; however, it is clear that Berry's fiction is meant to display some kind of vision that is worked out in other terms in his essays, and again in other terms in his poetry, and in other ways on his farm, and yet all of this is of a piece, if I understand him correctly.

What is that vision? Bill Kauffman notes that a home place is central to the possibility of a good life, and that Berry is striving to work against what he sees as the deadly illness of humanity—an unholy mélange of selfishness, violence, placelessness, and greed, the answer to which is not some kind of humanitarian universalist vision.[3] Kimberly Smith thinks that Berry is trying to help us to live a fully human life in a dangerous and unpredictable environment, not by seeking godlike control over the conditions of our existence but by cultivating the virtues that allow us to live gracefully in the presence of fear, namely moderation, prudence, propriety, and fidelity.[4] Berry works at these matters by displaying before us and by inviting us into the life and history of Port William. Make no mistake, Port William is not a perfect place—the Port William stories include murder, infidelity, waywardness, greed, sloth, greed, sloth, but the reader will also see love, mercy, faithfulness, forgiveness, and redemption.[5]

In *Jayber Crow*, we see life in the Port William membership through the voice and eyes of the town barber. Jayber's life basically spans the twentieth century, which provides a way for Berry to map the developments of that century with its so-called progress, technological and otherwise, the move from agricultural base to urbanization, the coming of the car and the

---

1. Berry has written about Port William in novels, poems, and short stories. See for example his recent collection *A Place in Time*.

2. The placement of the "Notice" is interesting; it appears prior to the table of contents, but following a page which declares that this is "The Life Story of Jayber Crow, Barber, of the Port William Membership, as Written by Himself." The reader is left to wonder if the "Notice" is Berry's voice or the fictional Jayber's strong assertion. Subsequent references to *Jayber Crow* will be included in the body of the essay.

3. Kaufmann, "Wendell Berry on War and Peace," 24, 30.

4. Smith, "Wendell Berry's Political Vision," 49.

5. Leax, "Memory and Hope in the World of Port William," 67.

concomitant expansion of highways, the increase in speed (not just in transportation, but in life more generally), the increase in mobility and the attendant fragmentation of communities and families. Poor Jayber is orphaned early but has the fortune of being raised by a series of good people. He grows into manhood, possessing an "obscure handsomeness," and for a while at least he lives a life that is not exactly profligate but rather that of a "cut-rate prodigal" (68). He thinks he hears the call to the ministry, but it turns out he is wrong about the nature of the call. Jayber gains clarity regarding his mistaken sense of call in a pivotal conversation with one of his professors, Dr. Ardmire, wherein Jayber's confession regarding his ongoing questions brings an unexpected answer, namely, that Jayber's call is to a life in which he will have to live out the answers to his questions, probably a little at a time (52–54).[6] Almost by accident, Jayber picks up the skills necessary to be a barber. He's smart, he likes to read, and he's a Christian, and he really believes that he is led of God (133).[7]

Despite the themes of conversion and calling, it would be a mistake to suggest that this is an evangelistic book in some conventional way. It seems to me that Berry is seeking throughout *Jayber Crow* and all of the Port William books and stories to bring to view an embodied sense of the concrete and the particular,[8] a look at life on a local scale. And insofar as his vision is religious, Berry's writing has a "radically incarnational character."[9]

I want to look at just a few of the dimensions of Berry's incarnational vision as seen through the narration of Jayber. First, community is primary to the individual and is crucial to the possibility of the life of virtue. There are many instances in Berry's stories where people are described as leaving Port William, and often it is the case where the person's departure is cast in a negative light, with some comment such as "people thought they could do better elsewhere."[10] But Port William is not just a town, it is a membership

---

6. Dr. Ardmire's influence remains strong throughout Jayber's life. For example, when Jayber is an old man, reflecting on his life, he frames his understanding in part on his long-ago conversation with Ardmire (250–54).

7. Jayber's "conversion" account is narrated as something that he cannot explain, but he believes that "I seemed to have wandered my way back to the beginning—not just of the book, but of the world—and all the rest was yet to come. I felt knowledge crawl over my skin" (79). This conversion account is reminiscent of Augustine's *Confessions*, and to some extend reminds me of Canadian philosopher George Grant's account of having an inexplicable experience that he spends the rest of his life trying to understand (and live in its light). Jayber's description of his life includes obvious echoes of John Bunyan's *Pilgrim's Progress*.

8. Smith, "Wendell Berry's Political Vision," 54.

9. Kroeker, "Sexuality and the Sacramental Imagination," 135.

10. Berry, *Fidelity*, 21.

(139, 205), an immersion in and commitment to a community, a reality that can never be reduced to the institutional life of that membership (33).

A second dimension of Berry's incarnational vision as seen in *Jayber Crow* includes a strong resistance to dualism, especially between body and soul/spirit. This dualism troubles Jayber greatly while studying at Pigeonville College, where "everything bad was laid on the body, and everything good was credited to the soul. It scared me a little when I realized that I saw it the other way around ... these preachers I'm talking about all thought that the soul could do no wrong, but always had its face washed and its pants on and was in agony over having to associate with the flesh and the world. And yet these same people believed in the resurrection of the body" (49). That the world is created by God and is there for the life and enjoyment of people is clear to Jayber (83). When this kind of dualism appears in the church, Jayber seeks to resist it there as well (165).[11]

Third, Berry's incarnational vision carries with it a strong anti-war dimension. Whether it's World War I, World War II, or the Vietnam War, the characters in Port William may well go to war, or send off one of their loved ones, lose several of them to one war or another, or welcome them home in whatever condition. However, this participation in war is cast in a negative light almost all of the time. Patriotism is fidelity to the land, not the taking up of arms to fight other confused young men. Often mention of war comes in the form of "The War," as though it functions as a thing or a power (142–43, 162, 287, 294).

Berry also treats the intertwined forces of technology, economy, and progress as powers that are exceedingly difficult to resist. Jayber finds himself seduced by the purported advantages of car ownership, believing at least for a time that the car is part of the abundant life (167, 171). His later rejection of this belief results in his abandonment of car ownership, and his growing realization that development of the interstate highway, so intimately connected with the proliferation of car ownership, brings with it the erosion of local community and carries the modern world into Port William in ways that even television is incapable (281, 282).

We get a sense of Jayber's relationship to technology when his barbershop is "inspected." His barbershop does not have hot running water, and so, by law, he cannot really charge for his haircuts, even though the technology used in the barbershop is adequately suited for the tasks at hand. So Jayber

---

11. See Peters, "Education, Heresy, and the 'Deadly Disease of the World,'" 270–71. It's an interesting exercise to keep an eye on the humor in Berry's fiction, the jokes his characters tell—they are often quite earthy, as when Athey Keith responds to a question about his health with his great line, "Well, sir, where I used to be limber I'm stiff and where I used to be stiff I'm limber. Do you know what I'm talking about?" (213).

gives haircuts away for free, and those whose hair he cuts leave a donation, a practice whereby the members of Port William subvert both the technological and economic juggernaut whose progress seems inexorable. Jayber's friend Danny gleefully participates in this alternative economy, because for Danny, "a barbershop in the woods on the riverbank, giving free haircuts in return for which people gave away dollars, a barbershop bootlegging haircuts in defiance of authority, dispensing and receiving lawless charity—that appealed to his fundamental dissidence and contrariness" (314). Jayber later reflects on these and other developments that he has witnessed, and poses several questions.

> I watch and I wonder and I think. I think of the old slavery, and of the way The Economy has now improved upon it. The new slavery has improved upon the old by giving the new slaves the illusion that they are free. The Economy does not take people's freedom by force, which would be against its principles, for it is very humane. It *buys* their freedom, pays for it, and then persuades its money back again with shoddy goods and the promise of freedom. "Buy a car," it says, "and be free. Buy a boat and be free. Buy a beer and be free." Is this not the raw material of bad dreams? Or is it maybe the very nightmare itself? (332)

A further dimension of Berry's incarnational vision that is evident in *Jayber Crow* is the relationship of people and land. Berry's characters are obsessed with the way the land of Port William is used or abused. In fact, it is impossible to think about fidelity and ignore the way people live on the land, or their relationship to those who live on the land. Jayber himself is always a gardener, whether in the back lot behind his barbershop or at the shack down by the river. But an understanding of what it means to be faithful on the land and to the land centers in this novel on the differing visions of Athey Keith and his son-in-law Troy Chatham. Troy avoids service in the war because of a trick knee sustained during his high school basketball glory days, marries Mattie Keith, and begins to farm in a way that could not be more different than the way Athey works the land. Whereas Athey uses his land conservatively, improving his land so that he could leave it better than he found it, Troy's philosophy is different: "Never let a quarter's worth of equity stand idle. Use it or borrow against it" (179). Athey keeps an eighty-acre stand of timber on his land, worth more to him than to anyone who would be willing to buy it—he calls it his "Nest Egg." The clash of visions between Athey and Troy (181–87) intensifies over the years and becomes even more acute when Troy's son, Athey's grandson, becomes more attached to Athey than to Troy, who is portrayed as someone who sees the world only in reference to himself (338). The vision that prevails at least in some ways is Troy's, as illustrated in the fate of the Nest Egg, which Troy seeks to "liquidate.'" However, as it happens, it is his last play in the "game of farming," since Troy finds that he simply has leveraged far too much, and even in his defeat it is possible to see Athey's vision of the land portrayed as the one that is sustainable, while Troy's vision collapses in on itself.

Another dimension of Berry's incarnational vision as displayed in *Jayber Crow* emphasizes fidelity to people. Instructive here is the relationship between Jayber and Mattie Chatham, that marriage in which Jayber gives himself in love's mystery to Mattie, even though she knows not a thing about it, or so it would seem. Jayber meets Mattie early in the arc of the narrative (9, 10). He is by then a barber in Port William while she's a giggling schoolgirl. "She was a pretty girl and I was moved by her prettiness" (10), says Jayber, who watches from a distance as Troy and Mattie begin to be together, and eventually get married and have a family. Jayber dislikes Troy; in fact, he manages to take offense at something he sees written in the flyleaf of a history book (135), so petty is his dislike. Indeed, there is almost a menacing tone to Jayber's intense dislike of Troy, fully on display when Jayber shaves Troy with a straight razor and cannot help but think about that razor in contact with Troy's soft throat (195).

But Jayber finds himself loving the married Mattie, a realization he finds deeply disorienting (191, 192). It takes some time for Jayber to come to the point of having some kind of grip on this bizarre situation. He begins his personal love affair with Mattie, to whom he does not declare his love, as a demand and trouble on his mind (193–94), and he longs for her in conventional ways. But this conventional vision of love comes to a crashing halt, since to get together with Mattie is ultimately an incomplete and unsustainable vision that would necessarily include the two of them running away from Port William. Having such a fantasy, where two people only have each other, is precisely what destroys his vision (196, 197). So Jayber's love for Mattie does not end, but his presumption and delusions fall away and in their place remains hopelessness, which becomes a sign of permanence. Poor Mattie experiences the death of a beautiful little daughter, and somehow we anticipate that Jayber and Mattie will get together, perhaps because we have been trained to expect just that sort of thing. It is tempting to want them to get together, to see Mattie to leave the unsympathetic Troy. But the novel offers no such satisfaction for the reader. Instead, we witness a wedding of sorts, wherein Jayber pledges himself to be a faithful husband to Mattie but without her knowledge of his fidelity to those vows. At the end of the telling, there is no mistaking the echoes of resurrection morning, the raising to new life as Jayber returns to his life after his "wedding" (242, 243).

That life, shaped and changed by his vows, allows Jayber to live with love in his heart; it connects him to eternity in a new way, motivates his return to the practice of prayer and renew his love for the world (247–54).

Jayber and Mattie meet from time to time, but their meetings are entirely chaste—it's as though their mutual embrace of certain views of life, of the beauty of certain things, and their love for the Nest Egg means that they will cross paths from time to time and so they do. "It is of utmost importance that you should understand that these meetings were not trysts" (348). But then Mattie is stricken with her final disease, just at the time that Troy is cutting the Nest Egg, and so we find Jayber in Mattie's hospital room, exchanging the briefest acknowledgment of their mutual chaste love, and Mattie gives Jayber "the smile that I had never seen and will not see again in this world, and it covered me all over with light" (363).

And thus ends the book; if I read it correctly, an attempt to envision a life of fidelity to the land, to community, to God, to people, to love, to virtue, to hope—the kind of faithfulness that calls for a lifetime of faithful practices. Finally a novel must not be reducible to a series of themes—it's a story, an account that is more than the sum of these themes.

8

The Year of Living Biblically

A.J. Jacobs. *The Year of Living Biblically: One Man's Humble Quest to Follow the Bible as Literally as Possible.* New York: Simon and Schuster, 2007.

> *Jacobs is a self-described secular journalist who tries to do something many Christians claim to do—obey the Bible. So, in addition to growing a really long beard, Jacobs finds that his quest creates some very awkward situations (have you ever stoned someone for committing adultery?) and generates surprising insights into the Bible. In addition, this book has the merit of holding up a mirror to our own approaches to the Bible—and it's funny.*

A few years ago, I was involved in an interesting conversation with a friend, solving some world problem or another with reference to what the Bible had to say, when he finally told me that it might be true that the Bible taught this or that but he no longer cared, since the Bible was no longer the source that guided him in his approach to the issue at hand, or any other issue for that matter—this despite the fact that he had previously been a pastor. A.J. Jacobs, on the other hand, moves in the opposite direction in the journey described in this book. He declares himself as secular, but no doubt a particular kind of secular in that he describes himself as a secular Jew, which I take to be very different than, say, a secular Mennonite. But the Bible has clearly *not* been his guide in any way, and now he embarks on what he calls a spiritual journey in which the Bible will be his guide, as he commits himself to taking the Bible as literally as possible for an entire year.

He claims to be motivated to undertake this spiritual journey by several factors: he wants to write a book, religious experience fascinates him, and he is interested in exploring the phenomenon of biblical literalism. More specifically, he intends to show that biblical literalism is necessarily a selective enterprise.[1]

What can one say about a secular Jew who decides to write about interpreting and living the Bible, and does so at least in part so that he can have a book contract? If I was to teach a course addressing the interpretation of the Bible, I would certainly consider starting with this book, but I might not conclude with it. The strength of Jacobs's book is his bringing to view of the many issues that surround a serious reading of the Bible; the weakness is the lack of depth on some important issues.

In analyzing a book, I usually begin with strengths and positive dimensions, a pattern drilled into me when I was being trained to be a teacher. But I want to break the pattern and start with a general complaint, although my treatment of strengths will be much more fully developed, as I do not want to be appear churlish, cranky, or God forbid, cynical.

My general complaint is that Jacobs sometimes brings up the right issues within this complicated field of biblical interpretation, but treats them too simplistically. For example, he knows that the issue of so-called original intent of the writers of Scripture is important, but his discussion of it is so underdeveloped and clunky that I wish he had just let it be. He also engages in a truncated bit of history regarding images, adds a throwaway comment about Pharisees that just confirms stereotypes, and attempts to describe the writing of the Bible as a process akin to Wikipedia—a comparison that falls seriously flat. For Jacobs to admit that some of these matters were beyond the scope of this kind of book, and certainly beyond the author's expertise, would have been perfectly acceptable.

However, despite those complaints, I like this book a lot. Jacobs's writing is clear, and he made me laugh out loud in with his descriptions of a meeting of atheists who just cannot get organized, the stoning of a mean adulterer, and his uncle Gil. His writing can also be very moving. He nearly made me weep as I read his account of the birth of his twins. These several pages were written in such a way that I was transported back to the birth of my daughters. Emergency surgery was performed, the room full of about ten experts who had gathered in the middle of the night to save both my wife and little girl; and then the second time, I had to be escorted out of the room so that there wouldn't be an additional patient. Jacobs brought me

---

1. Jacobs, *Year of Living Biblically*, 289. Subsequent references to the book will be included in the body of the essay.

back to those mind-bending, soul-altering, life-changing moments by the power of his writing—I like that about a book.

However, it is primarily what he brings to view about the Bible—its power, the fragility of faith, and the vagaries of interpretation—that I want to highlight. Jacobs's journey, all of his struggles, his wide-eyed wonder at what is actually in the book he has neglected so fully for so long brings him to the realization that one has to grapple with the Bible. There is a real sense in which there is no such thing as just reading the Bible; reading always requires interpretation. For Jacobs, there is no denying a strangeness within the Bible that he recognizes early in his journey. "I didn't expect to find such strangeness in the Bible" (7). Jacobs does not seem to realize that this discovery puts him in good company. After all, Karl Barth, who was quite a bit more familiar with the Bible than Jacobs can ever hope to be, declared a long time ago that there is a "strange new world within the Bible," and it is this world that we must struggle to become familiar with, which is a good thing to remember for those of us who grew up with the Bible and have come to believe that we're familiar with the Bible, or worse, that the Bible is familiar.

As Jacobs struggles to understand and live the Bible, he brings into relief a number of instructive issues. For example, often even while he tries to obey the Bible in the most literal fashion, such as following the injunction to "not join hands with a wicked man," Jacobs finds that this fits nicely into his own phobias, and thus on a literal level, he can avoid shaking hands with people because they might be wicked (and who isn't, he figures). He combines that with the practice of evading handshakes with males who have engaged in sexual intercourse within the previous day. But here, as in many other places, Jacobs struggles to understand the relationship between the act and some underlying principle, and in so doing often finds ways to justify a watering-down or even avoidance of the specific biblical instruction with which he is struggling. This brings to light one of the common interpretive moves that many folks use precisely to avoid actually following the Bible, or to "get a handle" on the narrative of the Bible. That is, we say something like, "The Bible says to do this or that, but the thing behind it is some broad principle." The Bible says things like "Give to those who ask," but it really means something like "Be generous and nice." Jacobs's book shows how that method of interpretation can often lead to our avoiding the performing of specific acts. In fact, it is interesting to read the book and see that it is often in while following the specifics of particulars that the biggest change happens in Jacobs. In Norman Wirzba's book *Living the Sabbath*, he argues that following the Sabbath is not about a specific day or particular rules addressing our behavior. By the time one has worked through his book, the notion of setting aside a specific day in which we act in a certain way has faded way into the background. Fair enough, but notice that Jacobs learns what it is to celebrate the Sabbath by following specific rules. This grappling with the issue of whether the Bible can be reduced to a set of "principles" or can be understood as calling for a primary focus on practices is an important part of the book.

A closely related issue raised by Jacobs is the nature of the relationship between action and belief; namely, must we believe before an action is authentic, or can we act ourselves into belief? A great example of this dynamic is his discussion of the principal of the school who started "mandatory volunteering," which as a young man struck Jacobs as ridiculous—"Mandatory volunteering is oxymoronic! You can't legislate morality! It must be cultivated naturally. Plus, the policy came from the administration, so it had to be wrong" (301, 302). Jacobs now concludes that mandated morality is a good idea. For Jacobs the move will have to be from action to belief, since he professes no belief, although he has had some inexplicable mystical experiences as a young man. Early on he signals that he is not the kind of person who can be debated into belief. So he will try out the theory of cognitive dissonance—"If I act like I'm faithful and God loving for several months, then maybe I'll become faithful and God loving. If I pray every day, then maybe I'll start to believe in the Being to whom I'm praying" (21). This approach is fascinating to watch; he continues to do things even when he does not understand them, or before he understands them, and even when he never comes to understanding them. This means that sometimes he just practices obedience, as in the rules about the mixing of fibers, and really never comes to any more understanding. At other times, the practice of some rule or another begins to change him as a person. For example, he begins to get "hooked on gratitude," sending up prayers of gratitude and, he claims, becoming a different person. Here action turns into an agent of change. Other times, the practice of this or that serves to deepen his understanding.

What is so interesting to me is that his practice of these various rules, which range from the sublime to the ridiculous, at least at first glance and often much beyond that, creates an ongoing inner struggle for Jacobs. He asks himself questions such as: What was I really doing when I just did *that*? How much of that action was motivated by pure thoughts and motives? Does it matter? The way this dynamic between action and belief is displayed is compelling.

Another important issue concerning the reading of the Bible brought forward by Jacobs is the question of authority. It is the rare Christian or Jew who would say the Bible is not the authority for life, but the question to be considered is just how that is the case. The issue surfaces in a dramatic way when Jacobs attends a meeting of atheists, a meeting presided over by

Ken, who asserts that atheists have to stop being polite and start getting their message out there without worrying about being politically correct, an argument I have also heard being used by earnest Christians. No one at the atheist meeting listens to Ken, and Jacobs, showing what I think is very keen insight, chalks this up to the fact that Ken does not speak with any authority: no one believes that his authority comes from God, and further, as Jacobs observes, "It's hard to be passionate about a lack of belief" (98). The question of authority has not only to do with whether or not one accepts the Bible as authoritative, it also has to do with what parts of the Bible function in this way. Jacobs returns to this question late in the book, when he shows that all of us pick and choose to a greater or lesser extent from the Bible, and in so doing, bring up this very question—does this not destroy the credibility of the Bible? Maybe not, suggests one of his advisors, since it is also the case that if you treat the Bible as some kind of depository of *all* that God has said and done, the danger of committing idolatry on the Bible itself becomes very real (328, 329).

Jacobs's reading of the Bible also forces us to reflect on the thorny question of the embodiment of faith. I love the fact that he begins to understand that "religion," as he puts it, enlists our bodies as an essential part of what it means to express that faith. It seems to surprise him that religion does not make you live with your head in the clouds, but that rather it grounds you in this world (172). Exactly right; in another spot he points out that this is not like studying sumo wrestling in Japan, it's more like the wrestling itself (119). Indeed, one cannot help but realize how bodily this entire experience of faith is throughout the book. Jacobs wears certain clothes, he does specific things with his hair and beard, he binds things to various parts of his body, he is much more aware of his bodily functions as part of faith; he is also aware of his wife's bodily functions, and she is not above using this against him, as she sits on every chair in the apartment when he refuses to sit on chairs which have been used by someone "impure" (51, 52). He realizes fairly early on that biblical living is about constant reminders, and many of these involve not only some interior notion but fully involve the body. But even here, Jacobs cannot quite keep things together when it comes to sex. His wife, hugely pregnant with twins, when asked if she would like to be intimate, replies, "I can't think of anything I'd rather do less" (285). This provides an opportunity for Jacobs to return once again to the issue of lust, which is a bit of a struggle for him. But here it seems to me that he misunderstands the body and faith, and makes the mistake made so often by Christians in that he seems to equate "putting the earthly nature to death" with practicing asceticism, with *not* having sex, and controlling his lust through some rather cheesy methods such as thinking of people as "out of your league," thinking of a woman as if she were your mother, and so on. This comes dangerously close to Gnostic dualism, wherein the body is seen as the enemy, as something that has to be defeated in order to be properly spiritual (286–88).

Another issue raised by Jacobs is that of a faith community. He realizes that this quest that he is on is being carried out in a radically autonomous way, and that without a real faith community his experience is doomed to be thin at best (213, 214). This lacuna is on display throughout and is in the end instructive for us, it seems to me. He does exactly what many of us do: he recruits a panel of advisors from here and there, some good, some a bit idiosyncratic, and draws what he can from them, but he's not committed to any or all of them, and in the end his drawing on them is part of deciding what to do with the information. Glaringly obvious is his very infrequent attendance of religious services, Jewish or Christian, and when he does attend, they serve as research trips. He misses the notion that understanding scripture, and understanding what kind of practices and life comes out of the reading of the Bible, is at heart a community-dependent process. Indeed, the notions of authority, tradition, change, interpretation, and ethics—all of these dimensions of faith have their genesis within a faith community, which is sadly lacking for Jacobs. Perhaps in seeing this in his experience, we can see it in our own experience as well.

All of this brings me to the observation that this entire book might be thought of as a mirror of sorts. We see that for Jacobs, the Bible functions like a mirror, showing him much about himself that he could not see before. For example, as he seeks to obey the biblical mandate to stone adulterers, and as we watch and laugh at the absurdity of it all, we are brought up a little short when Jacobs recognizes that what is disturbing about stoning an adulterer is how much he (Jacobs) likes to do this. He recalls a scene from *All in the Family* where Meathead punches somebody and is so upset because of how good it feels to commit violence. Jacobs confesses that it feels good to chuck rocks at the particular adulterer he is punishing, since the man is a nasty bully and to stone him feels good. This is like getting revenge, getting him to feel pain, and all under the guise of doing the righteous thing (91–94). Friedrich Nietzsche accuses Christian morality of being just like this at its very heart, a morality of revenge, weakness, and resentment thinly papered over by the self-righteousness. But time and again, the attempt to follow some imperative or another shows Jacobs more about himself than he knew previously.

Further, I contend that the book itself holds up a mirror to our own practices of Bible reading and interpretation, and our claims to want only to obey. In fact, Jacobs finds so many different kinds of readers and interpreters whom he puts on display that surely we can see ourselves both in Jacobs's own experiences and in the approaches held by some person or movement consulted for guidance in the book. I saw myself a number of times, the picking and choosing, the self-justifications, the fragility of faith, the struggle to know what to do next, the surprising and humbling insights about myself found just by reading the Bible seriously, the strong desire to consult whomever I want for guidance if I think I need it, and the tendency to draw other people into my way of seeing things.

I learned a lot from this book, and some of Jacobs's insights into the nature of faith as it is nurtured by serious Bible reading are every bit as edifying as many a book written by someone other than a secular journalist. The kinds of personal changes Jacobs describes are deeply insightful. For example, he describes a change in himself as geographical, that is, his sense of geography changes as he comes to understand the significance of place differently, and what he looks for and therefore what he sees is shaped by his reading of the Bible. Even his method of calculation changes, as he comes to realize that the story of the prodigal son does not make sense as long as one thinks quantitatively, if life is seen as a balance sheet.

Jacobs talks about a "religion-soaked life" and soon begins to feel more at home with the ultra-religious than with secular folks. He begins to see just how odd many of the things done *outside* the religious community are when you stop to think about it. How weird is it to handle snakes as act of faith? Well, perhaps it's less strange than being intimately aware of the personal lives of celebrities or less weird than scheduling one's life around some television show.

So, as we watch Jacobs on his journey, we're a bit suspicious. This is, after all, in part about selling books, about pitching an idea to a publisher, about following up a related book contract in which some other iconic text was read to see what would happen. But if Jacobs is to be believed, he begins as an agnostic, and then something changes about him—he becomes a grateful, reverent agnostic.

9

Atheist Delusions

David Bentley Hart. *Atheist Delusions: The Christian Revolution and Its Fashionable Enemies*. New Haven: Yale University Press, 2009.

The so-called new atheists (e.g. David Dennett, Richard Dawkins, Sam Harris, Christopher Hitchens) have captured the attention of many readers. Theologian David Bentley Hart contends that these atheistic writings are based on profound conceptual confusions and facile simplifications of history. He attends to many issues that the "new atheists" address, seeking to bring into focus the truth about the most radical revolution in Western history: Christianity. Sometimes theology is considered a blood sport, and Hart's book is a fine example of this very thing.

In recent years, authors such as Dennett, Dawkins, Harris, and Hitchens have captured the attention of many. Various Christian writers have attempted to reply to these "new atheists" by taking on their arguments in a direct fashion, seeking to point out specific errors in fact, reasoning, and argumentation. The purpose of this essay is not to rehearse such arguments but to provide an extended review of another approach to the new atheists, one that responds substantively without reverting to direct refutation of some specific line of argument.

American Eastern Orthodox theologian David Bentley Hart contends that these atheistic writings are based on profound conceptual confusions and facile simplifications of history. In his book *Atheist Delusions: The*

Christian Revolution and Its Fashionable Enemies, he attends to many issues that the new atheists address, seeking to bring into focus the truth about the most radical revolution in Western history.¹ Considered by some to be one of the most brilliant scholars in the Christian world, Hart is nothing short of prolific, writing for the popular press and for theological journals while also producing a steady stream of books, both short and long.² The blurbs on the back cover of *Atheist Delusions* are given by a veritable who's who of the theological and intellectual elite, commenting on things such as Hart's "impressive erudition, polemical panache; devastating dissection; one of America's sharpest minds; learned, provocative and sophisticated; original and intellectually impressive." All of these lofty compliments combine with John Milbank's assessment that the new atheists "would never have dared put pen to paper had they known of the existence of David Bentley Hart. After this demolition job all that is left for them to do is to repent and rejoice at the discreditation of their erstwhile selves."

If theology is a blood sport, as it is sometimes described, then this book is a fine example of just that dynamic. What we have here, according to reviewer Matthew Feldman, is a "hyperventilating apologia for Christian humanism that might leave more mild-mannered readers somewhat uncomfortable."³ And Hart starts quickly with the new atheists in his sights, describing them variously as "manifestly moral idiots, extravagantly callow, borderline illiterate, guilty of intellectual caricature, failure of consecutive logic" and accusing Richard Dawkins of being a "tireless tractarian with an incapacity for philosophical reasoning" (3, 4).

However, my point is that despite such rhetorically incendiary material, which has come to be expected to some extent by readers of Hart, the new atheists are *not* at the center of the book. That is, the new atheists and their writings are not the topic of the book—at most, they and their ideas are the occasion for this book. So, as a response of sorts that does not consist of a point-by-point refutation of any particular writer's case, Hart offers a book that "concerns the history of the early church, of roughly the first four or five centuries, and the story of how Christendom was born out of the culture of late antiquity" (x). This central concern provides the material for Hart to argue "that among all the many great transitions that have marked the evolution of Western Civilization, whether convulsive or gradual, political or philosophical, social or scientific, material or spiritual, there has been only

---

1. Specific references to *Atheist Delusions* will be included in the body of the paper. I also gratefully acknowledge permission to use this essay, previously published as Doerksen, "Responding but Not Replying," *Directon* 40 no 1 (Spring 2011) 80–89.

2. For example, see Hart, *In the Beauty of the Infinite*; and Hart, *Doors of the Sea*.

3. Feldman, Review of *Atheist Delusions*, 379.

one—the triumph of Christianity—that can be called in the fullest sense a 'revolution': a truly massive and epochal revision of humanity's prevailing vision of reality, so pervasive in its influence and so vast in its consequences as actually to have created a new conception of the world, of history, of human nature, of time, and of moral good" (xiii). The negative side of his argument consists of his rejection of the myth or ideology of modernity, of the Enlightenment. He wants to shine a light on the grand narrative of the Enlightenment and replace it with a different narrative. Here Hart puts on display not only the content that he will deal with, but perhaps more significantly, also brings to view the way in which he understands theology ought to be pursued. In *The Beauty of the Infinite*, his earlier tour de force, Hart asserts that "Christian theology has no stake in the myth of disinterested rationality: the church has no arguments for its faith more convincing than the form of Christ; enjoined by Christ to preach the gospel, Christians must proclaim, exhort, bear witness, persuade—before other forms of reason can be marshaled."[4] Therefore, theology in its original condition is that of a story, "thoroughly dependent upon a sequence of historical events to which the only access is the report and practice of believers, a story whose truthfulness may be urged—even enacted—but never proved simply by the processes of scrupulous dialectic. What Christian thought offers the world is not a set of 'rational' arguments . . . rather, it stands before the world principally with the story it tells concerning God and creation, the form of Christ, the loveliness of the practice of Christian charity—and the rhetorical richness of its idiom."[5] For Hart, this earlier framing of the condition of theology, the way theology ought to be pursued, now functions without much comment or explicit defense as the impetus of the form of his response to the new atheists.

The overall structure of the book is simple enough—it begins with a brief description of the current situation, explores the way modernity has the story wrong, and then explicates the true nature of the Christian revolution, which is the advent of Christian humanism, or, as Hart puts it, "the Christian invention of the human," the section that he declares to be the heart of this book (xiii).

Hart's purpose in part 1, entitled "Faith, Reason, and Freedom: A View from the Present," is to set the table, to whet our appetites for his constructive work, and so he begrudgingly acknowledges the new atheists. But the purpose of introducing them is not to take them seriously, because they don't deserve to be taken seriously. Indeed, the strongest emotion that I

---

4. Hart, *In the Beauty of the Infinite*, 3.
5. Ibid., 3, 4.

sense in this section, especially in chapter 1, is a certain wistfulness and melancholy, a longing for the good old days when atheists were formidable opponents. When Celsus or Porphry challenged the early church, there was a challenge of substance; when David Hume, Voltaire, Denis Diderot, or Edward Gibbon would put pen to paper, at least there was a modicum of elegance, a dash of moral acuity. And then—Hart can hardly contain his admiration—then there's Nietzsche, that greatest atheist of them all, who had the good manners to despise Christianity for what it actually was. Ah, those were the days, when atheists were something to be reckoned with; now all we have are "gadflies [who] seem far lazier, less insightful, less subtle, less refined, more emotional, more ethically complacent, and far more interested in facile simplifications of history than in sober and demanding investigations of what Christianity is or has been" (6).

The salient point, according to Hart, is to see if a world devoid of religious belief would be better than a world in which the Christian revolution at least has some sway. The world we currently live in, insofar as it is modern, is one that Hart characterizes as an "age of freedom," but it's freedom of a particular kind. We have largely embraced a nihilistic notion of freedom whose ultimate horizon is nothing—perhaps of the kind Janis Joplin sang about, where "freedom's just another word for nothin' left to lose." When religion is understood within that model of radically autonomous individualist emancipation from all things transcendent, religion itself becomes what Hart calls something that is indistinguishable from interior decoration, insofar as "spirituality" is undemanding and therapeutic, pursued by purchasing any or all religious symbols ranging from dream catchers to Andean flutes (24). That kind of freedom is much different than the sort passed on to us by Christians such as Augustine, and so much the worse for us.

The second section of the book, entitled "The Mythology of the Secular Age: Modernity's Rewriting of the Christian Past," is really Hart's entry into what he calls "a struggle for the past." After all, as he points out in chapter 3, modernity gives an account of the past that has a so-called age of reason emerge from and overthrow the age of faith. This account, which we get from popular historians, is very misleading, Galileo's fate being just one of the stories used to paint the Christian faith in a negative light—but this tale is too simple, embraced by too many, and promoted by people who should know better.

But who hasn't heard this story—the one that suggests that Christianity introduced a "night of reason" into Western civilization? This narrative has Christianity, in an attempt to become fully dominant, plunge the world into a millennium of mental squalor, killing folks and generally wreaking all manner of havoc in order to keep the faithful ignorant, to exert power—after all, didn't Christians burn that big library? Hart takes notice of this way of reading history and carefully tries to reframe the story, not to refute each point. Christianity did not in fact violently burn anything and anyone opposed to it; it's simply not true, says Hart, and it's simply too simple. Allowing for some culpability on the part of Christians, Hart nevertheless argues that what we had in the ancient world was pagans versus Christians, but to a great degree they got on, conducted business, studied together, and so on (44). What was *not* the case was some kind of binary scenario in which we had in this corner pluralistic pagans who were open to rational and scientific inquiry, and in that corner irrational fideists who reveled in ignorance, and indeed *depended* on ignorance and violence precisely in order to perpetuate their Christian religion.

And neither is it true, argues Hart, that scientific knowledge and all manner of scholarship disappeared from the Christian world, only to survive, just barely, because of the Islamic religion, which meant that it survived in the Arabic language and had to be retranslated and brought back to the West when the influence of Christianity waned sufficiently. Simply put, Christianity did not reject all of classical civilization, seek to root it out and inaugurate the "Dark Ages."

All those accounts of Christianity trying to suppress science, of the church's "war against reason" that brought scientific inquiry and discovery to some screeching halt have been largely discredited, says Hart—discredited but still widely embraced. He lines up the amateur historian Charles Freeman in his sights and points out that Freeman "attempts long discourses on theological disputes that he simply does not understand, continually falls prey to vulgar misconstruals of the materials he is attempting to interpret, makes large claims about early Christian belief that are simply false, offers vague assertions about philosophers he clearly has not studied, and delivers himself of opinions regarding Christian teaching that are worse than simply inaccurate" (57). The case concerning faith and science rather is something like "Christian scientists educated in Christian universities and following a Christian tradition of scientific and mathematical." And Galileo—well, this was "one episode of asinine conflict among proud and intemperate men [which] does not exactly constitute a pattern of Christian intellectual malfeasance" (66).

But further, "the most splendid and engrossing of modernity's self-aggrandizing fables is that of Western humanity's struggle for liberation, of the great emancipation of Western culture from political tyranny, and of Europe's deliverance from the violence of religious intolerance" (75). Hart's burden here is to show that Christianity is guilty of violence, but that this is not necessarily because it is inherently violent. Rather, there is plenty of evidence to show that the state is violent, and that the tragedy occurs when Christianity is assumed into temporal power, when it becomes responsible for national or imperial unity. What we see in history is a constant struggle between the power of the gospel to alter and shape society and the power of the state to absorb the church into itself and make it useful to the ends of the state. Hart wonders whether we really think that if the church had stepped aside and allowed a fully secular society to emerge that violence would fade into the annals of history to be replaced by a long, soft summer of peace and safety. In fact, many of the so-called wars of religion, especially those of the sixteenth century, were in fact the birth pangs of the modern state, a point he takes from William Cavanaugh.[6]

Hart's transition into his constructive section is found in chapter 9, "An Age of Darkness." The burden of this chapter is to resist being drawn into an argument that defends Christianity but in so doing makes Christianity responsible for things such as "scientific progress," as though scientific progress is an unmixed good that itself need not be brought into question. To fall into this trap would be to act in a similar fashion to the kinds of apologists who claim that Christianity should not be reduced to science and reason, and then use only science and reason to make that very point.

And so we turn to the heart of the book—the Christian revolution, the Christian invention of the human, where Hart shifts gears considerably. In part 2, we saw him involved in polemics, in apologetics of the sort that encourages people to get the story straight. If that section may be understood as apologetics, then this section should be labeled as evangelism, the spreading of the word of the gospel. Frankly, this material, while difficult to reduce to sound-bite-sized pieces, nonetheless seems to me to be much more authentic as evangelistic material than some of the tools or techniques I've been exposed to in the past. For my money, rather than sharing *The Four Spiritual Laws* or being trained by folks like Bill Hybels to share my testimony over coffee within sixty seconds or so, when I get a chance to share the content of the Christian faith with someone, I'll say: Here, sit while I read pages 111 to 215 of this book to you. And when I'm done, all that will be left for that person to do is repent and embrace the truth that is theirs in the Christian revolution!

In his chapter "The Great Rebellion," Hart attempts to do several things: first, to show just how outrageous the gospel was in its time and place, and further, to show how the cataclysmic event of baptism initiated the believers into a community that held to a gospel that was seen as an

---

6. See Cavanaugh, "'A Fire Strong Enough to Consume the House'"; Cavanaugh, *Theopolitical Imagination*; and Cavanaugh, *Myth of Religious Violence*.

outrage. He identifies a spirit of rebellion, of sedition that we find difficult even to imagine today. We're not seen as rebellious now, just intolerant, as though the Roman world in its day was somehow tolerant. To say that the difference between Christianity and the Roman world was one of tolerance versus intolerance Hart identifies as anachronistic. The Romans, says Hart, were tolerant of what they found tolerable. The real problem was that the Roman pagan world had no social morality of which to speak; it deserved to be replaced, and Hart sees in the ancient world then a gradual ascendancy of Christianity before the days of Constantine, a new faith that was seen as preferable by many. It was not just Constantine's conversion that spread a faith that otherwise would have wallowed in obscurity only to finally disappear as a historical and ephemeral curiosity. Further, while Constantine's conversion, along with the subsequent legislations and so on, may have hastened the spread of Christianity in some ways, it is also true, argues Hart, that Constantine retarded the growth of the authentic faith in many and real ways.

Hart characterizes the Roman world as having "a glorious sadness." He sees there a "prevailing mood of cosmic disquiet," evidenced in the rise of certain Gnostic sects that were "a particularly acute and colorful expression of a spiritual yearning that was omnipresent in the empire" (141). As Hart puts it, Christianity

> entered into a twilit world of pervasive spiritual despondency and religious yearning, not as a cult of cosmic renunciation (pagan religions and philosophical culture required no tutelage in that) but as a religion of glad tidings, of new life, and that in all abundance ... the principal gift it offered to pagan culture was a liberation from spiritual anxiety, from the desperation born of a hopeless longing for escape, from the sadness of having to forsake all love of the world absolutely in order to find salvation, from the morbid terror of the body, and from the fear that the cosmic powers on high might prevent the spirit from reaching its heavenly home (143, 145).

Against this prevailing mood we find the gospel message, which is a liberating one. Christianity was not just another mystery cult that happened to have the most engaging myths, nor was it simply a series of threats and promises that suckered ignorant folk into believing, but a faith in which train follows social and moral difference. For Hart, the fact that hospitals appear wherever Christians have a significant presence, or better, the way Christians have a significant presence by building hospitals and hospices—that is evidence of a revolution. And, he claims, women, slaves, and the poor really feel the difference that the Christian revolution brings about—imperfectly to be sure, but the law of charity is one that cannot be swept away.

And then, perhaps my favorite chapter: "The Face of the Faceless," in which Hart's exposition of the significance of Peter's tears is achingly beautiful. We are heirs, Hart says, of a culture that sprang from Peter's tears (167). This frames his moving discussion of what he calls a "total humanism," the notion that all people, slaves, handicapped, weak, poor, women, have a face, because "Christians were willing to grant full humanity to persons of every class and condition, of either sex" (169). It is precisely this humanism wrought by the Christian faith that Nietzsche gazed upon with dismay and Julian the Apostate complained about. But "the scandal of the pagans, however, was the glory of the church" (170). This has often itself been compromised by the church, especially when the "church became that most lamentable of things—a pillar of respectable society" (171), but the early Christian faith is an essentially subversive movement. Alas, this radical nature we cannot recognize precisely because we are already Christian (173).

The following chapters 14 and 15 trace the continuing development of the revolution, one that converts, reshapes, reorients, and overthrows previous understandings. The Christian revolution was gradual, subtle, small, inchoate, but nonetheless real. Constantine's work probably retarded the revolution; in fact, if Hart had his way, Constantine the Christian emperor should have been more like the emperor Julian the Apostate, and perhaps the Christian revolution would have been more radical and thorough than it was. Nonetheless, Hart soldiers on, tracing the production of a moral vision of the human that has, as he puts it, "haunted us ever since."

Hart traces the development of this vision by looking at some of the great theological debates. The real issue in the nasty debate between Arius and Athanasius, according to Hart, is the nature and possibility of salvation as deification. This possibility (deification) ushers in a new "grammar of faith"—all of which makes a huge difference to our personal and psychological selves, as well as to the shape of our social lives. After all, this is a new metaphysics of the self, one in which our physical bodies are of utter importance; where we are gifted with immense dignity and infinite capacity. All of this is so much more than the liberal autonomous self put forward by modernity and postmodernity, wherein we essentially become walking choices—the bearer of freedom that has no horizon—whereas the Christian view cultivates an "unimaginably exalted view of the human" (213). And so, asks, Hart, what will happen to us if we actually become post-Christian—does that mean we will in a real sense also become post-human?

I believe that Hart's work, in both form and substance, is important theologically for the Christian church. If my assessment is correct, his work will linger and be read in the next generation and beyond, and I'd rather read him than most of the books that pass as Christian or spiritual writing today.

Nonetheless, several cautions are in order. In a lengthy review of this book in *First Things*, Paul Griffiths expresses considerable worry about the possibility that Hart has been seduced into playing a game that no one should play, that is, counting corpses and attributing blame. For example, when Hart says that Christianity is guilty of some violence but not nearly as much as the secular state, Griffiths thinks this is a move that is fundamentally pagan in flavor. In other words, for all of Hart's profundity, all of his provocative and brilliant prose, Griffiths thinks he detects a "world-weary, deeply ironic, . . . heavy sigh, weary shrug . . . the question 'You mean I have to engage this idiocy yet again?'"[7] This is a pagan flavor—a stance that Griffiths claims is a mixture of Eeyore and Hamaan, a trace of Chrysostom, and it trails clouds of paganism (echoing Wordsworth's poem). Griffiths also complains that Hart emphasizes the novelty of the Christian revolution to the detriment or oversight of the Jewish people and their scriptures. In the end, Hart also veers close to a certain idealism of the sort that privileges ideas and concepts above practices or loves.

Of course, it remains to be seen if Hart's work will have the kind of long-term influence of which I think it is capable. It seems that every time some putative threat to the Christian faith appears, there are those who are willing to challenge such challenges *seriatim*, and it would be churlish to dismiss such efforts out of hand. However, the kind of constructive theology on display here in Hart's book, which seeks to narrate the beauty of the story of the Christian revolution, offers a way of responding to such threats without allowing "fashionable enemies" to set the agenda in perpetuity. Come to that, neither should "'fashionable friends" be allowed to set the theological agenda.

---

7. Griffiths, "The Face of Civilization: Review of *Atheist Delusions*," 55.

10

Original Sin

Alan Jacobs. *Original Sin: A Cultural History*. New York: Harper, 2008.

> G.K. Chesterton famously states that original sin is the only provable Christian doctrine in existence. Alan Jacobs, in this cultural history of a doctrine that is often misunderstood, shows how the notion of original sin has shaped our political structures, how we teach and raise children, and especially how we understand ourselves. Does our Christian faith really require us to believe that all of us are bad to the bone?

What does it mean to be human? In the previous chapter, I tried to summarize a theologically generated view of the human put forward by David Bentley Hart, who says that we are heirs of a culture that sprang from Peter's tears.[1] This frames his moving discussion of what he calls a "total humanism," the notion that all people—slaves, handicapped, weak, poor, and women—have a face.

So to now turn to a consideration of original sin might seem a bit depressing. As I prepared this reflection, I recalled a hymn written by Isaac Watts that we used to sing in church.

> Alas! and did my Savior bleed
> And did my Sov'reign die?

---

1. Hart, *Atheist Delusions*, 167.

Would He devote that sacred head
For such a worm as I?

Refrain:
At the cross, at the cross where I first saw the light,
And the burden of my heart rolled away,
It was there by faith I received my sight,
And now I am happy all the day!

They don't write stuff like "for such a worm as I" anymore, and if they do, we don't sing it. After all, we believe that to promulgate that kind of theology is to make people think poorly of themselves; we'll raise kids with lousy self-esteem, we as adults will be unable to sustain positive relationships, and it'll be hell on evangelism, if that matters to us. So we ask, how can a message like that be relevant, how can it be seeker-friendly? How can it help us be the church in today's world? And on and on the reactions go, including a strong resistance to the notion that children are born in sin.

In the previous chapter we read a book occasioned by the so-called new atheists, in which we observed Hart setting out a case for belief based on a certain telling of the Christian story. And now we look at a particular doctrine that has fallen in disrepute, or is perhaps just largely ignored, at least in the church. Some of these questions are of course explored in literature and movies, such as *Dexter, East of Eden, No Country for Old Men,* but tend to be resisted in church.

The first question to consider is simply the nature of the doctrine. Perhaps as good a place as any to begin is by attempting definitions and descriptions, positively and negatively. There is a temptation that Jacobs almost falls into in this book, namely, to suggest that original sin is empirically verifiable, as suggested in those great aphorisms by G.K. Chesterton and Reinhold Niebuhr that describe sin as "the only doctrine for which there is physical evidence." But to understand original sin as verifiable, observable data is surely to warp the discussion from the get-go. We are not talking about some banal observation that bad things happen; original sin is not the first sin; it's not the point at which everything started to go wrong for you or me; it's not some tragedy. Rather, it is best understood as *peccatum originalis,* "sin that's already in us, already dwelling in us at our origin, at our very conception."[2] It's an "inherited affliction, collective and inherited responsibility, universally shared circumstances" (xiv). Put another way, "sin came into the world through one man; many died through one man's trespass; the judgment following one trespass brought condemnation; because of one

---

2. Jacobs, *Original Sin,* xiii. Subsequent references to the book will be included in the body of the essay.

man's trespass, death reigned; one trespass led to condemnation; by the one man's disobedience the many were made sinners" (47). Other terms used include "total depravity" and "primeval contagion." So *peccatum originalis* is a serious attempt to answer the question *Unde hoc malum?* Whence this evil?

If that's the doctrine described in brief, we have to ask if we believe it, and if so (or not), what difference does it make? There are after all a number of options available to us, such as Panglossian optimism. The figure of Pangloss (the name itself tells the tale of seeing everything as shiny) is given currency by Voltaire in his funny but caustic novel *Candide*. Panglossian optimism is a reference to the widely held and widely spread belief that we live in the best of all possible worlds (Leibniz), a belief that still holds significant currency in many circles. A Christian version of such a belief might be expressed as "everything will work out for the better"; or that "'God would not allow anything to happen that isn't somehow going to add up to good once everything is weighed in the balance."

Another available option might be labeled as Rousseauian idealism. Jean-Jacques Rousseau is famous for arguing that "man is born free, but is everywhere in chains," thus putting forward the notion that we are innocent and good. It is our relation with others, it is society that is corrupting, and thus presumably if we are left to pursue our own devices, we will flourish

We might also pursue revolutionary aspiration. We often find ourselves set about by barriers that have for one reason or another been erected before us; these might be in the form of moribund institutions, hidebound thinking, capitalist pigs, and if only we would be given the chance to fire up a revolution, we could sweep all that stands before us out of the way. Then when the coast is clear, because of who we are, we would flourish in ways not seen before. Such revolutionary aspirations have been expressed and acted upon many times throughout history, and radically so in the twentieth century. Or, we might embrace Victorian meliorism, the belief that the world can be made better through human effort.[3]

However, we want to consider what happens if we take seriously the doctrine of original sin, especially the one promulgated by Augustine drawing on Paul. Augustine is a key figure in Jacobs's account—even though this is a cultural history and an exemplary one, the fact that Augustine is at the center of things so often means that at least some theology has to be part of the conversation. And so it is here: Augustine takes Paul's writings, especially in Romans, and seeks to have them shape his own thought. We see this already in *Confessions*, wherein Augustine muses about the level

---

3. Jacobs discusses these and other kinds of views throughout the book; see pp. 226–27 for a brief summary statement.

of selfishness he sees within himself as when he is an infant suckling at his mother's breast. When he is confronted by the erstwhile Pelagius and the Donatists, Augustine continues to refine, and some would say harden, his views to the point where he makes us more than a little uncomfortable. Pelagius is concerned that Augustine's emphasis on grace, on loving God and doing as you please, creates a soft faith that simply excuses immoral behavior by papering it over with some vague belief that we cannot do any better. After all, we are all flawed. And if God then simply covers us with his grace, so much the better. And, complains Pelagius, where is the real free will if we are born with original sin? Further, it's not as though Pelagius is suggesting that God does not offer us his grace. What other than God's grace would have created a being who actually has the capacity to do right, who has the opportunity to do right, and who assumes personal responsibility? Pelagius is a formidable opponent, although no match for Augustine when it comes to gaining the upper hand in the halls of power.

The Donatists, another formidable opponent to Augustine, argue for the purity of the church, for the integrity of the sacraments and the priestly office, wanting to make sure that those who had denied the faith during the great persecutions could no longer be considered appropriate to baptize or to ordain. The primary concern was for the purity of the church. Not so, says Augustine; the sacraments are Christ's sacraments, and the one administering the sacrament can no more denigrate the reality of grace than deny the sacrifice of Christ. The church, says Augustine, is *corpus permixtum*, a mixed body of believers and unbelievers, and we know that this will always be the case because we are all sinners, all of us; we're born in it, why, we're even conceived in sin, according to the psalmist—"In sin, did my mother conceive me."

Consider what happens if we take the doctrine of original sin seriously. First, I think we have to admit that seen a certain way, there can be a bizarrely toxic mix that intertwines sin, sex, and condemned babies that just seems wrong. Augustine, no stranger to the pleasures of sex, comes to see it so closely related to an expression of sin that one cannot help but begin to understand why he turned to the monastic life when he embraced this very robust understanding of sin. Add to this his rather repulsive view of the damnation of unbaptized children, who, if unfortunate enough to die before being baptized may well find themselves crawling around for eternity on the floor of hell. It's all too easy to imagine that Augustine intends for us to have sexual intercourse only for the purpose of procreation and that without experiencing lust; then if a child is born from this union, you hope you can get the infant to a priest quickly; if and when you do, what you have is an original sinner. Add to that the way Augustine understands eating and drinking and all in all, this is not at first blush the formula for much fun.

However, Jacobs argues that this is surely not the whole story. Rather, he suggests that the doctrine of original sin can be curiously liberating. As Jacobs points out very nicely, Pelagianism writes the recipe for profound anxiety when the original encouragement of "You can do it" quickly leads to "But *am* I doing it?" The only true Christian life quickly becomes the life of severe asceticism and self-scrutiny. By contrast, says Jacobs, Augustine's emphasis on the depravity of human nature of curiously can be liberating precisely because it fosters a kind of total dependence on the grace of God. This reality gives hope to the backslider, the waverer, the slacker, and the putz. His focus on original sin allows and indeed shapes Augustine to be tolerant; the primeval contagion brings a paradoxical light (243).

Here I must bring Mennonites into the discussion (after all, Jacobs does not). Traditionally, Anabaptists have not embraced Augustine very enthusiastically, in part because we like to blame him for crystallizing and justifying the Just War Tradition, but not only that. We have tended to resist fairly strongly the line of Augustine that leads to Luther and John Calvin and their spiritual progeny. Some strict notions of predestination, original sin, and so on led to some of the abuses of the so-called Magisterial Reformation, that branch of the Reformation that dismissed Anabaptists as Enthusiasts that deserved persecution. So our Anabaptist forebears were sometimes seen as being pretty close to Pelagius's views of sin and grace, something like semi-Pelagian. Jacobs looks to be correct: isn't it true that our emphasis on choice and free will has led at least sometimes to a certain legalism, a tendency to try really hard, to want our churches to be made up of true believers, to describe those who disagree as "outside of the perfection of Christ" (Schleitheim Confession)? To rectify some of these negative tendencies, perhaps we should not work at having a more positive anthropology but a more robust view of original sin.[4]

---

4. The Mennonite Brethren Confession of Faith does not mention original sin; see Canadian Conference of Mennonite Brethren Churches, MB Confession of Faith Detailed Edition. Article 4 on "Sin and Evil" teaches the following:

Sin and Its Consequences

"We believe that the first humans yielded to the tempter, Satan, and fell into sin. Since then, all people disobey God and choose to sin, falling short of the glory of God. As a result, sin and evil have gained a hold in the world, disrupting God's purposes for the created order and alienating humans from God and therefore from creation, each other and themselves. Human sinfulness results in physical and spiritual death. Because all have sinned, all face eternal separation from God."

Notice the emphasis on the choice in sin.

It's interesting that we still carry the tendency to focus on the possibility of doing good works. So when Mennonites forsake the faith, when they no longer really believe in Jesus, they often still stay in the church, or at least remain connected—but in what capacity? As workers in the fields of justice, peace, environmental issues, and so on. From time to time someone like Stephen Dintaman[5] writes about the spiritual poverty of Anabaptism, but one might say that much of Anabaptist work would carry on even if you took Jesus out of the mix. If my diagnosis carries with it a modicum of truth, then it may be the case that we need more emphasis on original sin, not less, especially if it drives us into the arms of a gracious God.

Another reason to consider a more positive embrace of the doctrine of original sin is a connection to the practice of democracy.

> Jacobs follows the twentieth-century social theorist, Eugen Rosenstock-Huessy, in characterizing the consequence of this new observance as "the Christian democracy of the dead and the dying," "the first universal democracy in the world." When we understand everyone in the economy of salvation as both giving and receiving, it levels the ground beneath. No one is useless. And everyone is needy. Or, rather, no one is useless because everyone is needy. Paradoxically, the understanding that we are all profoundly flawed creatures disposes us more charitably toward one another. Or it can. Taken to heart, it means no one can scorn another from a position of essential superiority . . . the doctrine of original sin proceeds from, or at least resonates with, this egalitarian spirit. . . . And the doctrine of original sin insists that we all live by grace. More subtly and sympathetically, the doctrine has been resisted by modern social reformers, who do not wish to believe in the limited and mitigating character of their projects.[6]

Jacobs also argues, drawing on Blaise Pascal, that original sin explains both our misery and our ambition for happiness, that is, it explains us to ourselves (117). By happy coincidence, our philosophy club here at Mennonite Brethren Collegiate Institute was reading some of Pascal's famous book *Pensées* during the time that I was working my way through this. He writes in aphoristic style in that book—"Man's greatness comes from knowing he is wretched: a tree does not know it is wretched. Thus it is wretched to know that one is wretched, but there is greatness in knowing one is wretched."[7]

---

5. Dintaman, "Spiritual Poverty of the Anabaptist Vision."
6. Lipscomb, Review of *Original Sin*, 58.
7. Kreeft, *Christianity for Modern Pagans: Pascal's Pensées*, 58.

And again, "What sort of a freak then is man! How novel, how monstrous, how chaotic, how paradoxical, how prodigious! Judge of all things, feeble earthworm, repository of truth, sink of doubt and error, glory and refuse of the universe!" Pascal goes on to explore these matters, arguing that our condition is dual, and that that realization itself is not possible unless we have faith—that is, you need faith to know that you are a sinner.[8]

What I find missing to a large extent in Jacobs is the notion that sin is essential for salvation. Stanley Hauerwas argues, for example, that the discovery that we are sinners is part of the good news of the gospel. The doctrine of original sin is in fact only made possible through the resurrection of Christ.[9] Put another way, "Fathomless depth of sin may only be glimpsed under the tutelage of the Redeemer."[10]

To the question of what difference this doctrine makes, one of the topics Jacobs deals with happens to be one that is close to my heart, namely, education. I have probably been more influenced by the notion of the image of God than that of original sin, a tension discussed by Jacobs.

> Why do we so often need a doctrine of shared guilt to convince us of universal kinship? Shouldn't uplifting doctrines like the imago dei accomplish everything the fierce Augustinian doctrine does, and more? But, Jacobs writes, "a genuine commitment to the belief that we are all created equally in the image of God requires a certain imagination." To see in others—all others—the image of God requires a hard and uncertain effort of self-overcoming, bucking a natural tendency to identify with the ingroup. By contrast, "it takes relatively little imagination to look at another person and think that, though that person is not all he or she might be, neither am I." Jacobs remarks that this fact—that we often need the fierce doctrine to bring us around to appreciating our kinship with one another—"could be read as yet more evidence for the reality of original sin."[11]

What would happen, I ask myself, if I swallowed the notion of original sin in its Augustinian formulation and applied it to my teaching? I think I do to some extent already; for example, I don't believe everything my students say, and yet hope that we can have some level of authenticity at the same time; I can't assume that they will do their best work without guidance, but the guidance they need should be gracious, not punitive; since they are

---

8. Ibid., 108. See also Chesterton, "The Paradoxes of Christianity."
9. Hauerwas, "Sinsick," 18, 19.
10. Anderson, *Necessarium Adae Peccatum*," 39.
11. Lipscomb, Review of *Original Sin*, 59.

sinners, they need grace. But I'm also a sinner, and therefore it is the case that what I think might be grace may well not be—so, that leads me to conclude that my dealings with them are never the final word, allowing me to sustain hope for all my students.

I conclude by suggesting that we need to beware of embracing an Augustinian anthropology without its attendant theology. We know that we're like a two-headed calf (223), or as Alexander Solzhenitsyn famously put it, "the line separating good and evil passes neither through states, nor between classes, nor between political parties either—but right through every human heart."[12] But it is entirely possible to allow this recognition to turn us into depressed and hopeless people. After all, this is a theological anthropology that is embedded within a larger theology—a theology of grace.[13]

Are we really bad to the bone? That surely would explain a lot, but that's not nearly the whole story, and I refuse to believe it unless it is framed by the cross of Christ. Thus for me, Jacobs's book is not theological enough in the end.

---

12. Solzhenitsyn, *Gulag Archipelago Two*, 615–16.

13. Hauerwas's argument in "Sinsick" is that our condition as sinners is bounded by the more determinative reality of salvation.

11

Acedia and Me

Kathleen Norris. *Acedia and Me: A Marriage, Monks, and a Writer's Life.* New York: Riverhead Books, 2008.

> *The poet Kathleen Norris deals with what is probably a fairly widespread phenomenon—spiritual malaise—which the ancient Christians knew as acedia, or alternatively, the "noonday demon." She believes that the restless boredom, frantic escapism, commitment phobia, and enervating despair so many of us experience is the "ancient demon of acedia in modern dress." This is not indulgence in outrageous speculation but a serious attempt to understand a spiritual condition deeply experienced by Norris herself.*

Kathleen Norris is a poet who has also published what might be called "spiritual writing." In some of her other books we find collections of short meditations, or a kind of spiritual autobiography, a kind of writing with longstanding historical precedence going all the way back to Augustine's *Confessions*.[1] *Acedia and Me* is actually an essay in the truest sense of that word, a genre of writing which distinct form has its origins in the work of the French writer Montaigne. The word itself is derived from the French, used to describe a "try," an attempt to get at something and fully realize that such an attempt will be neither the beginning nor the end of the discussion. As such, an essay is not necessarily a conventional research paper or an

---

1. See Norris, *Dakota*; Norris, *Cloister Walk*; Norris, *Virgin of Bennington*; and Norris, *Amazing Grace*.

opinion piece but a serious attempt to bring forward some topic and work with it in an intelligent way. It is not so much the length that determines whether some piece is an essay, but the style. In that sense, *Acedia and Me*[2] is not a book but an essay, an attempt at understanding the interrelationships of several things such as acedia, a personal life, monastic discipline and teaching, marriage, and the craft of writing, and all of this within a Christian framework.

Before I consider the content of Norris's book, I want to be confessional (to some extent). Given that Norris is open about her life and relationships (although of course we have no idea just how open she really is; she chooses what to include or exclude for specific literary purposes), I thought I would try using her essay as a model for my musings. Instead of being coldly academic, or (God forbid) going into oversharing mode, I also want to, as kind of an experiment, be somewhat open about my own life. I'll insert some reflections along the way, but my experience will not be the center of attention.

I begin my confessional mode by letting you in on two very personal things, namely what I've been reading while I prepared for this evening, and secondly, what my family has experienced while I read, thought about, and then wrote this lecture. Let me begin with the family experience: I am the exact age that my dad was when he died very suddenly of heart trouble. Our family always holds its breath when someone reaches Dad's age of death, and sure enough, a younger brother recently experienced a heart attack, had to undergo an angioplasty, and is now on the slow road to recovery. However, his medical situation moved from the center of our attention, because another brother of ours has been in intensive care in Winnipeg's St. Boniface Hospital for the past three weeks or so, on a ventilator and very near death.[3] So, death and disease have been my companions in a very intense way over the past month especially. Along with that has come a stark face-off, as it were, with my own mortality. And while all of that has been going on, I have been reading some interesting material. I have re-read some of David Foster Wallace's work; he is considered by some to be *the* great American novelist, and sadly, a recent suicide. Reading him is a disturbing experience for me, because he sees beneath the surface of much of what passes as life, and what he sees is not comforting. I have also been reading Søren Kierkegaard by happy coincidence, since Norris refers to him quite a bit. Specifically, I was

---

2. Specific references to the book will be included in the body of the essay.

3. I originally presented this material on April 7, 2010. My younger brother is doing well; sadly, the other brother I mention here died in 2013.

reading *Works of Love*,[4] and those of you who know Kierkegaard realize that he is also keen to see the beneath the surface of our lives, especially our putatively Christian lives, and what he sees is also less than comforting. Indeed, once he was done with me in that book, I realized that much of what I consider to be loving may well be a thinly disguised, delusional form of selfishness and self-righteousness. Finally, I have been reading a wonderful book entitled *The Imaginative World of the Reformation*,[5] wherein Peter Matheson tries to sustain the argument that it might be best to understand the Reformation as the shattering of certain images, which are then replaced by other world-defining images; it is traumatic to have your imagination rocked and then replaced. My point is modest: while I've been working through *Acedia and Me*, I keep seeing myself in some of it, and I read almost hungrily, hoping that whatever form of acedia, of spiritual malaise I might be experiencing, might be addressed constructively and positively.

Acedia is one of those words that resists strongly a definition that comes anywhere near certitude. I like the way Norris circles around the concept, using ancient and modern sources, dictionaries, and so on, and it is within this circling that we get some sense both of what acedia *is* and what it *is not*.

Acedia used to be considered a sin, a deadly sin at that, and then it became a disease, and then a kind of lyrical emotion that can be fruitful for inspiration, and therefore can even be pursued in the name of creativity (121). According to Norris, there's some kind of connection of acedia to sin; she calls it a "vice that is best countered by spiritual practice and the discipline of prayer" (3). Norris has little time for any kind of discussion of original sin. Augustine's view of original sin, which undergirded Western Christianity's concept of sin, does not play much of a role here. Nonetheless, the doctrine of sin is important; after all, hope is the heart of the doctrine of sin. For Norris, the definition of sin is a very pragmatic one, encapsulated in the understanding that "to comprehend that something is wrong, and choose to do it anyway" (206). It is important that we do not ignore sin, or at least our sinfulness, because in doing so we run the risk of deluding ourselves in an infantile way by convincing ourselves that we do not need to take responsibility for our actions. Such an undeveloped self-consciousness is a manifestation of acedia.

As Norris points out, before the seven deadly sins became just that, there were eight "bad thoughts," and the difference between the one list and the other is acedia, which was classified as a bad thought but not one of

---

4. Kierkegaard, *Works of Love*.
5. Matheson, *Imaginative World of the Reformation*.

the deadly sins. Nonetheless, Norris argues that acedia is sin, which is to her a "viable concept, one that helps us explain the mess we've made of our battered, embattled world, and the shambles we make of so many personal relationships" (34). While in my view, Norris has a less-than-robust view of sin (God, Jesus, and the cross do not loom large in her discussions of sin), she sees it as important to categorize acedia as sin instead of as depression or despair. The categorization is important precisely because the treatment is determined at least in part by what we understand our condition to be. It is important also to recognize that Norris, following the early desert monks, uses the language of the demonic to capture the meaning of acedia—the "noonday demon." We do not get the sense that the demon is some kind of gargoyle-like creature that has an autonomous moral existence, some "thing" that floats around and does things to us. Rather, it seems that the demonic is something like a power, an influence that works primarily on the soul, on the thoughts and mental processes.

So, if acedia is not depression or despair or a disease but rather related to bad thoughts, sin, and "demon activity," what does it look like? Put another way, how is it manifested in our lives? Here Norris is slippery, and purposefully so. She in fact argues that acedia has a liminal status in the history of Western culture, "persistently eluding our attempts to comprehend it" (44). However hesitant she is to define or freeze acedia within some definition, she nonetheless does not hesitate to describe various dimensions of this spiritual condition. A partial list of her descriptors includes: noonday demon, apathy, torpor, boredom, vice, absence of care, the monk's temptation, malaise, soul-sickness, indolence, distraction, parody of leisure, carapace of sloth, ennui, despondency, paralysis of the soul, aversion of the appetite from its own good, ubiquity of indifference, rejection of a divine and entirely good gift, weariness of soul, deadly solipsism, thorough disengagement, chronic dissatisfaction, listlessness, being a spectator at life's banquet, caring too little about the right things, willful rejection of loveliness, refusal of joy, distorting mirror, sadness corroding our desire for God . . . and so on.

However, Norris is far too good a thinker and writer to simply list, describe, and explain these terms in some pedantic fashion. Rather, these descriptions make their way onto the page as parts of broader discussions of monastic teaching and practice, and alternatively as part and parcel of her depiction of her writing life and her marriage to David, and poignantly, his death. As her story unfolds, we as readers are placed into the position of participating in the story, and in so doing we learn how acedia works.

Acedia manifests itself as a confused heart that has lost joy within itself and so seeks consolation outside of itself. We find ourselves seeking exterior goods, perhaps never realizing that our seemingly insatiable desire for one thing or another—fashion, electronic goods, more books, a bigger and better house, more education, whatever—may well be the result of acedia, a spiritual condition that attaches itself to certain kinds of behavior by way of our bad thoughts. Indeed, even the pursuit of spiritual practices can itself become self-indulgence that results from a spiritual malaise, a search for novelty that simply will not go away, because the nature of the desire for novelty is that it can never be satisfied.[6]

Acedia also manifests itself as the failure to escape from the closed circle of the self (145). Here Norris is really interesting as she tries hard to find her way through the differences between therapy and healing. It is hard to say if she's successful, but she is compelling on one point. That is, she refuses to reduce the response to malaise as simply an intensified search for sincerity. Here she refers to Oscar Wilde (sincerity is the worst vice of the fanatic) and Henri de Lubac. "It is not sincerity, it is Truth which frees us, because it transforms us. To seek sincerity above all things is perhaps, at bottom, not to want to be transformed" (143). Put another way, we need more self-knowledge and less self-consciousness.

Another way in which acedia manifests itself is in a certain kind of openness to things that we would not otherwise embrace. So, for example, when one is afflicted by acedia and then is confronted with an experience of grief, it may be the case that grief attaches itself to the acedia, creating the kind of sadness that ultimately corrodes our desire for God (261, 324).

Further, we find the version of acedia that cannot come to grips with the quotidian dimensions of everyday life. The kinds of things that make up everyday life become somehow impossible to carry out, since it seems to us that those things are without significant meaning and since they are so seemingly insignificant, they do not deserve any of our attention. If one is struggling with such malaise, it seems useless to make the beds, take out the trash, plan ahead for this week's menu, and so on. It may even be the case that those very quotidian dimensions of life loom over us as the cause of our malaise, and we think that other people are saving the world while here I am picking up dog shit in the back yard.

Connected to the manifestations of acedia is the fact that we live in a world in which the "perfect vehicles" of acedia have emerged. According to Norris, in our hyped-up world, broadcast and Internet news media by their very nature demand that we care equally and all at once about celebrity divorce, terrorism, technological advances, and so on, giving us no way

---

6. This is one of the main complaints that I have of the so-called Emerging Church movement, and especially Brian McLaren. See my article, "The Air Is Not Quite Fresh."

to discern between truly horrific events and those that are merely gossip. Our world has been flattened and we are incapable of giving appropriate *gravitas* to anything because we do not know to what we ought to pay attention. Norris draws on Thomas Merton for this material, but she could just as easily have drawn on Neil Postman and his classic *Amusing Ourselves to Death* (1985), wherein he argues that media are a form of epistemology that actually shape the way we think and indeed what we are capable of thinking about. Thus we are ultimately guilty of idolatry.

But what to do? That is the question. We know we're dealing with some kind of spiritual malaise, some soul-sickness, sin, or demonic power that leaves us incapable of seeing the truth, of connecting with people, of pursuing our desire for God; it deadens our souls, leaves us feeling out of sorts with a strong sense of being adrift. All the while, we seem to be perfectly capable of carrying on, but things are not right, and we and those close to us know it all too well.

For Norris, the way through and beyond the spiritual condition of acedia is through spiritual discipline, beginning with the analysis of our thoughts, which, according to some ancient monks, would allow us to "take hold of our souls."[7] The point here is to experience our emotions, to embrace what we are facing—not in the sense of refusing to do anything about our feelings, but refusing to ignore what is actually going on in our souls. This is difficult, humbling, humiliating even, but absolutely necessary. Norris returns to this notion a number of times in the book, showing how the early monastics would study their own thoughts as they arose, noting which thoughts were life-giving and which were destructive (88). They noted, too, how these thoughts come upon us, which of them are easily resisted, and which are "vexatious." Norris also refers to this process as "spiritual discernment" (147), the practice of asking ourselves how it is that one thought can beget another, and how these thoughts interconnect.

In addition to the spiritual discipline of self-knowledge, Norris also asserts the importance of "looking beneath the surface of things." "It is hard to look beneath the surfaces presented to us" (129), to examine cultural and historical forces underlying current conditions. Norris herself doesn't do much of this in the book; nonetheless, her point is well taken. In fact, if I were to apply this advice to my own discipline of teaching, I would say that one of the primary shaping initiatives of my teaching is to teach students to look beneath the surface of things, to read and think, to think about what they read, to think about what they think, to guide them to the kinds of

---

7. Miles, *Word Made Flesh*, 86.

writers and thinkers who might help them and me to see beneath the surface of things.

As we try to resist and respond to acedia, Norris suggests that we turn to constructive sources. She quotes the old saying, "Life's a bitch and then you die" (132), but not as a conclusive assertion. Instead, she continues by saying that even if that's what life is like, why not find a psalm and sing it anyway? She also suggests reading early Christian theology as a source for addressing acedia. One of the strongest reasons for her own use of Kierkegaard is that he turns to early Christian writings as the taproot for his work, which in Norris's view is what makes Kierkegaard's writing so fecund for the resistance to acedia. Instead of trying to keep up with all of the latest and most popular Christian writers via live satellite feeds and other social media, why not read some of the ancients? asks Norris.[8]

Further, Norris returns a number of times to the notion of repetition and routine as basic to resisting acedia. For example, if she finds herself avoiding the basics of life such as making her bed because she knows she'll just go to bed again anyway, she recognizes this as an early warning sign of the approach of malaise. Or sometimes she can't seem to see any meaning in these quotidian tasks even if she does them; this too is a sign of an imbalance. Then she may use the mundane tasks of life as a way of resisting the onset of acedia. As she puts it, routine is the scaffolding of a life, repetition a saving grace (chapter 10). Therefore, instead of looking to novelty, unique interventions, and what not, she returns again and again to the basic things that make up a life, seeking to understand the significance of such tasks and disciplines and resisting the temptation to think that it is only the non-mundane that makes up a faithful life. According to Norris, it is not the exotic travel experiences (and the like) that make up a life, but in thinking that those things make up a life that we are succumbing to the temptation of acedia. After all, Norris argues at some length (40, 41), boredom is important. Closely related to all of this is the quality of attention (190), a concept that has been addressed with great clarity by the late French philosopher Simone Weil in her fascinating essay entitled "Reflection on the Right Use of School Studies with a View to the Love of God."[9] In it, Weil begins her argument by noting the key realization that prayer consists in paying attention; the quality of attention accounts for much of the quality of prayer. School exercises can be an integral part of developing a lower kind of attention, but one that nonetheless increases the power of attention available at the time of

---

8. Some of Norris's books display the kind of reflection on early sources she is so keen to promote here.

9. Weil, "Reflection on the Right Use of School Studies."

prayer. According to this argument, the intrinsic interest of a subject is secondary to the capacity for paying attention; even if we have no aptitude for geometry, nevertheless our faculty of attention can be developed by studying a theorem or solving a problem. Every time a human being succeeds in making an effort of attention with the goal of increasing the grasp of truth, she acquires a greater aptitude for it. "Students must therefore work without any wish to gain good marks, to pass examinations, to win school successes, without any reference to their natural abilities and tastes, applying themselves equally to all of their tasks with the idea that each one will help then to form in them the habit of that attention which is the substance of prayer . . . happy are those who pass their adolescence and youth developing this power of attention."[10]

Norris's engaging and provocative book should also be subjected to constructive critical analysis. First, I confess to significant ambivalence about the level of self-referential material in the book. Given what Norris has taught me in this book, I want to practice some discernment—where does my ambivalence come from? Perhaps I'm reacting to her level of self-disclosure (also very evident in *Dakota* and *The Virgin of Bennington*) simply because of my own reticence to share my life on the page for fear of being far too vulnerable; perhaps my reticence is nothing more than self-protection. However, perhaps my ambivalence here has something to do the feeling that I'm being played just a bit. After all, as open as Norris claims to be, I know that as a writer she chooses about what to be open, and that what she reveals is shaped by her agenda for each of the books in which she is putatively open.

However, I hasten to add that the fact that Norris takes spiritual experience, especially malaise, seriously is very compelling, because her way of taking it seriously does not reduce it to some "triumph of the therapeutic." Put another way, her descriptions of experience are mostly diagnostic and constructive, taking the Christian tradition into account but without reducing that tradition to a series of devotional platitudes. Norris's book, overall, is a gift to those who struggle to confront the noonday demon that comes in the guise of spiritual malaise.

---

10. Ibid., 108, 114.

12

Shop Class as Soulcraft

Matthew B. Crawford. *Shop Class as Soulcraft: An Inquiry into the Value of Work*. New York: Penguin, 2009.

> What does one do with a PhD in political philosophy from the University of Chicago? Why, become a motorcycle mechanic, of course. It is this kind of work that requires real mastery of real things, the kind of work that cannot easily be outsourced. Further, practice of the "useful arts," which seeks to resist our increasing manual disengagement, may well provide the crucible in which our souls can and should be shaped in important ways. Or so claims Crawford, in this "beautiful little book about human excellence and the way it is undervalued."

Matthew Crawford is an electrician, political philosopher, and now owner of Shockoe Moto in Richmond, Virginia, where he is a motorcycle mechanic specializing in repairing imports. The front cover of the book displays a vintage BMW, the back a picture of Crawford insouciantly leaning against the doorframe, wrench in one hand, the other resting nonchalantly on the handlebar of some other cool bike. This is not your typical author photograph, especially if the author is a philosopher (pipe-smoking, Scotch-drinking, leather-patch-on-elbow-wearing old guy whose image screams irrelevance and obscurantism).[1]

---

1. Dineen, "Whole Hog."

Crawford worries about the disappearance of tools, the "creeping concealedness" of machines. His ideal is manual competence, not only as some end in itself but for the stance it entails toward the built, material world. His is a project concerned with the experience of making things, fixing things, and how this is related to human flourishing. Along the way, he wants to interrogate the assumptions that lull us all into accepting manual disengagement.

Crawford would approve I think, of my friend Myron, who recently sold the house his family had been living in for some time. As he left, he walked through the house, running his hand over all of the things that he's built with his own hands in that house. Crawford would not approve of me so much, I can't help but think. I can't do a damn thing with my hands. I try to be funny when people talk to me about this kind of thing and tell them that the only tool I can actually handle is a shovel (although in actuality I also can work a rake). Some time ago, my neighbor helped me with something practical, and when in good neighborly fashion I told him to ask me if he ever needed any help, he asked, "What are you going to do—write me a paper?" Coincidentally, while reading this book, my brother Mark and I together tried to repair an old garbage trailer. With seven university degrees between the two of us and a trip to Princess Auto for various parts, we managed to kind of get the thing working—if you consider the fact that the signal works only when you press the brake at the same time as the signal is on. In fact, any part of that process that was successful was due to my brother. I'm afraid Matthew Crawford would consider me part of the problem, not part of the solution.

Crawford's concern has to do with dimensions of the human experience such as individual agency, competence, usefulness, ethics, meaningful work, and the intelligibility of the world to ourselves. So he makes a case for the useful arts in which he is keen to deny or resist the dualism that he sees between knowledge work and manual work. His alternative account gives credit to the cognitive richness of the skilled manual trades. His point is that elaborate potential for human flourishing exists in the manual trades. The craftsmanship pursued within them is not some precious pursuit of luxury items within an otherwise manually disengaged way of life. Rather, craftsmanship—grappling with material things and processes, repairing things, dealing with durable objects—calls for embodied manipulations. Craftsmanship puts us in the service of others, it chastens the easy fantasy of mastery that permeates modern culture, it makes us aware of our interdependence, it refers to objective standards that do not issue from the self and its desires, and thus posits a direct challenge to consumerist culture.² But somewhere along the line a dualism has been created between mental and manual labor, between blue and white collar work, the history of which Crawford traces in the first chapter of the book.

In seeking to understand, embrace what we can, and resist what we should, I want to bring to view three dimensions of Crawford's treatment of the "useful arts," the practice of which seek to resist our increasing manual disengagement, and which he claims may well provide the crucible in which our souls can and should be shaped in important ways. These dimensions include a) epistemology—the theory of knowledge, its method and validation; b) anthropology—an understanding of the human being; and c) morality—some notion of what's right or wrong, what constitutes the good life in which the human being flourishes. These three dimensions or categories aren't entirely discreet from one another; the boundaries are permeable, and we won't make too much of it if the discussion of one leads into another and back again, but I'll use these dimensions as a kind of heuristic device to give some shape to the material.

When we speak of the acquiring of knowledge, it feels natural to think in terms of thinking; the task seems as if it consists primarily in brainwork. But to think like that is itself a product of a dualism that has arisen contingently, and in Crawford's view, it's a false dualism. Simply put, the modern world (and Descartes is often seen as the original sinner here) has separated thinking from doing, and in the process has elevated thinking and thus denigrated and degraded manual work. The result is that we are getting stupider every day. Crawford offers a standard treatment of how blue collar work has been degraded; much more interesting is his bringing to view the degradation of white collar work with its mind-numbing routinization, resulting in a rising sea of clerkdom, as he puts it. In a fascinating section entitled "Everyone an Einstein," Crawford takes on what the practice of "harnessing creativity," wherein everyone from the top to the bottom of the employee scale is apparently free to offer creative solutions to problems, implement initiatives, and so on. But even here Crawford sees not so much real creative possibilities as managerial ass-covering. Creativity is really something that is a by-product of mastery of the sort that is cultivated through long practice (47–52).³

---

2. Crawford, *Shop Class as Soulcraft*, 16, 17. Subsequent references to the book will be included in the body of the essay.

3. I am reminded here of a speech Wynton Marsalis delivered during a jazz concert, in which he claimed that improvisation is possible only if the musician knows her scales cold.

Crawford is interested in reuniting thinking and doing, in order to change our conception to "thinking as doing." Thus the acquisition of knowledge has to do with confronting real things in real situations, on a personal basis, wherein an individual takes responsibility and in so doing learns in a particular way. This kind of knowledge is neither fully formalizable nor essentially rule-like. Real knowledge, argues Crawford, comes from confrontations with real things, and it is in these kinds of dealings with real things that we move away from the abstract and also confront our narcissistic refusal to grapple with material work. In addition, in such attempts to gain real knowledge, we confront the experience of being wrong as an important and real part of what it means to actually gain knowledge. The opportunity to be wrong has largely been edited out of the education experience, complains Crawford (204).

Part of discussion of thinking as doing includes a reference to "tacit knowledge," wherein Crawford draws heavily on the work of the great twentieth-century thinker Michael Polanyi. To illustrate the notion of tacit knowledge, we are given the example of the firefighter. Algorithms can't always represent the states of the world and its vagaries formally by some sort of code that claims to be able to explain it all. Part of the problem is that while those kinds of representations of the states of the world carry significant amounts of factual information, they disseminate such information precisely as *information*, and thus treat it in isolation from the context in which the *meaning* of that information arises. Sometimes a firefighter can tell when a building is about to blow; this kind of knowledge comes from accumulated experience and often unarticulated or even unarticulatable account of things—this is tacit knowledge. Therefore, theoretical knowledge is open to radical critique on these grounds (171). So, Crawford is really joining an initiative to place epistemology on a footing that joins thinking and doing, places the knower within a tradition, and calls for the embodied participation of the human in learning the useful arts.[4]

You can't read this book without being confronted with the term "individual agency." I confess to a default position that arises in me when I run across such a term: I'm afraid that we're about to get some impassioned defense of freedom understood as having all barriers to self-expression removed, some version of "let me do whatever the hell I want to do" emancipation from the strictures of society. But this is not the case here. In fact, Crawford is at pains to distance himself from an ideological notion of choice, freedom, and autonomy that results in some warped version of the

---

4. Mitchell, "Tacit Dimension of Shop Class."

"Unfettered Self" (63). This whole discussion makes him realize that nothing less than an anthropology is at stake.

> Thinking about manual engagement seems to require nothing less than that we consider what a human being is. That is, we are led to consider how the specifically human manner of being is lit up, as it were, by man's interaction with his world through his hands. For this a new sort of anthropology is called for, one that is adequate for our experience of agency. Such an account might illuminate the appeal of manual work in a way that is neither romantic nor nostalgic, but rather simply gives credit to the practice of building things, fixing things, and routinely tending to things, as an element of human flourishing. (63–64)

So, what does manual engagement have to do with this? According to Crawford's account of things, meaningful work and self-reliance inhabit overlapping territories as ideals that are tied specifically to the struggle for individual agency (7). His definition of agency is "activity directed toward some end that is affirmed as good by the actor" (206). Or as he puts it in chapter 3, we want to and should be "masters of our own stuff;" we want the world to be intelligible so that we can be responsible. It's important to Crawford that we recognize and embrace the "concrete heterogeneity of human experience" (55), which flies in the face of the presumption held by some, that is, the fungibility of human experience—that all of our activities are equivalent or interchangeable, as they seem to be when reduced to clock time or to repeatable actions that don't require any kind of real engagement.

A very interesting feature of this discussion is the notion that to be master of one's own stuff entails the "prideful basis of self-reliance," but Crawford is quick to move on to show that neither pride nor self-reliance is the end of his idea of agency. Instead, he is at pains to demonstrate that we necessarily encounter a paradox, namely, that to be the master of anything also calls for the individual to be mastered by that thing. That is, our agency arises within concrete limits that are *not* of our own making. Repairing a motorcycle is an example of this paradox. To fix a motorcycle is not just to impose our will on that thing; it calls for judging rightly, paying attention, being part of bringing the motorcycle to do what it was designed to do by somebody external to us. Therefore, embodied agency is not simply something like "self-esteem" or "self-expression," and it certainly calls us to move beyond the temptation of solipsism that is so endemic to our modern society (57ff.). The negative example of being masters of our own stuff is a place like Build-A-Bear, wherein the consumer chooses between predetermined alternatives, offered presumably because someone else has judged these available options as "good" (68–71).

Somewhere within this discussion of both epistemology and anthropology belongs at least a mention of Gnosticism, that ancient heresy that dogged the ancient church and in certain forms continues to do so. The Gnostics split asunder many things that belonged together—Old Testament from New, Jewish faith from Christian, body from soul, and here the work of the mind and the work of the hands.[5] According to Mark Mitchell, "the result of this elevation of the mental over the physical is what amounts to a practical Gnosticism whereby the body is denigrated or ignored and the mental faculties are given a prestige that exceeds their capacity." Mitchell then quotes Wendell Berry: "It is clear to anyone who looks carefully at any crowd that we are wasting our bodies exactly as we are wasting our land. Our bodies are fat, weak, joyless, sickly, ugly, the virtual prey of the manufacturers of medicine and cosmetics. Our bodies have become marginal; they are growing useless like our 'marginal land' because we have less and less use for them. After the games and idle flourishes of youth, we use them only as shipping cartons to transport our brains and our few employable muscles back and forth to work."[6] In these discussions of epistemology and anthropology, Crawford seeks to make an argument for manual competence as the way to orient ourselves so that our knowledge along with our understanding of what it means to be human can flourish.

Closely related to both of these concepts is that of morality. Crawford argues that the stochastic arts that he's put before us work in such a way as to diagnose and fix things that are variable, that are not of our own making, not fully knowable. All of these matters require a disposition that is both cognitive *and* moral. As far as I can see, his notion of the moral has to do with human flourishing. Getting things right requires that we be attentive in the way of a conversation rather than assertive in the way of a demonstration (82). That is to say, the mechanical arts have a special significance for our time because they cultivate the virtue of attentiveness, a way of seeing. He writes of trying to bushwhack his way through a thick undergrowth of perception with no apparent way forward to comprehension (while trying to draw a skeleton). Crawford tries to argue that seeing rightly, developing vision, is something that must be done without literally being an "idiot," in the old sense of the word (i.e., private). What is required is to see clearly and unselfishly, recognizing the possibility of being wrong, what Iris Murdoch

---

5. Dineen, "Whole Hog."

6. Mitchell, "Tacit Dimension of Shop Class." Mitchell is quoting from Berry, *Unsettling of America*, 108.

calls "unselfing." We don't just sit back and look, but we see *and* do—and thus move ever closer to actions that are just and bring them into conformity with a vision that is just. This calls for perpetual iteration between seeing and doing—"our vision is improved by acting, as this brings any defect in our perception to vivid awareness" (100). As Crawford puts it, to respond to the world justly, you have to see it clearly, and for this you have to get outside of your head (103). This quality of vision isn't something that I can take for granted in myself, says Crawford, but needs to be achieved on a moment-by-moment basis. Here the source being drawn on most explicitly is Iris Murdoch, and especially her wonderful book *The Sovereignty of Good*.

> I can only choose within the world I can *see*, in the moral sense of "see" which implies that clear vision is a result of moral imagination and moral effort . . . One is often compelled almost automatically by what one *can* see. If we ignore the prior work of attention and notice only the emptiness of the moment of choice we are likely to identify freedom with the outward movement since there is nothing else to identify it with. But if we consider what the work of attention is like, how continuously it goes on, and how imperceptibly it builds up structures of values around us, we shall not be surprised that at crucial moments of choice most of the business of choice is already over. This does not imply that we are not free, certainly not. But it implies that the exercise of our freedom is a small piecemeal business which goes on all the time and not a grandiose leaping about unimpeded at important moments. The moral life, in this view, is something that goes on continually, not something that is switched off between the occurrences of explicit moral choices. What happens in between choices is indeed what is crucial.[7]

A similar kind of argument can also be seen in Michael Polanyi:

> Personal knowledge . . . is not made but discovered, and as such it claims to establish contact with reality beyond the clues on which it relies. It commits us, passionately and far beyond our comprehension, to a vision of reality. Of this responsibility we cannot divest ourselves by setting up objective criteria of verifiability—or falsifiability, or testability, or what you will. For we live in it as in the garment of our own skin. Like love, to which it is akin, this commitment is a "shirt of flame," blazing with passion and, also like love, consumed by devotion to a universal demand.[8]

7. Murdoch, *Sovereignty of Good*, 37.
8. Polanyi, *Personal Knowledge*, 64.

In response to Crawford's work, I would like to raise several issues. First, there is at least some concern that in the end, Crawford's own work is useful only insofar as it enables men to ride motorcycles, an activity about which he waxes positively poetic. Motorcycle riders have gotten something right—it's a "kingly sport that is like war made beautiful" (196). Kalefa Sanneh claims that Crawford may have set out to write a book about work but has succeeded only in writing about consumption, about men riding motorcycles—import bikes no less, and this despite his criticisms of outsourcing. He's a connoisseur, says Sanneh, and more concerned about shoddy workmanship than shoddy working conditions.[9] As clever as Sanneh's review is, and as concerned as he is with Marxist analysis, this is patently unfair to Crawford. It's as though Sanneh missed the point that what is being argued for is a disposition that finds a place in the world. In other words, it's a strength of the book that you can put it into practice without being a motorcycle mechanic. This doesn't let Crawford off the hook entirely, and part of the problem is exactly that his is a manly book in a certain kind of a way. The crew or the shop are settings where men can be men, and where part of being apprenticed into a craft includes the learned skill of using foul language (which we are also exposed to here in this learned book), telling dirty jokes, and learning how to be the butt of filthy discourse and learning then too how to use it appropriately.

I'm not sure how to articulate this next observation, because no doubt I'll appear defensive. I'm not sure where I fit in as a teacher. You all know the old adage about teachers: Those who can, do; those who can't, teach. (Those who can't teach, teach teachers.) What happens, if anything, to the sensibilities, ideals, practices that Crawford sees as so important to human flourishing? He does mention teachers (and medical workers) ever so briefly, almost tangentially (182). I like the emphasis on "focused attention," but I wonder what else might be learned. What is it about teaching that calls on me for the shaping of epistemology? Anthropology? Morality? Is it the case that when I confront a student (in the broader sense of having the student before me, kinda like a bike on a bench) that I must now open myself not only to master the situation/student, but also to be mastered by that student? What might it mean to assert my embodied agency in a way that calls for my judgment? My engagement? In what sense, if any, can I be understood to be part of making something here? Of fixing something?

I confess that I often feel as though I'm preparing students to be knowledge workers. I have noticed over the years that when a former student I happen to meet responds to the question of what they're up to, they look

---

9. Sanneh, "Out of the Office."

decidedly sheepish if they're not somehow involved in academics. What have I done, I ask myself? And so, where am I in Crawford's vision? I came away from this book wondering where those in the so-called caring professions, such as teachers, childcare workers, medical workers, and pastors, might fit in.

As far as secular, liberal visions of the world, of the good, and of human flourishing go, this is one of my favorites. In the end it's still a liberal, secular vision, but it's one that draws on at least some Christian sources, such as Michael Polanyi and Alasdair MacIntyre. I'm not trying to make some sort of move that counts up Christian sources versus non-Christian sources, and then based on that kind of calculus declares this to be a Christian book or not. That's not the point; that's never the point when we read! But surely, a Christian reader who confronts a vision that addresses issues such as epistemology, anthropology, and morality will think about where the shape of the Christian faith comes to bear. There will surely be some overlap, often in unexpected and wonderful places; if we maintain the kind of openness to which our Christian faith calls us, we may well be confronted with ways in which we have to change our thinking and doing.

So I want to at least pose the question that I so often pose to students when we're studying Christian theology or ethics: "What's *Christian* about that?" I won't answer that question here, but let me display briefly what it might mean to push Crawford in the direction of faith. In the discussion of epistemology, for example, I'd like to know what role belief might play in the pursuit and shape of knowing. For centuries, Christians have claimed something along the lines of "I believe in order to understand," which has functioned in different ways in different times, but at the very least calls into question the overblown trust in the unaided power of reason, of rationalism to be the basis of all knowledge. And what about love and/or worship? What about peace as an epistemological shaping power? Polanyi hints at this in his work—we come to know that which we love. As for Crawford, his work is potentially fruitful as a way of teaching us to embrace neglected practices that have the power to shape us.

13

Following Jesus in a Culture of Fear

Scott Bader-Saye. *Following Jesus in a Culture of Fear*. Grand Rapids: Brazos Press, 2007.

The world is a formidable place, and it is easy to let fear rule the day. What will happen to our children? Are we safe from terrorism? Who profits from our fear? And how does confessing Jesus Christ address our fears, at least some of which surely are legitimate? What we need is some clear, sensible reflection on fear: how to acknowledge it without being manipulated by it, how to resist it without assuming we should (or could) be fearless, how to receive it as a gift (if it can be a gift) without letting it dominate our lives. After all, Jesus does not promise safety to those who follow him.

Julian Barnes's book *Nothing to Be Frightened Of* offers a great opening line, "I don't believe in God, but I miss him." The book is an extended memoir of sorts, dealing with one of the threads that prevails throughout Barnes's life, namely, his lifelong fear of and obsession with death, and his refusal to embrace that great consolation of religious belief. After all, it appears that sometimes we do just that: we use belief as a way to dispel fear. Barnes cites the example of the great philosopher Ludwig Wittgenstein, who for a time taught elementary age children. He supervised a school hike and, noticing the fear that was beginning to be expressed as night began to fall, Wittgenstein apparently went from pupil to pupil saying quietly, "Are you afraid? Well, then you must think only about God." Quite aside from questions of truth/reality, to believe in God in the midst of such an instance is portrayed by Barnes as harmless, and maybe even helpful. Belief in a nonexistent god can at least dispel fear of nonexistent elves, sprites, and wood demons.[1]

Even if fear of death is not the particular issue, it seems there is plenty of fear to go 'round—fear of the economy, of global warming, extremist terrorism, disease, species extinction—and the list goes on. In an article entitled "How Complex the Culture of Fear," addressing the fear of immigration, Irshad Manji argues that "the culture of fear isn't merely one in which the natives fear the immigrants. It's one in which people of all backgrounds fear being branded for their sincere worries about whether unity can be extracted from diversity. After all, if you don't know who you are, to what are you asking newcomers to adapt?" The concern in this article is the Swedish experience, wherein there doesn't seem enough of a connection to tradition to be able to deal with the "other."[2]

As is obvious, fear is not just a personal, existential condition, it is also political, public, and global in scope. Further, it is seen by some influential thinkers as constructive, as the basis on which to organize society. Thomas Hobbes, writing in post–Reformation England, produced a number of political, philosophical, and theological works but is most closely identified with *Leviathan*, in which he draws on all of these streams of thought to produce his vision of a commonwealth that could produce peace, one that would avoid the gruesome violence of the so-called wars of religion, especially that of the Thirty Years War (1618–48). Life is tough; Hobbes claims that in its natural state, not only is life solitary, nasty, brutish, and short, but that what we see in nature is quite simply a "war of all against all." Left to our own devices, we will turn on each other and all hell will break loose. Therefore, what we need is some way to construct a peaceful commonwealth. Hobbes's concern for this kind of peaceful commonwealth that avoids religious warfare is the heart of his project, which develops a theological justification for a society created through a *social contract* in which the people hand over, by consent, the right to govern to a civil sovereign (either an individual or a group). The commonwealth thus artificially created is known as *Leviathan*.[3]

---

1. Barnes, *Nothing to Be Frightened Of*, 21–22.
2. Manji, "How Complex the Culture of Fear."
3. Hobbes, *Leviathan*. Among the many issues that Hobbes must face in the manufacturing of this artifice is that of Christianity, and more specifically, the role of the church. If the Christian faith, which Hobbes believes cannot be discarded, when socially organized into the church poses a threat to the commonwealth, then Hobbes has to find a way for the church to have an appropriate place within *Leviathan*. He does just

For a more recent political vision centered on fear, we might turn to Judith Shklar, who argues that "liberalism has only one overriding aim: to secure the political conditions that are necessary for the exercise of personal freedom . . . every adult should be able to make as many effective decisions without fear or favor about as many aspects of her or his life as is compatible with the like freedom of every other adult . . . apart from prohibiting interference with the freedom of others, liberalism does not have any particular positive doctrines about how people are to conduct their lives or what personal choices they are to make."[4] Fear is a political notion, according to Shklar, because the fear and favor that have inhibited freedom are overwhelmingly generated by governments, formal and informal. She argues that fear has again become the most common form of social control, and that the liberalism of fear is a response to these actualities, concentrating primarily on damage control. Liberalism in this register does not rest on a theory of moral pluralism, it does not offer a *summum bonum* toward which all political agents should strive, but it certainly does begin with a *summum malum*, namely cruelty, which all of us know and would avoid if only we could. Fear is as universal as it is physiological—it is mental and physical, common to humans and animals. To be alive is to be afraid, and much to our advantage in many cases, since alarm often preserves us from danger; yet what we fear most is a society of fearful people.[5]

As comprehensive as Shklar's work may be, it largely ignores the spiritual dimension. Adding that dimension to the discussion is not meant to simply meet fear with some consolatory belief, since to include spiritual reality does not *a priori* eliminate other factors such as the psychological, political, or personal in our thinking about fear, but it does change the discussion considerably.

Rowan Williams's book *The Truce of God* (2005) provides a concrete example of a project in which spiritual issues are explicitly included in matters that are most often understood as primarily political. His concern is to treat war and peace as spiritual issues, and so he begins his first chapter by probing the religious dimensions of our inner fears, and the connection of those fears to the violence we accept, promote, or even promulgate.

---

that, radically reinterpreting Christianity and the role of the church on a theological basis so that it cannot pose a threat to the unity of the commonwealth. That is, Hobbes places the church within his created artifice so that the church can continue to function as an institution that deals with questions of salvation, faith, and so on, but in such a way that it is controllable and controlled by the civil sovereign. Hobbes's church is to be a tamed, domesticated institution that cannot threaten the peace of *Leviathan*.

4. Shklar, "Liberalism of Fear," 3, 4.
5. Williams, *Truce of God*, 3–11.

Williams's first chapter, entitled "Fears and Fantasies," connects our fears to the causes of violence. Our fears as depicted in the movies often take the form of catastrophes or forces unleashed against us and out of our control, such as a possessed child, a psychopath, somebody or something not quite human (such as Hitler). If violence is done to us by agencies over which we have no control, it's never something humans *decide* to do—violence is out there and can be reacted to in much the same way. But such an understanding makes us incapable of seeing violence as a moral problem; instead we see ourselves as innocent and vulnerable. This is a fatalism that calls for defensive action, we think, but not for assuming full responsibility, by which Williams means penitence. When we see ourselves as victims, such as was the case in the Cold War (it's *their* fault)—that is, if violence is forced on us—it's hard to assume responsibility. All of this has the tendency to lead to cynicism and passivity, even within democracy (despite the fact that we often associate these attitudes with totalitarianism). But instead of assertions of innocence, victimhood, powerlessness or omnicompetence, Williams wants admission of guilt, responsibility, penitence, and radical dependence that must be combined with responsibility, vision, and strength. Hopelessness, on the other hand, is a kind of peace that needs unmasking. Throughout this chapter, Williams seeks to bring to view the reality that war and peace are spiritual issues, given the importance of penitence, "conversion," hope, and rejection of illusory control. A key element in his discussion is the central role of the church, its sheer, bare existence. It is not a program but the church that shapes the Christian response to fear as one not based on violence that itself appears as something for which we are *not* responsible; that is, Williams wants to resist illusory fear that gives way to delusional violence.[6]

These observations serve as an extended introduction to Scott Bader-Saye's *Following Jesus in a Culture of Fear*. Bader-Saye wants to address both personal and political fear, where they do or do not overlap, and do so within a theological framework, giving us not only the solution to our fears but a way to make fear itself intelligible. Without the Christian faith, any account of what to do about fear and how fear is to be understood is incoherent at its heart. You have to be able to know what's going on, you have to have some way of knowing what to fear, what not to fear, how to be courageous, how to resist without being controlled, and how to be prudent without being paralyzed. And so Bader-Saye states the purpose of his book in the following way: "We are in need of some clear, sensible reflection on fear—how to acknowledge it without being manipulated by it, how to resist

---

6. Ibid., 7–20.

it without assuming we should (or could) be fearless, how to receive it as a gift (if it can be a gift) without letting it dominate our lives. This is especially important among Christians who seek to follow Jesus, for Jesus' words, and more so his life, do not promise safety . . . risky discipleship can hardly be described as 'safe.'"[7]

The argument appears in three parts. First is the diagnostic: trying to understand fear, the shadow virtues that it generates, and then the "placing of fear," all of which diagnosis is generated through Thomistic analysis. The second part goes beyond the diagnostic toward working out what it means to follow Jesus, pursuing a constructive vision, central to which is an understanding of providence. The third section details the practices that we are called to cultivate, which themselves hold the potential of generating fear, based as they are on vulnerability.

The first four chapters provide the diagnostic material, showing first how fear in the particular forms we experience it is no accident. Fear is a lucrative business that creates anxieties that its stimulators are ready to quell. Fear causes us to buy products in order to secure our identity, to support political decisions that do not serve us well in the long run, and to trust the superficial answers of our religious leaders that do not satisfy. In short, people profit from our fears. Bader-Saye analyzes the pursuit of security that exchanges the Christian virtues of hospitality, peacemaking, and generosity with the counter values (which he labels "shadow virtues") of barring strangers, waging preemptive violence against potential enemies, and accumulating wealth for one's own future. The author invites us to be "reflective about fear, to reinscribe fear in a larger vision in which fear has a place but can also be kept in its place" (50). The moderation called for by Aquinas leads us between recklessness and paralysis, a way of "putting fear in its place."

The second section begins Bader-Saye's constructive vision. This middle way between recklessness and paralysis finds its place in a community whose members speak of their fear to each other honestly, but which also provides a web of support in which risk is possible.

Central to such a pursuit is a new understanding of God's providence. Bader-Saye calls for "a way of narrating our lives in light of God's larger purpose" (76). To do this we need to attend to the scriptural narrative patterns of God's presence and providence in the world, facing the horrors that have been perpetrated in our lives and in our world. It is important to own up to human sin and not blame our violence on God. Yet we also must realize

---

7. Bader-Saye, *Following Jesus in a Culture of Fear*, 21, 22. Subsequent references to the book will be included in the body of the essay.

that Christian hope asserts that the story is not yet ended. God will yet act to redeem what has been lost. Drawing on the work of Samuel Wells, Bader-Saye divides history into five acts: creation, the call of Israel, the incarnation, the calling and sending of the church, and the consummation. We live in the fourth act, but in the fifth act God will transform our tragedies into destiny. We anticipate this by placing our stories within God's great drama. In God's story, no earthly event can *finally* be seen as utterly tragic (82). However, Bader-Saye is a long way from some naive notion that "everything is gonna be alright." We tie up what loose ends we can; we discern something of the patterns we've been taught in Scripture; but we also recognize that the pattern as a whole may be much deeper and more complex than we ever imagined (84). And so, Bader-Saye argues that perhaps Christians ought to affix two bumper stickers to their cars, the first declaring that "Shit Happens," and the other claiming that "God is my co-pilot" (92). That set of stickers makes perfect sense to me.

In the third section, Bader-Saye outlines the practices that we are called to cultivate, which themselves hold the potential of generating fear, based as they are on vulnerability. Bader-Saye maps out the risks that the church community faces when it embraces the call to follow Jesus. We risk hospitality to strangers when we find our center in God and thus can live with open borders. We "renounce unjust violence and false patience in order to embrace the vulnerable and patient discipline of peacemaking" (131). We hold loosely the abundance God offers and allow it to flow through us to those in need.[8]

I am generally compelled by this *kind* of book, which is part of The Christian Practice of Everyday Life series (Brazos Press). The authors in this series attempt to make the issue at hand intelligible and to find a way forward in our lives. This is done not by dumbing things down but by a process I call distilling. So here we have a book where a good theologian writes in a way that is accessible, drawing on complex sources and taking up complex issues such as the role of God's providence in the world without getting hopelessly obscurantist. In part Bader-Saye does this by drawing on all manner of more popular sources, from newspapers to films, television series, popular music, novels, and so on. The problem with using contemporary cultural references is that they quickly become dated and thus ironically, the attempt to be relevant results is being irrelevant in a very short time. However, in Bader-Saye's case, I think that the critical weight of his argument is generated by sources that have and will stand the test of time; that is, his argument is generated

---

8. This succinct summary of the structure of the book is based on Ruge-Jones, Review of *Following Jesus in a Culture of Fear*.

biblically and theologically. He does not begin with some mention of whatever popular source and then attempt to give that thing a theological veneer. But there are times, too, when he spends much more energy on contemporary culture than on theological issues, which are relevant in different ways. For example, in his treatment of hospitality, he broaches the Trinitarian argument that the *perichoresis* of the Trinity might serve us as a way to understand radical hospitality. However, that complicated and potentially fecund discussion is truncated into a single page, while his discussion of a movie immediately following takes up much more space. I wish he would have turned that around; with Bader-Saye's gift of clarifying and distilling solid theological work and making it accessible and intelligible, it would have been even better to explore the Trinitarian argument more fully.

Bader-Saye's book addresses an important issue, one that was directly addressed very early in the pontificates of both John Paul II and Benedict XVI; I include excerpts from the two addresses here as concluding words of encouragement.[9]

> Homily of His Holiness John Paul II for the Inauguration of His Pontificate
>
> St. Peter's Square, Sunday, 22 October 1978
>
> ...
>
> 5. Brothers and sisters, do not be afraid to welcome Christ and accept his power. Help the Pope and all those who wish to serve Christ and with Christ's power to serve the human person and the whole of mankind. Do not be afraid. Open wide the doors for Christ. To his saving power open the boundaries of States, economic and political systems, the vast fields of culture, civilization and development. Do not be afraid. Christ knows "what is in man." He alone knows it.
>
> So often today man does not know what is within him, in the depths of his mind and heart. So often he is uncertain about the meaning of his life on this earth. He is assailed by doubt, a doubt which turns into despair. We ask you therefore, we beg you with humility and trust, let Christ speak to man. He alone has words of life, yes, of eternal life.
>
> Mass, Imposition of the Pallium and Conferral of the Fisherman's Ring for the Beginning of the Petrine Ministry of the Bishop of Rome

---

9. See John Paul II, Homilies, Mass at the Beginning of the Pontificate; and Benedict XVI, Homilies, Mass for the Inauguration of the Pontificate.

Homily of His Holiness Benedict XVI

St. Peter's Square, Sunday, 24 April 2005

...

At this point, my mind goes back to 22 October 1978, when Pope John Paul II began his ministry here in Saint Peter's Square. His words on that occasion constantly echo in my ears: "Do not be afraid! Open wide the doors for Christ!" The Pope was addressing the mighty, the powerful of this world, who feared that Christ might take away something of their power if they were to let him in, if they were to allow the faith to be free. Yes, he would certainly have taken something away from them: the dominion of corruption, the manipulation of law and the freedom to do as they pleased. But he would not have taken away anything that pertains to human freedom or dignity, or to the building of a just society. The Pope was also speaking to everyone, especially the young. Are we not perhaps all afraid in some way? If we let Christ enter fully into our lives, if we open ourselves totally to him, are we not afraid that He might take something away from us? Are we not perhaps afraid to give up something significant, something unique, something that makes life so beautiful? Do we not then risk ending up diminished and deprived of our freedom? And once again the Pope said: No! If we let Christ into our lives, we lose nothing, nothing, absolutely nothing of what makes life free, beautiful and great. No! Only in this friendship are the doors of life opened wide. Only in this friendship is the great potential of human existence truly revealed. Only in this friendship do we experience beauty and liberation. And so, today, with great strength and great conviction, on the basis of long personal experience of life, I say to you, dear young people: Do not be afraid of Christ! He takes nothing away, and he gives you everything. When we give ourselves to him, we receive a hundredfold in return. Yes, open, open wide the doors to Christ—and you will find true life. Amen.[10]

---

10. In our Take and Read Group, we ended the discussion of this book with a concluding litany, taken from Bader-Saye's introductory material (10): "Most loving Father, whose will it is for us to give thanks for all things, to fear nothing but the loss of you, and to cast all our care on you who cares for us: Preserve us from faithless fears and worldly anxieties, that no clouds of this mortal life may hide from us the light of that love which is immortal, and which you have manifested to us in your Son Jesus Christ our Lord; who lives and reigns with you, in the unity of the Holy Spirit, one God, now and forever. Amen."

Collect for the 8th Sunday after Epiphany, *Episcopal Book of Common Prayer*.

14

Confessions

Saint Augustine. *Confessions*. Translated by Henry Chadwick. Oxford: Oxford University Press, 1991, 2008.

Long considered one of the great masterpieces of western literature, Confessions *is both a confession of praise as well as confession or acknowledgment of faults. Even though this is an ancient book, the twenty-first-century reader who picks up this recent translation may well be surprised at its power to speak to our contemporary situation. This personal narrative includes deep and moving meditations on the nature of desire, the power of temptation and sin, memory, time, grief, and so on. And the central question of all of this is: what does it mean to love God?*

Frederick van Fleteren introduces *Confessions* in the following way:

> *Confessiones* . . . is a literary, theological, and philosophical masterpiece. The most-studied of all Augustine's works in the twentieth century, it continues to attract the attention of historians, theologians, philosophers, philologists, and psychologists. Because of it, the facts of Augustine's youth are more well-known than those of any other figure in antiquity. The description of his decisive encounter with Neoplatonism recorded in *Confessiones* 7 has attracted theologians and philosophers. His conversion to monastic Christianity has attracted artists, as well as theologians and literati, to the present day. His attention to, and descriptions

of, interior states of the human being have attracted philosophers and psychologists. His use of rhetoric continues to be studied both in itself and as a liturgical, literary, and theological tool. Though many works lay claim to the title of first "modern" literary work, *Confessiones* stakes its claim to this title on the fact that it is the first work to explore extensively interior states of the human mind and the mutual relationship of grace and free will, themes dominant in the history of Western philosophy and theology.[1]

In addition to these kinds of superlatives, it is also important to note Augustine's own life is examined in order to investigate and elaborate on any number of theological themes; more accurately, God's work in Augustine's life is what provides the material for reflection and analysis. Many topics have been suggested as *the* unifying theme of this book: it is the story of the journey to conversion; it is the odyssey of the soul; it is the fall and return to God; it is really an extended version of the parable of the prodigal son; or it is an account of the ascent of the soul to God. One could argue that the unifying theme is that wonderful line in the very first paragraph of the book, where Augustine declares that "you have made us for yourself, and our heart is restless until it rests in you."[2] Or one could argue that the unifying theme is confession itself in its various forms on display in the book: confession of sin, confession and witness to a present state, or confession of belief and praise of God. At any rate, the entire book is directed to God and therefore should perhaps be understood as a prayer.

Augustine is interested in framing his life as a product of free decisions that nonetheless have been guided by God's grace to their proper conclusions. That is, he is more interested in a biblically based theology of grace than he is in autobiography.[3] Indeed, his narrative can only take on coherence within the coherence of the biblical narrative.[4] Augustine wants readers to see our lives as *less* intelligible than we may have previously thought. That is, we cannot understand ourselves without trying to find ourselves in the biblical narrative. To think that we already know ourselves, that we know what is going on, is to not be open to the kind of transformation that Augustine wishes for the reader. After all, he is someone who has lost his certain future when we meet him, and he is obsessed by the need to

---

1. *Augustine through the Ages*, s.v. "Confessiones."
2. Augustine, *Confessions*, 1.i.1. Subsequent references will be included in the body of the essay.
3. *Augustine through the Ages*, s.v. "Confessiones."
4. Mathewes, "Book One: The Presumptuousness of Autobiography," 9.

understand what had really happened to him in the distant past.[5] Further, as we read through *Confessions*, we find the entire work is "speckled with warm patches of light,"—those wonderful accounts of relationships, moments, people, and happiness.[6]

Confessions was written in approximately AD 397 and generally follows a chronological path, beginning in Augustine's infancy and continuing into his mid-thirties. Augustine sees the workings of God in many ways. God takes an active role in moving him toward faith, even in his infancy. This divine intervention, according to Augustine, predated his faith and his awareness of God, and is considered much more than some vague sort of protection. Rather, Augustine claims that "I wandered away in conceit and was carried about by every wind (Eph 4:14). Yet very secretly you were putting a check on me" (4.xiv.23). This notion of sensing the direct intervention of God in his life marks *Confessions* in a way that serves to tie it together as a literary unit. Whether this work of God is turning what appeared to be vain childhood learning into something useful for Christian service, or answering the ongoing pleas of Monica, Augustine's mother, little question remains regarding the direct hand of God in Augustine's life.

This spiritual autobiography, aside from revealing Augustine's view of the intervention of God, shows in fascinating detail a slow but steady journey toward faith. In one sense, this *Confession* might be seen as the recitation of pre-conversion sinfulness that tends to mark the testimonials of zealous converts. However, this is no cheap rendition of tawdry facts designed to titillate readers. Augustine draws us along by weaving together strands of his life that eventually lead to his dramatic conversion experience in his thirty-second year. These strands include his mother's continued, passionate, and prayerful intervention on Augustine's behalf, as well as an ongoing struggle against sexual sin. However, the struggle against sin does not stop at sexual temptation. Augustine seems to be acutely aware that he is facing sinfulness at some base level that is deeply disturbing to him.

A further strand that compels the reader is Augustine's ongoing search for truth. This search leads him to align himself with the Manichees from the age of nineteen to his twenty-ninth year, and then reject them. Faustus, a leading figure among the Manichees, unintentionally shows Augustine the ignorance of the cult. Despite his rejecting the Manichees, Augustine does not immediately convert to Christianity. He continues to move toward conversion aided by the impact of people such as Ambrose, Alypius, Nebridius, Simplicianus, and Monica. When Augustine ultimately comes to faith

---

5. Brown, *Augustine of Hippo*, 149.
6. Ibid., 17.

through a dramatic encounter in which he hears and obeys a voice that tells him to pick up a book and read, the experience is described as one where "all shadows of doubt were dispelled" (8.xii.29). It is clear from Augustine's narrative that the search for truth has been a long, arduous journey, one that was directed by God and not always welcomed by Augustine.

Perhaps the most compelling element of *Confessions* is the ready identification of the modern reader with Augustine's experience. The ongoing struggle with sinful physical desires connects in a remarkable way with the licentious world of the twenty-first century. For example, it seems that Augustine could be speaking in our time when he pleads for God to give him chastity, but not yet.

Augustine's drive for finding answers to the large questions of life also rings true to me. As he looks for an explanation for the existence of evil, considers the errors of astrology, struggles with what kind of a person can be a carrier of truth, and attempts to find solace when confronted with the death of a friend who is too young to die, Augustine strikes many chords that ring familiar. This then is perhaps the strongest attraction to *Confessions*—a sense that despite a sixteen-century chronological gap of sixteen hundred years, a strong connection exists between a fourth-century saint and a twenty-first-century Christian.

However, I fear that I am being too general here, and so I want to do some closer reading, focusing on three dimensions of the book: desire, pride, and sin. In much of Christian writing, there is often a very close relationship between human desire and our relationship to God.[7] As Augustine puts it, "The whole life of the good Christian is a holy desire."[8] Indeed, it is sometimes the case that when we read Christian thinkers or listen to Christian hymns and choruses, or read or listen to a religious poem, we are witness to the writer pouring out their emotions to God in such a way that sometimes it's difficult to tell if this expression is religious or romantic. To provide just one example, St. Bernard of Clairvaux, who wrote so many sermons on the Song of Songs, in his "Three Kisses" describes his relationship with Christ in terms of evermore intimate physical contact, first kissing his feet, then his hands (once the supplicant has been raised up by Christ), and then the ecstasy of the face-to-face kiss.[9]

Desire is overwhelming and has the power to mislead every one of us. Four of the seven deadly sins directly involve desire that has gone astray:

---

7. I return to the issue of desire in a sermon included in this book entitled "Simultaneously Satisfying and Insatiable," reflecting on some of these same sources.

8. Augustine, Fourth Homily of the First Epistle of John, 4.6.

9. Bernard of Clairvaux, "Three Kisses."

envy, gluttony, lust, and greed. Desire has the power to control, it has the power to utterly frustrate, but at the same time it can provide the impetus necessary to cultivate passions, to order and invigorate relationships, and to energize our lives. So as a Christian, I want to identify and embrace desire and yearning; I want to also learn about the intensity that can lead to danger. However, one thing I do not want to do is to extinguish desire or to assume that to follow Jesus Christ requires the eradication of all of our passions or the detachment from all of our loves. Yet it is also true that as a Christian, I will no doubt find it necessary to detach myself from some desires and to cling to others, and to cultivate others that should be overwhelming and provide focus for my life. In other words, it is not the case that I have to abandon all of my desires if I want to be a Christian, which is sometimes the way things are put to us, formulated something like, "Just give it all up and follow Jesus and then your real needs will be met." Rather than thinking about the abandonment of desires, I believe we should think in terms of the ordering of our desires. This means that we will want to abandon some of our sinful desires, we will try to detach ourselves from others, we will surely want to cling to some, and we will also want to cultivate some desires that currently are not part of our lives but should be.

I believe that the ordering of our desires can only find be found in relation to God. The Christian life at its most faithful is one both of detachment from sin and an intense desire for God.[10] True desire is patient, able to grow with time in ways that can be sustained. Augustine has much to teach us about the nature of desire in *Confessions*, since he was a man of robust passions. As a young man, this pursuit of passion led him to a number of illicit sexual relationships, but upon conversion he seemed to realize that the intensity of those passions is not simply to be abandoned. "Give me a man in love: he understands what I mean. Give me a man who yearns: give me a man who is hungry; give me a man traveling in the desert, who is thirsty and sighing for the spring of the eternal country. Give me that sort of man; he knows what I mean. But if I talk to a cold man, he does not know what I am talking about."[11]

Augustine returns often to these kinds of thoughts and nowhere more poignantly than in book 10 of *Confessions*. In some intensely moving passages regarding spiritual desire, Augustine tries to make sense of these matters. He struggles to understand and live with the interplay of physical, emotional and spiritual realities.

---

10. This is the view of St. Gregory, known as the "Doctor of Desire." See Leclercq, *Love of Learning*, 29.

11. *On John's Gospel*, 26.4; quoted in Rist, *Augustine*, 157.

> My love of you, O Lord, is not some vague feeling ... But what do I love when I love my God? Not material beauty or beauty of a temporal order; not the brilliance of earthly light, so welcome to our eyes; not the sweet melody of harmony and song; not the fragrance of flowers, perfumes, and spices; not manna or honey; not limbs such as the body delights to embrace. It is not these that I love when I love my God. And yet, when I love him, it is true that I love a light of a certain kind, a voice, a perfume, a food, an embrace; but they are the kind that I love in my inner self, when my soul is bathed in light that is not bound by space; when it listens to sound that never dies away; when it breathes fragrance that is not borne away on the wind; when it tastes food that is never consumed by eating; when it clings to an embrace from which it is not severed by fulfillment of desire. That is what I love when I love my God (10.vi.8).

Notice that Augustine wants us *not* to think that we can find satisfaction in the earthly pleasures of life, and yet only in loving God does it become possible to truly find pleasure in the things of this world that are meant for us to enjoy. It is in loving God that our desires can be ordered, sorted out. Our embrace of God makes possible our embrace of his world, a truth I wish I had come across much earlier in life and wish I could embrace ever more completely.

Augustine himself mourns the fact that he went too long without this ordering of his own desires:

> I have learnt to love you late, Beauty at once so ancient and so new! I have learnt to love you late! You were within me, and I was in the world outside myself. I searched for you outside myself and, disfigured as I was, I fell upon the lovely things of your creation. You were with me, but I was not with you. The beautiful things of this world kept me far from you and yet, if they had not been in you, they would have had no being at all. You called me; you cried aloud to me; you broke my barrier of deafness. You shone upon me; your radiance enveloped me; you put my blindness to flight. You shed your fragrance about me; I drew breath and now I gasp for your sweet odor. I tasted you, and now I hunger and thirst for you. You touched me, and I am inflamed with love of your peace (10.xxvii.38).

This is Augustine talking about getting his life right—recognizing that his desire for God is simultaneously satisfying and insatiable.

Augustine's treatment of the multi-layered problem of pride provides a second focus for reflection. In book 10, Augustine turns to I John 2:15–16, focusing on three temptations: the lust of the flesh, lust of the eyes, and the pride of life. The discussion of the first two sins is interesting enough, but when Augustine turns to pride, we see him at his finest, probing with penetrating insight into the psychology of the sin of pride in his own life, the life of a devout believer and influential church leader. To some extent, he believes that he can test himself on those first two sins and see if he has made some progress (or not), and see them for what they are. Not so with pride. The frustration comes through clearly. Pride is a temptation that has not passed from me, he says—will it ever pass? Augustine sees it as a "wish to be feared or loved by people for no other reason than the joy derived from such power, which is no joy at all" (10.xxvi.59). Augustine is a powerful leader, and he recognizes that in his case, by holding certain offices, just by virtue of holding the office, one may be loved, admired, obeyed, even feared perhaps. This realization that in doing the job he is called to he may be succumbing to pride brings a vast flood of tears to Augustine, since he "cannot easily be sure how far I am cleansed of that plague" (10.xxxvii.60). What then might be the cure? he asks himself. Should we live wicked lives, so that we won't be praised, and therefore at the least not be proud? He answers himself, "Nothing more crazy can be suggested or imagined" (10.xxxvii.60). Augustine admits that in this matter he knows less about himself than he does of God. "There is a temptation to me even when I reject it, because of the very fact that I am rejecting it. Often the contempt of vainglory becomes a source of even more vainglory. For it is not being scorned when the contempt is something one is proud of" (10.xxxviii.63). The onion metaphor is obvious here—I reproach myself for pride and find myself guilty of an even emptier pride, and presumably if I reproach myself for that, I might find emptier pride still. Tellingly, Augustine simply cannot solve the problem and leaves it hanging there.

A third focus for discussion is the nature of sin. Book 2 includes Augustine's famous account of stealing pears with his teenage buddies. He analyzes this incident with what has been called "fascinated repulsion."[12] Peter Brown, who calls Augustine "a great connoisseur of the human will," suggests that what we are witness to is a gratuitous act that is a sad paradigm for free will—in our eagerness to embrace false notions of freedom, we "throw ourselves headlong," as he puts it.[13]

Clearly this story connects us to all of the mysterious elements of the biblical account of Genesis 3, that narrative of forbidden fruit and its plucking—Augustine's narrative acts as a conduit into that larger biblical

---

12. Brown, *Augustine of Hippo*, 166.
13. Ibid.

narrative.[14] Just as Adam and Eve had everything they needed—food, comfort, companionship—they had nothing to fear in Eden. The point in the pear story seems to be at least in part the trivial and motiveless character of the act itself. "Such was my heart, O God, such was my heart. You had pity on it when it was at the bottom of the abyss. Now let my heart tell you what it was seeking there in that I became evil for no reason. I had no motive for my wickedness except wickedness itself. It was foul, and I loved it" (2.iv.9).

Augustine seems to need to acknowledge that what he really enjoyed was the sin itself, which is the nature of sin itself. The age-old question, "How could he/she do that?" is answerable in many ways that make some sense, but in the end, none of those answers goes as deep as this account of stealing pears. It had to be something seemingly trivial precisely to make that point—to bring to view the nature of sin, the depths of our depravity in ways that conventionally heinous sins would not be able to.

Of course many, many things have to be left unsaid here. We haven't noted the battle with the Manicheans, which is another important theological thread; Augustine's relationship with his mother is also really interesting. What are we to make of their shared vision at Ostia? What is the proper way to grieve the loss of your mom? Or of a close friend who dies young? What about the role of memory in our present lives? In preparing for the future? Should Genesis 1 be read allegorically? Just how misogynist (or not) was Augustine? Why not give us the name of that lover, the mother of his beloved son, who when she was torn from his side caused him to bleed? How reliable a guide is Augustine for our sexual mores? Our eating habits? What is the nature of conversion—the intellectual conversion of book 7? The spiritual conversion of book 8? How should we read the Bible—pick it up and read whatever presents itself? What about the way Augustine treated those with whom he disagreed—the Donatists? Pelagians? Is his ethic of "Command what you will and give what you command" adequate? And then there's his theological justification of the Just War Tradition—how can we possibly embrace that?

Perhaps the best way to end such an incomplete discussion of *Confessions* is to agree with the opinion of John Cavadini when he says, "The *Confessions* is one of those texts whose beauties emerge gradually to the person willing to read and reread over time, to one who is willing, too, to see its various facets from different perspectives, Sometimes, if you are looking in just the right direction, one facet glimmers out and seems to illuminate

---

14. Cavadini, "Book Two: Augustine's Book of Shadows," 29.

all of the others, and it is a source of further enjoyment and understanding to share these discoveries with others."[15]

---

15. Ibid., 25.

15

Just War as Christian Discipleship

Daniel Bell Jr. *Just War as Christian Discipleship*. Grand Rapids: Brazos Press, 2009.

The Just War Tradition (JWT), while widely embraced by Christians, has often been criticized for failing to have enough of a pastoral dimension. That is, the JWT does not provide a shape to life, or guidance for the life of the Christian disciple, since the tradition has become primarily a matter of statecraft. Daniel Bell wants to reinvigorate the JWT and hopes to do so by recentering the tradition in the church rather than the state. It will be interesting to attempt a pacifist reading of Bell's important project.

I describe myself as a Christian pacifist, and therefore I want to read and discuss this book in a manner congruent with pacifism. Chris Huebner in his book *A Precarious Peace*,[1] addresses the issue of epistemology, acutely aware of the role of power and control in issues of acquiring and disseminating knowledge. Huebner uses the language of vulnerability, openness, giving up control, reticence toward closing discussions and toward drawing hard and fast conclusions. His phrase "pacifist epistemology" alerts us to the fact that we often think of pacifism, peace, just war, and so on only in terms of war and peace, violence and non-violence. We proceed as though we know what all those things mean, and what's at stake. To use his term, he wants to

1. Chris Huebner, *Precarious Peace*.

"complexify" things; that is, he asks what it is about knowledge—learning, acquiring, teaching, and passing it on—that could be construed as pacifist? Huebner draws on the work of John Howard Yoder for at least some of the direction of this work.

As part of Yoder's pacifist stance, which extends to the dialogical engagement with other traditions and positions, he attempted to take the JWT seriously on its own terms through respectful dialogue.[2] This dialogue is an attempt to hold the JWT accountable on its own terms. The extent of the engagement is quite remarkable, ranging from Yoder's involvement on the campus of the University of Notre Dame with Catholic interlocutors amidst the military officer training program there to an extensive number of essays that directly engage just war thinking.[3] Yoder makes the claim that in none of this respectful dialogue is he being disingenuous, but is simply calling the JWT to its own best principles. He couches his exposition and critique of the tradition in terms of seeking an ecumenical way of giving "the benefit of the doubt to the mainstream theological tradition," and in doing so "is not advocating backhandedly my own pacifist ideals," an exercise that "would call for a biblical and a pastoral argument."[4]

Despite such disclaimers, a reading of Yoder's dialogue with the JWT reveals a distinct reservation of positive judgments for those occasions when the tradition acts like pacifism. Put another way, Yoder is willing to approve of the JWT when that tradition leads, on its own terms, to conclusions that coincide with pacifism. At most, his respectful dialogue is an attempt to acknowledge the tradition as credible, but that attempt will never extend to a concession that it is right or faithful.

Yoder's treatment of the JWT includes several dimensions. First, he argues that pacifism and the JWT are part of the same universe of discourse, that they interlock in several ways: "a moral presumption against violence (although they differ on whether it may be over-ridden); a stake in the rejection of total war, which issues in politically making common cause against unacceptable national policies; support for maximizing the potential of nonmilitary means of pursuing just social objectives, including national

---

2. This is Yoder's own description of his initiative in a book-length engagement with the Just War Tradition. Yoder, *When War Is Unjust*, ix. Much of the discussion of Yoder and O'Donovan in this essay is taken from my book *Beyond Suspicion*.

3. Yoder, "Bluff or Revenge"; Yoder, "Challenge of Peace"; Yoder, "Credibility of Ecclesiastical Teaching"; Yoder, "How Many Ways Are There to Think Morally about War?"; Yoder, "'Just War' Tradition: Is It Credible?"; Yoder, "Military Realities and Teaching the Laws of War"; Yoder, "Reception of the Just War Tradition"; and Yoder, "Surrender: A Moral Imperative?"

4. Yoder, "Credibility of Ecclesiastical Teaching," 37.

defense."[5] Given these areas of overlap, Yoder believes that pacifism and the JWT can work together in resisting less restrained views.

Nonetheless, whatever the commonalities that can be embraced within a common universe of discourse, Yoder is clear in all of his forays into the JWT that even if such thinking is honest, "Just War discourse deceives sincere people, by the very nature of its claim to base moral discernment upon the facts of the case and on universally accessible rational principles. It lets them think that their morality is somehow less provincial and more accessible to others than if it referred specifically to the data of Christian faith, including the words and the work of Jesus."[6] Herein the shape of Yoder's dialogue with the JWT becomes clear—he finds specific flaws that ultimately bring to view the fact that the tradition needs to become more credible by being true to its own best principles. However, it seems equally clear that in the event that the JWT were to be credible, by which is meant that the tradition would be able to say that some wars are not justifiable, Yoder would still declare it to be unfaithful to Jesus Christ. He is quite specific about some of the flaws in the tradition, especially in his book *When War Is Unjust*, but not only there. Many of the shorter pieces cited above show Yoder assessing the credibility of the tradition in historically specific cases, and in each case finding it wanting in some way. Some of his complaints include his fear that the restraints of the tradition are continually being weakened as exceptions are ruled out, as war becomes total, as technology escalates, and as less and less rigor is required to determine what is considered acceptable.[7]

The purpose of this lengthy treatment of Yoder's thought is to display the kind of pacifist reading that I want to perform in taking up Daniel Bell's book *Just War as Christian Discipleship*—I intend to be open and vulnerable, and call the reader to its greatest strengths, trying not to forcefully impose my agenda on the book and then criticize it for not matching up to my preset expectations. It is important to begin by acknowledging more generally that pacifism has problems, and therefore we must not begin with the triumphalist notion that pacifists have it all right. A brief look at a prominent critic of pacifism, namely Oliver O'Donovan, will bring to view some of the criticisms facing those who claim to embrace pacifism.

O'Donovan's criticisms of pacifism are most closely related to his belief that it cannot discharge the calling of Christian political discipleship in the theater of the *saeculum*, that place where can be found "a time to love, to believe, and to hope under a regime of provisional judgment; here, too, it is

---

5. Yoder, "Just War and 'Non-Violence': Disjunction or Dialogue?," 172.
6. Yoder, "'Just War' Tradition: Is It Credible?" 298.
7. See especially chapter 5 of Yoder, *When War Is Unjust*.

possible to practice reconciliation, since God's patience waits, and preserves the world against its own self-destruction."[8] According to O'Donovan, pacifism cuts off responsibility to the world outside of the church, because it can only offer suspicion and criticism without engaging in constructive work. Indeed, O'Donovan suggests that pacifism has much in common with the kind of deterrence based on massive arms build-up. That is, both pacifism and deterrence seek to banish force entirely from human history, and as such pacifism is merely a mutant form of deterrence, "transformed by a technological and historicist vision of human progress."[9] Instead, O'Donovan insists, Christians are called to offer to the world a counter-praxis to the violence that is based on the praxis of unmediated conflict. For O'Donovan, pacifism is a Christian strategy that limits counter-praxis to the pastoral theater and can offer nothing more than endurance and martyrdom in the theater of the world. In this sense, he rejects any notion that there are many and variegated forms of pacifism but claims that "in the face of a praxis of unmediated opposition, it [pacifism] holds that an evangelical counter-praxis of judgment is not to be looked for."[10] Pacifism contains a serious flaw in that peace is seen only as a gift from God, and therefore nothing can be done in the secular realm (understood as the opposite of the eternal) to create peace. Pacifism thus amounts to a *via negativa*, a praxis whose watchwords seemingly all begin with the prefix "non," circumscribing the possibility of action in the world. In sum, pacifism warns people away from war with the attendant effect that it becomes impossible to think practically about the tasks that are necessary for building stable peace and justice.[11]

---

8. O'Donovan, *Just War Revisited*, 6.

9. O'Donovan, *Peace and Certainty*, 28–29. O'Donovan returns to this argument several times throughout his essay on deterrence, arguing that pacifism has unwittingly found itself intertwined with total-war strategy in the search for total peace, and because it is unwilling to engage in a search for the conditions for a sustainable just and stable peace, which might call for *appropriate* use of force. The deterrence O'Donovan refers to in this essay "is the name we have given to the stance of perpetual armed threat with which the two great political blocs of the post-war world confront each other" (1).

10. O'Donovan, *Just War Revisited*, 7.

11. Ibid., 9–15. In a 1985 public debate with Anabaptist thinker Ronald Sider regarding peace and war, O'Donovan presents a number of disagreements with Sider's position as presented, and argues that the real question on the table is whether resort to force is ever justified. O'Donovan suggests that if Sider and other pacifists assume such an *a priori* position, then it becomes impossible to move beyond a discussion of face-to-face confrontation to a consideration of the protection of others, which may entail the use of force, according to O'Donovan, even while remaining faithful to Jesus. See Sider and O'Donovan, *Peace and War*, 13–17.

What I have been attempting to this point is to set up a pacifist reading of Bell's book by acknowledging the complexity of the task itself. Bell's book is important in that it aims to address one of the main lacunas of which the JWT has been accused, namely the lack of a pastoral dimension. I will not rehearse the argument Bell makes in the book other than to say that we are given a fine account of the history, theology, and various dimensions of the JWT, and he works his way through it patiently, all the while seeking to show how we can be "just war people."

Here are some of the strengths of the book as I see them (no doubt there are more). First, this is a specifically Christian treatment of the issues. It is often said that the JWT is not specifically Christian, that it was co-opted from Cicero by Ambrose but especially by Augustine, who needed to make that move because of Constantine and because of the church's eagerness to participate in the secular exercise of power. However, Bell seeks to refill, as it were, the tradition with explicitly Christian content in a sustained way.

Second, Bell gives us at least some traction for how to live as Christians—that is, how to be shaped as "just war people." Part of this is the recentering of the tradition in the church and not in the state. The JWT treated in this way is not just about politicians trying to make decisions and bishops writing formal letters of support or criticism. Rather, the whole enterprise is shifted away from a checklist that poses questions such as: Does this war fill these criteria? Do the soldiers fight properly? According to Bell, instead of seeing its task as asking those questions, the church should pay attention to being part of an embodied tradition that is lived out in faithful form of discipleship whether a war is on or not. He draws the shape of many of these community-forming practices from the long-standing moral tradition of the virtues.

Third, Bell gives a solid account of how "times change." In the first three centuries after Jesus's life, death, and resurrection, the church was pacifist, but then things changed. According to Bell, God did not somehow change his mind, but prophecies were fulfilled, rulers were converted, and the church was in a new position that called for certain kinds of action. This is not a defense of self-defense, says Bell, but an embodiment of enemy-love, a kind harshness.

Fourth, Bell challenges those who claim that what Christians are called to is some kind of "realism," of the sort espoused by Reinhold Niebuhr and more recently by John Stackhouse.[12] In Bell's account, we are never called to some notion of the "lesser evil." To reduce the JWT to that is to reduce God's call to faithfulness to something considerably less than that. Rather

---

12. See Stackhouse, *Making the Best of It*.

than understanding the JWT as a lesser evil, Bell's primary move is to retrieve just war as Christian discipleship.

While these features of Bell's account are all strong contributions to the discussion, I nonetheless have a few questions. After all, pacifism is still engagement, but engagement in a certain way. First, then, is Bell's account of Constantine, Augustine, and the change in the church's understanding of violence an accurate one? Is it really the case that Jesus's teaching, especially in the Sermon on the Mount, should be construed as a series of "inward dispositions" and not outward actions? And in any case, is Augustine's development of the JWT really an organic development and faithful extension of Jesus and early Christianity? Of course things change, people change, influential people become Christians, and so on. We know that many things we believed and practiced in the first three centuries were wrong, or undeveloped, and so we change and move, and try to remain faithful—what was the case with *these* questions?

Further, it strikes me that Bell holds a rather optimistic view of war.[13] Is it really the case that war is anything but chaos, basically speaking? Bell seems to have a bit of a tin ear for the psychological dimensions of warfare.[14] This is closely related to his focus on character formation. The church shapes our characters, no doubt, and this emphasis is one of the strengths of Bell's work. But what happens when we sign up to be a soldier? Is it not the case that we are then shaped by the hands of the military? What does that look like? Won't at least some of the formation that has taken place in the church be re-formed, maybe even deformed?

Bell's book raises but leaves unanswered a number of questions regarding the relationship of church and state. For example, we need to ask if the church should be a "just war people" in any case. What does this say about the nature of the church? The role of the state? The relationship between the church and the state? Does God "work," as it were, through the church or through the state? What kind of authority does the state carry?

Finally, Bell's book must be given its due attention precisely because it seeks to frame questions of peace and war in terms of Christian discipleship, a welcome and important contribution to the church's ongoing search for spiritual guidance.[15]

---

13. See Bell, *Just War as Christian Discipleship*, 40, for an example.

14. For provocative treatments of the psychological dimension of warfare, see for example Hedges, *War Is Force That Gives Us Meaning*; and Bourke, *Intimate History of Killing*.

15. My reading of Bell's book is shaped by Siggelkow, "Just War Is *Not* Christian Discipleship: A Review of Daniel Bell Jr.'s Just War."

16

Love Wins

Rob Bell. *Love Wins: A Book about Heaven, Hell, and the Fate of Every Person Who Ever Lived*. New York: HarperOne, 2011.

> *Bell's theological voice is seemingly ubiquitous—heard in NOOMA videos, popular books, Mars Hill sermons, and so on. His style is distinctive, his influence widespread, and he is certainly not afraid to address big issues. So we'll see what happens when we read this theological voice theologically.*

James Gustafson, the American theologian and ethicist, describes what often happens when people find out that he is a theologian. They ask him to "say something theological," as if being a theological is a party trick or some such thing. I've always loved his reply: he claims that he has the presence of mind to simply say "God," about as theological an answer as one can give.

Roman Catholic theologian Gerald O'Collins expands this notion in his definition of theology, describing it as "watching your language in the presence of God." Over the last number of years especially, I have become more and more aware of the difficulty of speaking about God. After all, if you use that word/name you've said a lot, but it is not entirely clear what has been said, whether too much or too little. Often I find that words fail just at the point where I need them the most, and so I sometimes find myself literally stuttering as I seek to complete a sentence, and on occasion, I have simply bailed out of a sentence as I realize that I am heading for a verbal and/or conceptual dead end.

My work, which includes occasional preaching and adult education, as well as the formal teaching of theology at Canadian Mennonite University, means that I am required to bring up the topic of God from time to time, but to do so is a complicated task not to be taken lightly. The recognition of its complexity means I have to resist several temptations that are constantly before me, beginning with the urge to project what we want God to be like, and then describe God as having just those characteristics. As Karl Barth put it, theology sometimes amounts to little more than speaking about ourselves, but in a louder voice. Another related temptation is to talk about God as though this is simply a matter of topping up what we know to be the case about humans. For example, in speaking of God as Father, all we have to do is imagine the nicest dad around, and God as a kind of an intensified version of that nice dad. It seems to me that both of these temptations need to be avoided at all costs. But again, even if I say that God is wholly "other," to use a Barthian term, I'm still not sure that I have said very much. So, "the theological task requires that we speak of God, but the God to whom and about whom we must speak defies the words we use . . . Yet it seems the closer God draws near to us the more we discover that we know not how to say 'God.'"[1]

I don't think that this leaves any of us with nowhere to go or nothing to do regarding the theological task. According to John Howard Yoder, the task of theology is "working with words in the light of faith."[2] Fair enough, but since I'm in a confessional mode here, I want to acknowledge that I find such a task terrifying. I am sometimes attracted to the apophatic tradition, wherein one does not make positive assertions about God but rather works at understanding what God is not. But that would be to deny the tradition of which I am a part, a tradition that seeks to transmit the heritage of the faith without deforming it, even while attempting to speak to questions that arise in a new context.[3]

I mentioned my terror in the face of this task—nobody describes this kind of fear better than Annie Dillard,

> Why do people is churches seem like cheerful brainless tourists on a packaged tour of the Absolute? . . . On the whole I do not find Christians, outside the catacombs, sufficiently sensible of conditions. Does anyone else have the foggiest idea what sort of power we so blithely evoke? Or, as I suspect, does no one believe a word of it? The churches are children playing on the

---

1. Hauerwas, *Working with Words*, x.
2. Yoder, *Preface to Theology*, 41.
3. I take this idea from Yoder's work in *Preface to Theology*.

floor with their chemistry sets, mixing up a batch of TNT to kill a Sunday morning. It is madness to wear ladies' straw hats and velvet hats to church; we should all be wearing crash helmets. Ushers should issue life preservers and signal flares; they should lash us to our pews. For the sleeping god may wake someday and take offense, or the waking god may draw us out to where we can never return.[4]

The locus of my fear is that the way I talk about God might lull me into blithely messing with power that I do not recognize, and that I in turn lull students and others into that same illusory state.

All this to say that the work of theology is a delicate matter, a fearful enterprise, not something to be taken lightly. To take the Lord's name in vain is the heart of the matter. I am not speaking here of using impolite, foul, salty language (although I am not advocating such speech either—it's just that assuming that taking the Lord's name in vain has something to do with polite speech is to miss the point). People will boast about never having used a "swear" in their entire lives, all the while not thinking twice about what is being said about God's work and ways in the world. In fact, I have over the past few years begun to use a warning tone with some of my students when they speak about God in a way that is questionable. "Watch your language," I say sternly, and I can see them scrolling back through previous sentences, struggling to remember whether they said "shit," or "damn," or "hell," or something similar.

That long introduction is a way of saying that over the next several chapters we will ask: How are these writers "working with words in the light of faith?" and in so doing, I hope that we learn to discipline our own speech just a bit, but always in light of faith.

The book to which we (along with a couple other million people) have turned our attention in this chapter is Rob Bell's *Love Wins*.[5] Bell is a theological rock star, an author, star of a series of NOOMA videos, former pastor of the Mars Hill megachurch in Michigan, who resigned in 2011 to move to Los Angeles in order to be a "speaker" and work on a television series. Bell disavows being a scholar or theologian, but nevertheless he is one: he is doing theology, he is influencing people, asking questions, making assertions, talking about God, all in a loud voice. It won't do to simply shrug and say, "Aw, shucks, I'm just a regular guy." In this book, he is addressing some of the big issues of the Christian faith, and we want to watch him at work. In order to do that, I need to clarify the nature my intentions, or rather, clarify what I

---

4. Dillard, *Teaching a Stone to Talk*, 40–41.
5. Specific references to the book will be included in the body of this essay.

will *not* do. First, I will not aim to settle the issues Bell raises, as if I can state with confidence everything there is to say about God's love, heaven, hell, the atonement, and the fate of everyone. Were I to articulate only my own views, they would not somehow conclude the inquiry into these mysteries, and what's more, God forbid that my views would either provide comfort in the form of "Ah, he really is a Christian," or conversely, "See, he really is just a pagan liberal who doesn't believe the Bible"—as though my yes or no answer to a question such as "Do you believe in a literal hell?" would be the definitive conclusion. The formulation of the question in that way itself would make me tell my questioner to watch her language.

Further to what I will not do: I will not create a category in which to place Bell—for example, you won't hear me call him a universalist (155) or a heretic. That way of talking about things stops conversation and too often functions as a shortcut, wherein you create a category and throw someone into it, which allows you to avoid the hard work of actually reading, thinking, or analyzing the content of an argument.

I want to watch Bell do his work, keeping in front of us questions such as: What does he think he's doing? What kind of language does he use? Who is his audience? What does he say? How does he say it? This won't be done *seriatim*, nor will I rehearse Bell's argument in any kind of detail, although I will briefly trace the trajectory of the book as a way to orient ourselves to the way he works.

In his preface, Bell begins by calling us to grant him his first move; that is, God is all about love, that's what the story is about, as he puts it. Further, "lots of people" think that this story has been hijacked. He claims to be writing on behalf of "us," "millions of us," a "staggering number of us," using words like lots, some, sometimes, often, may, and perhaps. That is, there's the *real* story which he identifies, but lot of people don't like what has happened to that story in his hands (vii–xi).

The introductory chapter raises a lot of questions (I count around eighty-seven of them). Sometimes they are derisive, dismissive, snarky, smart-ass, facile, and unfair (7). They are also intuitively correct, insightful, and I would say representative of fairly widely held views, at least anecdotally. In a detailed commentary on this book, Ben Witherington III calls these questions irrelevant, since they don't ask the right theological questions,[6] but I think that charge isn't quite right. Even if Bell's questions are not theologically right, they are relevant because people seem to be asking them, and so he asks them on behalf of "many people." More worrisome is that the

---

6. See Witherington, "Do Not Ask for Whom the Bell Tolls . . . A Chapter by Chapter Review of 'Love Wins.'"

question of sin does not really make much of an appearance in this chapter, a problem that dogs this book throughout.

In chapter 2, Bell turns his attention to heaven, using compelling cultural references (21). While his targets are somewhat amorphous here (24, 57), Bell will not accept some literalist notion of streets of gold. Rather, he complexifies things considerably regarding location, identity, hope, judgment, and certainly on the question of who is in or out.

In his controversial third chapter, on hell, Bell shows the same pattern. That is, he ranges from being deeply insightful (Jesus talks about hell to religious people), to frustrating because of a lack of seriousness (70), to being too simplistic (71), to promulgating a concept of sin that isn't theological enough (72, 78–79). It's just not true that people who hold to a traditional view of sin do not care about life on this earth.[7] Overall, Bell keeps the notion of hell but by the time he's done with it, it has been reworked considerably from a "traditional" view.

In chapter 4, Bell asks if God gets what God wants. I dislike this question intensely because of the way it is asked, and because of what it makes God sound like. He formulates the question in a way that offers the answer in the question: "Will all people be saved, or will God not get what God wants (98)?" Further, he often uses questions to avoid answers, creating false dichotomies in the form of "this or that" questions (see page 102 for a number of examples).

The fifth chapter consists of his treatment of the atonement, and those who like the substitutionary form of the atonement will find this chapter very unsettling indeed. However, his treatment of the pattern of cross and resurrection as something akin to the changing of the season makes me much more nervous than does his discussion of atonement itself.

In chapter 6, Bell presses us to see the work of Jesus as extending far beyond what we might think, focusing on the notion of water coming from the rock, and that rock being Christ. Here Bell is clear that he is not a universalist (155), but whether his argument regarding Jesus as Rock points where he thinks it does is up for debate. In addition, his ecclesiology is less than robust; I think a much more developed view of the church is necessary to hold up his broader view of God's work in the world beyond the church.

What are we then to make of the way Bell uses language to talk about God and the things of God and faith? Let's begin with his stance: how does he approach things? He certainly is not afraid of questions, either those asked by others or those he raises himself from his experience as a child or as a pastor. This kind of openness is itself an act of faith in his view, or

---

7. Ibid.

so it would seem. This is not only intellectual curiosity for its own sake; rather, we are encouraged to think, to ask, to discern, and to pursue honest questions as part of the expression of Christian faith. This stance seems to me to be something that Bell finds in the biblical text itself; he finds it in the Gospels and in Paul, and so Bell's approach is deeply dependent on the form of speech we call the question. He interrogates things, notions, concepts, and practices, and, if read generously, all of this in order to understand and be faithful to Christianity. When he goes forward with his questions, Bell can bring to view numerous prejudices and misconceptions to which people cling, often without realizing it. By the time he is done posing questions about heaven, it's hard to assert that heaven is a place where we go at the moment of death, where we get to do and eat all the things we like without any negative repercussions.

However, to identify Bell's stance as openness characterized by the raising of sometimes very uncomfortable questions does not say enough. Not all questions are created equally; questions are tools of control as well as of inquiry. The person who sets the question exerts significant power, whether that be in setting an exam, setting the direction of a conversation or the tone of inquiry, or setting up the conversation partner for a specific kind of answer before the question ever gets asked. In other words, just because someone is asking questions does not mean that person is not actually teaching you something or asserting things. Bluntly put, "Bell argues through his use of question."[8] To provide one example from his book:

> And whenever people claim that one group is in, saved, accepted by God, forgiven, enlightened, redeemed—and everybody else isn't—why is it that those who make this claim are almost always part of the group that's "in"? Have you ever heard people make claims about a select few being the chosen and then claim that they're not part of that group? Several years ago I heard a woman tell about the funeral of her daughter's friend, a high-school student who was killed in a car accident. Her daughter was asked by a Christian if the young man who had died was a Christian. She said that he told people he was an atheist. This person then said to her, "So there's no hope then." No hope? Is that the Christian message? "No hope"? Is that what Jesus offers the world? Is this the sacred calling of Christians—to announce that there's no hope? (3)

Sarah Flashing responds to this kind of writing by arguing, "While I'm quite sure the scenario described here isn't the best Christianity has to offer,

---

8. Flashing, "An Indefensible Faith: Another Review of *Love Wins*."

it is hardly helpful to conflate this tasteless interaction with the exclusive claims of Christianity. This is a tactic of distraction used frequently by those set out invalidate Christianity, but Bell has validated the tactic and empowered those who use it by adopting it for his own use."[9]

All this to say that one of the ways that Bell talks about God, namely, through the use of questions, hides in part the content of his teaching, and thus is somewhat disingenuous and misleading. This is illustrated by what I would call his promiscuous use of the rhetorical question, since this form of the question often stops conversation, makes things sound as though they can be reduced to "this or that," a binary form of questioning that in the end is not nearly as open as Bell wants it to appear, and maybe even less open than he himself knows.

Another important thing to watch when we are looking at the way someone talks about God is to note the way scripture is part of the conversation. In a number of places, Bell shows himself to be a sensitive and interesting reader of the text, as in his reading of prodigal son and the discussion of "the age to come." He goes to the text and finds what we thought was not there, and sometimes he shows that what we thought was there is not there after all. He reads carefully, examining words used to discuss hell and heaven, questions of who is judged and how, how Jesus talks and to whom. But this is not the whole story. Without arguing about content, there are times when Bell seems lazy, whether that takes the form of using simple lists of verses as proof-texting, or by being far too simplistic, as in his brief discussion of the significance of Egypt in the history of Israel (88–89). At times he simply uses passages of scripture as trump cards, or as assertions the meaning of which he assumes are self-evident. I often found myself longing for him to give a full account of what he was arguing—an account, a thick reading, not just plopping a verse down in the book and saying "See?" Many times I felt like scrawling in the margin comments such as "explore further," "explain," "give evidence," and so on. I am not criticizing him for being what he's not, namely, a technical biblical scholar. Rather, it's his *use* of the text that is troublesome at times. After all, words can be weapons, both defensive and offensive, even if they are found in the Bible.

Further, we need to look at his use of the Christian tradition: the teachings of the church across time found in sources such as formal creeds, less formal confessions of faith, received opinions, influential writings, and the

---

9. Ibid. Ben Witherington agrees, claiming that some of the questions Bell uses are actually references to Christians behaving badly rather than to the content of the Christian faith, but the form of the questions hide this important distinction. See Witherington, "Do Not Ask for Whom the Bell Tolls."

like. Here Bell's practice in this book is, to my mind, dismal.[10] I'm dismayed by his lack of a decent bibliography, not because I want him to be a formal scholar but because I want to see how, where, why, and when he is part of the conversation that is constitutive of the church's orthodox or unorthodox beliefs and practices. Bell sometimes makes it look as though the topics under discussion have only recently been taken up. I acknowledge his claims to be part of the tradition (xi), but he does not really show how that is the case.

Far be it from me to say that this is useless writing, that Bell should not be read, that he's a heretic, or that he's not a Christian. I do think it's important to see that what Bell offers is poetic probing of the parameters of orthodoxy.

What we face, then, is the question of how to process this: what do we do with Bell, with the content, the questions? It seems to me that we need to take into account much more seriously than does Bell the community of faith, the church. In an important essay, John Howard Yoder reflects on the hermeneutics of peoplehood; in part of that essay he makes reference to the "shape of the conversation." Yoder suggests that the body of Christ has members with distinct roles who contribute to the process understanding faith: a) Agents of Direction—prophets—a trust that God is at work, and that whatever is said will be weighed by the community; b) Agents of Memory—people who remember expertly memorable, identity-confirming acts of faithfulness, of repentance—a collective scribal memory; c) Agents of Linguistic Self-Consciousness—teachers; d) Agents of Order and Due Process—leaders.[11] It is this kind of deliberate placing of oneself within the peoplehood of the church that seems to be missing in Bell's book, replaced by a largely maverick approach that while widely popular does not provide the kind of sustenance both the church and the world need.

---

10. See for example pp. 106–8, where the work of people ranging from the era of early Christianity to the Reformation are mentioned but ultimately glossed over in what amounts to a facile treatment.

11. Yoder, "The Hermeneutics of Peoplehood: A Protestant Perspective."

17

Working with Words

Stanley Hauerwas. *Working with Words: On Learning to Speak Christian.*
Eugene: Cascade Books, 2011.

Once dubbed "Best Theologian in America" by Time *magazine (his response: "Best" is not a Christian category), Hauerwas focuses here on the central challenge, risk, and difficulty of working with words about God. The content of his writing and the way he writes about writing about God are important dimensions of Hauerwas's attempt to discipline his (and our) Christian speech.*

To begin, I should disclose that I am not completely neutral when it comes to Hauerwas's work. I have met Stanley here in Winnipeg and at conferences, he has written a blurb for the back of my book, acted as a reference for me the last time I applied for a job, and contributed an essay to the last edited book I have published. I feel as if I knew him long before I met him, because I wrote my master's thesis on his thought, have been deeply influenced by his writing, and remain so to this day.

One immediately evident characteristic of Hauerwas's writing is that the form he uses deliberately and almost exclusively is the essay.[1] As I noted in an earlier chapter, an essay is a relatively short piece of writing that

---

1. Hauerwas makes reference to John Milbank's blurb for *Hannah's Child,* wherein Milbank states that "Hauerwas's work of writing and his work on himself are so clearly, as with Michel de Montaigne, one and the same." Hauerwas, *Working with Words,* ix. Subsequent references to the book will be included in the body of the essay.

does not pretend to begin at the beginning of some issue and stick with the matter until it is definitively concluded. It begins in the middle, as it were, of an on-going conversation, carries on with it, and contributes something to it, but never assumes that the end of the is the end of the conversation. As Hauerwas claims for this book, "It is a good place to begin . . . to remember that there is no place to start" (xii). For Hauerwas (and others), this is the way theology ought to be done because that is the nature of theology itself. The form of the essay embodies the theological task to some degree; style and content ought never to be extricated from each other. Many of Hauerwas's books begin with an introduction in which he explains how these essays happened to land together in a book, and he even manages to group them thematically, but really he is collecting the last fifteen or twenty things he has written and packaging them up for the purpose of publication. As he puts it,

> So this kitchen sink of a book hopefully provides some examples of my writing, my work, and, in particular, my attempt to work on myself so that I might become a more adequate Christian speaker. I do not intend to make a long book longer by "explaining" why I have included this or that essay or sermon. This is a collection, not a book, though I am not sure how to control that distinction. What is here is here because it is my work. I make no apologies. (xiii–xiv)

As was the case with my discussion of Rob Bell's book, I want us to watch Hauerwas at work. The book's title asserts that these essays address what it might mean to work with words, to learn to speak Christian. As Hauerwas puts it, he offers a reflection on *and* an exhibition of what it means for theology to be work with words, wherein the task involves watching Christians at work doing theology to see what can be learned from those who have tried to do theology in the past (x).

> "Tried" is a crucial word, because the theological task requires that we speak of God, but the God to whom and about whom we must speak defies the words we use. This defiance seems odd because the God about whom we must speak is, we believe, found decisively in Jesus of Nazareth, very God and very man. Yet it seems the closer God draws near to us the more we discover that we know not how to say "God." (x)

But how do you "watch" other people doing theology as part of doing the work of theology now? The answer for Hauerwas, in part, has to do with reading. In his commencement address to Eastern Mennonite Seminary, entitled "Speaking Christian," Hauerwas reflects on the nature of the work of the ministry. This sermon includes some great lines, including the one where he hopes that one day, in answer to the question of what they did that day as a pastor, the graduates will be able to answer: "I think I wrote one good sentence in the sermon for Sunday" (93). At any rate, his claim to these seminary students is that what they have done in the pursuit of their degrees, in ministry training, is to learn to read (86), and in so doing have also been trained to speak Christian. If that has not happened, and if it does not continue to happen as they move forward and take on the task of being "a teacher of language," then the church is in real danger of "losing the grammar of the faith" (87). It is through reading that we learn to discipline our speech, to say no more than needs to be said. Hauerwas believes that there is an essential relation between reading and speaking. Indeed, the very first paragraph of the book takes up the role of reading in Hauerwas's work. The only explanation for the fact that he has written so much is that "my writing is determined by my reading" (ix).

Hauerwas's reading habits have influenced me significantly. I have been reading him for years, and have always been at least as interested in his footnotes or endnotes as I am in the essays themselves. His notes consist of personal comments, arguments with this author or that, references to other issues that might be taken up; the notes are lively, often personal, and always interesting. It is an understatement to say that Hauerwas reads a lot. The bibliography of *Working with Words* includes approximately 250 sources,[2] ranging from Jewish theologians to Protestants, Catholics, social theorists, political theorists, ancient writers, his own previous writings, secular philosophers, poets, current and former students, John Howard Yoder, and so on. Reading is for Hauerwas essential to writing, all of which is crucial to the work of theology, to the work of being trained to speak Christian.

Closely related to the importance of reading in the task of doing theology is the claim that friendship is also central to theological work for Hauerwas. The way he pursues the theological task is part of the practice of friendship. By reputation, Hauerwas is very generous as a professor, mentor, and friend,[3] and *Working with Words* provides positive evidence of such a reputation, and of the importance of friendship to the work of theology. A number of essays include a final note in which he thanks somebody; these individuals are often students, former students, or colleagues, and it's important to note that what Hauerwas thanks them for is their criticisms

---

2. I returned to Rob Bell's *Love Wins* for comparison: there wasn't really a bibliography, but a source list for "further reading" consisting of a total of seven books.

3. I've experienced a bit of this—his willingness to read my book, and his personal touch when I asked him to be an employment reference for me.

and suggestions. In the case of chapter 3, he includes the essay written with Brian Goldstone "to celebrate our friendship" (33), and least five of the essays book are written with someone else. In another essay, he takes up the topic of Jean Vanier and the work of L'Arche, an international group of communities that consider friendship with people with disabilities to be the center of their ministry.[4] Hauerwas's final essay in the book is a theological reflection on the friendship cultivated between Dietrich Bonhoeffer and Eberhard Bethge.

Further, the work of theology, of working with words, is part of the task of what it means to be a missionary people. The gospel always seeks for ways to be incarnated in new contexts, and the very character of God is such that those who worship God must be witnesses. "The missionary character of the church, therefore, means that the testing of the words we use as well as their grammar can never be finished" (xi). The kind of witness Hauerwas is talking about, the way of working with words, is not a kind of desperate shouting but rather seeks to display an essential relationship between what we say and how we live. He cites the example of the philosopher Ludwig Wittgenstein, who upon hearing a street evangelist shouting to passersby is said to have commented, "If he really believed what he was shouting he would not use that tone of voice" (169). So throughout the book, Hauerwas time and again brings to view the importance of practice, of training, of being shaped, of worship—all of which take a lifetime of doing—of being involved in the missionary task of working with words.

Having taken note of what Hauerwas claims he is doing as he works with words, it is important to look at the work itself. Does he in fact do what he says he is doing? Here I want to take notice of the kinds of things he writes in this book and how he approaches his work, and then we will see what kind of theology appears when one works the way Hauerwas works. Several of his essays consist of extended conversations with ancient Christian writers, such as Augustine and Thomas Aquinas. The interesting thing to observe is *how* Hauerwas does this; after all, essays in conversation with Augustine and Aquinas are a dime a dozen. His Augustine essay (chapter 2) is a reflection on evil, written because Hauerwas was involved in an interdisciplinary seminar on evil and goodness. The essay was written for a specific occasion, which gave him a chance to read Augustine, which is not a sterile exercise of ivory-tower speculation. Rather, he drives the discussion to include his rationale for being against Nazism, and ultimately concludes that Christians do not have a way to explain evil—what we have is the church.

---

4. Hauerwas has written about Vanier before, and has also coauthored a book with Vanier; see Hauerwas and Vanier, *Living Gently in a Violent World*.

His essay on Aquinas, focusing specifically on the virtues, is coauthored with Sheryl Overmyer, but they are not just giving an account of the lists of virtues. Hauerwas and Overmyer refuse to read Aquinas as just another philosopher or moral thinker. A substantial part of the essay keeps in front of us a reflection on how Aquinas wrote, the "shape," or "architectonics" of the *Summa* itself. They are watching how Aquinas works with words. The chapter is a close reading of important and well-known ethical thought that keeps pushing the discussion back onto God. That is, a discussion of the virtues cannot be considered apart from God. The way that Hauerwas and Overmyer are able to make that move, at least in part, is to watch how the great scholastic thinker works with words.

Hauerwas also participates in an extended conversation with modern Catholic social thought. Again he coauthors this piece, this time with Jana Bennett. The conversation entails reflection on the papal encyclicals from 1891–1991, serving as a very fine introduction to this important and influential stream of work. After all, Catholics all over the world take these teachings from the papal office very seriously, as do others who are not Catholic. In other words, this essay is a reflection on a body of work that had and continues to have considerable shaping force. But we must note again the way it is written—not as a simple summing up, or liberal critique, but as an attempt to understand these encyclicals on their own terms. It is important to understand that "their own terms" are fundamentally theological. The encyclicals are referred to as social teachings, but what is at stake in this essay is the thesis that these writings cannot be absorbed unless their theology is understood. Indeed, the encyclicals "demonstrate(s) some of the best theological argumentation found concerning the Christian life" (251). This is important in a number of ways, according to Hauerwas; to give just one example, any discussion of gender in this context means that we must first think of "woman" as a theological matter, and then read political issues of rights in that light (254).

In addition to conversations with and about ancient thinkers and Catholic social teaching, Hauerwas also collaborates with a secular atheist, Romand Coles, in an essay about secularism, with reference to Canadian philosopher Charles Taylor. Chapter 15 begins by noting the poetry of Gerard Manley Hopkins, a Jesuit poet cited by Charles Taylor. What difference might it make for a Christian theologian and a secular atheist political theorist to reflect on a Christian philosopher's work on the secularity of the Western world? Romand Coles and Hauerwas are very interested in how to affect change in the world, and both are clear about their respective and differing faiths, and yet they work together in ways that are fascinating. Many of the statements in this essay use the first person plural pronoun "we," signaling the possibility of working and thinking together. This kind of work is fascinating to watch.

I want to use chapter 17 as an example of another way that Hauerwas works with words. In this chapter, he writes what amounts to a very useful introduction to the thought of Alasdair MacIntyre, a ground-breaking philosopher of our age and a force to be reckoned with. MacIntyre has confessed Christian faith in recent years, but writes as a philosopher. What is interesting about this essay for our present discussion is that Hauerwas does not really do much critical work here. I understand him to be giving appropriate credit to MacIntyre for the way that he has influenced Hauerwas, from a very early time in his career. In other words, Hauerwas is trying to introduce *his* readers to what *he* reads in a very explicit way, as if he is saying: "If you want to understand me, the way I work, the way I think, and the emphasis of my work, you ought to know that here's one of the people who has shaped me. So, once you put this book down, go read MacIntyre." And it works to some extent—for example, I have read MacIntyre because of Hauerwas. That influence is easy to see in part because Hauerwas is so confessional, so open about that influence. There is no sense here that he is claiming originality or novelty in his own thought, since to do so would be to allow distraction from the task of theology.

In chapter 7, Hauerwas engages the work of Richard Hays, one of the world's leading biblical scholars. This is also a very interesting engagement, in part because Hauerwas is defending himself to a certain extent, in response to the way Hays characterizes his work in *The Moral Vision of the New Testament* (1996). Hauerwas shows in this essay that he can engage with his critics, and take the criticism seriously. But that's not the interesting dimension of this chapter. The engagement with Hays gives Hauerwas the opportunity to write about how commentaries should or could be written. Hauerwas is not a trained biblical scholar, and so his own attempt to write a commentary proceeds a bit differently than does Hays's—that is, Hauerwas tries to display "the ways the words run" (108). The reason for this approach is to let the words shape our imaginations in a manner that forces us to read the world scripturally, and not the other way round (108). So, Hauerwas's engagement with a major biblical scholar becomes an occasion to pursue the question of what reading scripture theologically might look like. He is resisting the notion that on one side of the street stand biblical scholars, who take the text apart bit by bit using historical critical methods that are unable or unwilling to address our lives, and on the other side of the street are theologians, who can write entire essays and books without actually taking the Bible seriously. He ends the essay by acknowledging that Hays is one who works both sides of that street.

Hauerwas also includes seven sermons in this book, most of which are shaped by the readings of the church year calendar or by some specific occasion. These are not nearly as dense as some of the essays and are considerably shorter, but clearly recognizable as his work. Hauerwas sees his sermons doing the same kind of work as his academic papers, and vice versa. That is the case at least for the first two sections of the book, in which he uses both papers and sermons to address the questions of learning to say "God" (section 1) and those dealing with normative matters (section 2). He does not include sermons in the last section, presumably because this comprises writing about his various intellectual influences, and so the form of the sermon would not be quite appropriate. Hauerwas claims that "the sermon is at the heart of our ability to speak as well as sustain speaking Christian. The sermon is not your reflections on how to negotiate life. The sermon rather is our fundamental speech act as Christians through which we learn the grammar of the faith" (93). For Hauerwas, at least, the sermon is theological work every bit as important as any academic theology, perhaps even more so.

I can't help but remark on the lecture Hauerwas includes from his address to the Youth Academy at Duke. To be assigned a talk to teenagers and to come up with this lecture is fascinating to me. He takes on the question of "Why Did Jesus Have to Die?" Instead of beginning with attempts to show that he understands teen culture, or making reference to some part of their experience, he begins by informing them that he is afraid that the Christianity they embrace is not authentic Christianity at all, and then carries on with serious theological material. Who knows how this talk landed in his audience, but my guess is that might not be Hauerwas's most important consideration. Rather, he takes both the theological task and the young audience seriously, and carries on by talking about the things of God.

I conclude by displaying a sample of an often-repeated criticism of Hauerwas's work, namely, that he is not careful with his own words. Chase Roden's review of *Working with Words* claims that

> Hauerwas writes at length on speech and language as a means and metaphor for living out Christianity. However, as the speeches and sermons in this collection show, Hauerwas is not always particularly careful with his own words. After reading the youth speech, one can hardly imagine that the kids Hauerwas spoke to had the faintest idea what the first half of the address was about. Experienced readers will be able to identify (if not agree with) Hauerwas's beef with churches celebrating secular holidays, but Hauerwas seems to use shock as a hook for his audience without actually enlightening them in any way. He

tends not to use this rhetorical strategy as often in his academic works, but Hauerwas's sermons and speeches are littered with examples of provocative overstatements that cannot possibly be expected to educate his hearers or readers. Where is the room for careful speech—for habituated truth telling—in such a strategy? Even when Hauerwas is not trying to shock his audience into listening, he often does not display great care toward the communication of truth; his arguments in sermons and addresses are sometimes exceedingly hard to follow on the written page, let alone when read aloud.[5]

Roden's accusation that Hauerwas uses "provocative overstatements that cannot possibly be expected to educate his hearers or readers" reveals what I consider to be a deep misunderstanding of Hauerwas's work. Prominent theologian William Cavanaugh, a former student of Hauerwas, addresses this kind of complaint, citing several of these kinds of provocations as examples. In one instance, Hauerwas asked a medical researcher who defends experiments on fetal tissue if he would eat fetal tissue if it were discovered that it was a delicacy. In another example, at a rally protesting capital punishment, Hauerwas declared that he was for the death penalty if it would be used to execute people for stock fraud. After expanding on Hauerwas's answers, Cavanaugh argues that such follow-up explanations "dull the impact of Hauerwas's statements. Stanley will commonly eschew such explanations and let the audience figure it out . . . a deliberate part of Stanley's pedagogy is to force people to think by jolting them out of their customary positions."[6] *Working with Words*, while provocative at many points, does serve to educate readers, and the provocation is intended to provoke faithful following of Jesus Christ.

---

5. Roden, "How Then Shall We Speak?" Review of *Working with Words*.
6. Cavanaugh, "Stan the Man," 29.

18

The Undoing of Death

Fleming Rutledge. *The Undoing of Death: Sermons for Holy Week and Easter.* Grand Rapids: Eerdmans, 2002.

> *Rutledge is one of North America's most well-known preachers. She has published a number of collections of her sermons, beginning with the popular* Bible and the New York Times. *In this collection, assembled around the central celebration of the Christian year, she "brings her formidable intellect and her wide reading to bear in saying what is nearly unsayable." Here we have an opportunity to read and discuss written versions of spoken sermons—another form of speaking about God.*

Rutledge's book is the third in a series of discussions organized under the theme of working with words. We're ostensibly trying to learn to watch our language in these discussions, as we watch how various writers and preachers use language to talk about God. In our first of these meetings, we looked carefully at the way Rob Bell made a big splash by taking on questions about heaven, hell, salvation, and atonement. Among other things we noted the particular use of the question, which not only raises issues and acts as actual inquiry, but can also function as a way of arguing that is every bit as assertive as putting forward propositional statements. We also paid attention to Bell's use of sources and tried generally to think about what he was doing, to whom he was writing, and whether this way of doing theology would stand the test of time. We asked, What would happen to the church if this is the way theology was done more generally?

Our discussion of *Working with Words* by Stanley Hauerwas took on a bit of a different tone. He is much more self-conscious about what it means to be working with words, and writes almost exclusively in essay form (the "try"), because he believes that the nature of the essay is the nature of the theological task. Whether he writes a densely argued theological piece, a commencement address, or a sermon, in his view these are all part of the same theological task, namely, disciplining speech about God. We looked at the importance he places on reading (it shapes the grammar of our faith), at the role that friendship plays in his writing; we noted that he sees writing as mission work, and that his writing is both a taking up and a carrying forward of conversations with all manner of sources, ancient to contemporary.

Hauerwas's book also provided a rationale for including a book of sermons within the wider discussion of working with words. "The sermon is at the heart of our ability to speak as well as sustain speaking Christian. The sermon is not your reflections on how to negotiate life. The sermon rather is our fundamental speech act as Christians through which we learn the grammar of the faith."[1] For Hauerwas, at least, the sermon is theological work every bit as important as any academic theology—perhaps even more so. Further, Hauerwas contends, following John Wright, that "preaching is the appropriate practice for biblical reading." Wright argues that contemporary preaching too often takes as its task to find "applications" for the text when its task should be to turn a congregation away from one narrative world to another.[2]

In reading Fleming Rutledge, we turn our attention to another way of working with words, of watching our language, namely preaching. I ran across a definition by Klaas Runia, who claims that preaching is a "monstrous monologue by a moron to mutes."[3] Note that the burden of the insult is not on the congregation, but on the preacher. I preach occasionally, and some of the most bizarre conversations I have had in my life have come on the heels of preaching sermons. After a Mother's Day sermon in which I argued that according to Jesus's teaching in the Gospels, Christians ought to hate their mothers and fathers, a fellow parishioner demanded that I come back the following Sunday, not to serve the congregation again but to retract everything I had said in the just-completed sermon. A more disturbing reaction came to me courtesy of a complete stranger, who called into question

---

1. Hauerwas, *Working with Words*, 93.
2. Ibid., 99.
3. Runia, *Sermon under Attack*; quoted in Williams, "Interactive Preaching."

whether I loved God. Even though this person had never met me before, or heard me say anything other than what I had preached during those twenty-five minutes, she approached me later with this assessment. After I feebly tried to direct her to some part of the sermon as a way of showing that I did in fact love God, she claimed that this insight of hers had nothing to do with the content; she could somehow tell in other (unnamed) ways that I did not love God.

At any rate, I do not want to talk about preaching primarily from personal experience, or abstractly apart from Rutledge's book, except to say that there is a strong stream of thought within the Christian world that insists that preaching is one of the most important practices of the church's ministry. John Stott, in a memorable opening line to his book *Between Two Worlds*, simply claims that "preaching is indispensable to Christianity."[4]

Pithy sayings aside, Christopher Schwöbel argues that preaching is one of the most important ways of doing theology, a practice in which both the preacher and listeners are involved together, and therefore the ultimate testing ground and field of application for theology. But the preaching must be theological, and to be that it must include four dimensions, says Schwöbel. Theological preaching must be done biblically through patient engagement with the text, and it must be done pastorally, doctrinally, and congregationally. Schwöbel concludes,

> Christian preachers knew already that every good sermon must, of necessity, be incomplete, open to the validation of the message through the testimony of the Holy Spirit in our hearts. When a sermon is complete in itself, a finished masterpiece of spiritual rhetoric, this betrays that the preacher does not expect the address begun by human words of witness to be completed by God the Spirit Himself. This is a failure both of preaching and of theology. The art of preaching theologically consists in offering a sermon that is open to being completed by God, it consists in telling an unfinished story—because God has so much more to tell us.[5]

If we take seriously our self-assigned task, to look not just at what Rutledge writes but also ask what she is doing and specifically how she is doing it, and if we take seriously the importance of preaching to the Christian faith,

---

4. Stott, *Between Two Worlds*, 15. He goes on to quote others: "Sermonettes breed Christianettes," and "Brevity may be the soul of wit, but the preacher is not a wit—a Christianity of short sermons is a Christianity of short fiber (P.T. Forsythe)" (294).

5. Schwöbel, "The Preacher's Art," introduction to *Theology through Preaching*, by Colin Gunton, 20.

we have our work cut out for us. Rutledge is first and foremost a preacher, and we mostly and rightfully think of preaching as an *event*, delivered in a specific setting at a specific time within a particular context. In *The Undoing of Death* we have sermons that are published as written texts, thus seeking on the one hand to preserve the content and on the other to extend the audience both in space and time, but in so doing perhaps changing the very nature of the thing itself. There are many layers to consider as we read published sermons separated from their original occasions by time and space.

William Willimon claims that

> the Reverend Fleming Rutledge works well that same conflicted, risky ground between us and the gospel. Her sermons are vivid demonstration that, all reports to the contrary, faithful biblical preaching is alive and well, interesting, engaging, demanding, and residing, of all places, in the Episcopal Church. Each of her sermons here takes seriously our contemporary congregational difficulty in hearing the gospel. Yet they are chiefly remarkable because her sermons take even more seriously the peculiar word to our time which is called Good News. That is, although she often begins by quoting the *Times*, very quickly in her sermons we realize that she is allowing the Bible to confront, unmask, and defeat the *Times* and everything it believes to be news.[6]

It is important to let Rutledge speak for herself—that is, what does she think she's doing? Rutledge thinks that the sermon is a unique kind of thing in that it has a power behind it like no other; "it has the character of an *event*." She sees a world of difference between public speaking and preaching, which is human activity but derived from God; preaching is an impossible activity; and finally, "in the preaching of the Word of God, the risen, reigning, living Jesus Christ has promised to be present in power."[7]

In an essay entitled "A New Liberalism of the Word," Rutledge argues for the rebirth of Protestantism. She pleads for Christians not to let the church become just another ministry that is indistinguishable from other secular social agencies. Key factors in any Protestant resurgence include the scriptures and the power of God. One of the reasons for the declining reliance on is the kind of preaching that emphasizes spirituality, religious activity, or the human experience, which are anthropological sermons, not theological sermons, precisely because the subject is not God. The task of the church is "to discern, through the study of the scriptures in the context

---

6. Willimon, foreword to Fleming Rutledge, *The Bible and the New York Times*, xiv.

7. Rutledge, *The Bible and the New York Times*, 1–6.

of the worshipping community, what God is doing in the world so that we can move where he is moving... My proposal is that the single most powerful factor in overcoming the liberal-conservative theological divide is the renewal of confident preaching and teaching of historic, Nicene, Biblical faith." What she wants, she says in her dramatic conclusion, is "a revivifying dose of Scripture and the power of God."[8] Rutledge also claims that "the working out of Christian ethics is best done in the Sunday teaching and the day in, day out life of the congregation."[9] Preaching is central to keeping the church the church.

If it is the case that the sermon is so important and that Rutledge has a high view of preaching, we might ask how she goes about preparing her sermons. How does she choose topics or find the impulse for writing sermons? The primary source for the setting of topics, or more accurately, the choosing of biblical texts from which the sermon will be generated, is the liturgical church year. The liturgical readings tell her what to read as she prepares. In the first sermon in *The Undoing of Death*, addressing Palm Sunday, Rutledge is able to say something about that strange Sunday specifically because of the liturgy: "Here is the purpose of the Palm Sunday liturgy: for the church to know the things that make for (her) peace, to know the time of (her) visitation" (6). So, in this book she groups the sermons according to the days (xvii) of Holy Week, beginning with Palm Sunday, then working through Monday, Tuesday, and Wednesday as a group, followed by a separate focus on Maundy Thursday, nineteen Good Friday sermons, then a number of Easter Sunday and Easter week sermons, and then several from the Great Fifty Days (Eastertide), and a sermon for addressing the events of September 11—a piece that is homeless in this collection, an issue to which I will return.[10]

---

8. Rutledge, "New Liberalism of the Word."

9. Rutledge, *Undoing of Death*, xx. Subsequent references to the book will be included in the body of the essay.

10. The liturgical year also figures prominently in Rutledge's other collections. *The Bible and the New York Times* is shaped by the church year explicitly; *Not Ashamed of the Gospel* is organized by a focus on the text of Romans, but even there, it's not as though she set out to simply work through those texts. Rather, she collected sermons she had preached across a number of years, and then organized them for the purpose of publication in this form, often signaling that this sermon or that was preached as part of the liturgical year. In similar fashion, the sermons in *Help My Unbelief*, "designed for the man or woman who wonders about faith," were *not* written to "answer a specific question or to address a specific issue. They were written, as all sermons should be written, as expositions of Biblical texts in specific situations." Rutledge, *Help My Unbelief*, xi, xv.

The importance of the liturgical tradition shapes the texts that Rutledge studies and gives shape to the sermons even before content is considered, and the texts make a difference in the content. For example, in another of her Palm Sunday sermons, she points out that the Palm Sunday tradition is disconcerting, seeing as how we enter the church in a festive mood but before the service is over we are confronted by catastrophe.

> It would be tempting on this day, to follow good American practice and tone down the depressing parts—"accentuate the positive, eliminate the negative." Many American congregations have attempted this. *Were it not for the ancient liturgical wisdom given to the church*, it would be perfectly possible to go to Sunday services two weekends in a row—Palm Sunday and Easter Day—without ever having to face the fact that Jesus of Nazareth was abandoned, condemned, and put to death as a common criminal on the Friday between. Our historic liturgy, however, guards against this fatal misunderstanding. From early times the Christian church has placed the Passion narrative squarely in the center of all that we do on this deceptively festal day. The proper liturgical name for this day is not really "Palm Sunday"; it is "the Sunday of the Passion." In this way, the church announces for all to hear that the Crucifixion of Jesus is the main event. There is no passage from Palm Sunday to Easter without Good Friday. (11)

Rutledge's focus on the liturgy means that she begins with biblical texts, but we find neither a pedantic repetition of the stories nor a glancing off from the text to some favorite topic of the day. Instead, we see the text taken seriously as a way of reading the world, the church, and ourselves. And so we find ourselves as readers, as were the original listeners before us, invited to come, to see; we are summoned, even begged, to look at what is placed before us by the biblical text when it is taken seriously and then allowed to cast light on the world in which we find ourselves.

However, these sermons are not only reflections on the biblical text. Rutledge brings many other kinds of sources to bear on what the text puts before us. The material is wide-ranging, and while there is some overlap with the sources Rob Bell and Stanley Hauerwas draw on, there are significant differences between the way she and Bell use them, and in what she and Hauerwas read. Even within her work, Rutledge tries to pay attention both to the congregation and to the occasion itself, meaning that sometimes a sermon may be considerably longer than another one, or one may being noticeably more dense than another. One thing we notice is that she does not proceed by way of questions, as Bell does, nor is she an academic along the lines of Hauerwas—she intends to preach.

From time to time, Rutledge refers to a movie, but not often, since "the movie offers a mere two hours of more or less thought-provoking entertainment, whereas the Bible summons us to a whole lifetime of study and transformation" (41). She refers to a number of books, but they are not all of a sort. She draws on the novels of authors such as Flannery O'Connor and C.S. Lewis; she references collections of sermons by preachers such as Alexander McLaren, Barbara Bradford Taylor, and her favorite, John Donne; she brings to bear material from collections of essays, formal theological works (for example, John Calvin, Bishop Tutu, Charles Marsh), biblical studies and commentaries, some philosophy and historical theology, ancient writers, the Book of Common Prayer and the Lectionary, and poetry. In addition, she refers to newspapers, music, magazines, hymns, and even *TV Guide*.

The Bible leads the way for Rutledge, but to say that is not quite enough—the choice of what to do with the Bible and what to focus on is shaped by the liturgical year, and then other sources follow along. Among these sources, her use of hymn texts stands out. In a number of sermons, she quotes hymns at some length, and often she will call the reader's close attention to their words, using them as theological mooring points. Her focus is on the lyrical content of those hymns, although she makes no mention of the music itself.

Publishing the sermons in book form allows Rutledge to add to the experience of reading them by including reproductions of paintings. There's no explanation of how these paintings were part of the services in which the sermons were delivered. But in the book, they add a great deal to the written content of the sermons. The brief explanations are often quite personal, and very helpful in understanding both the painting and the content of the sermon, all of which extends the experience of reading text and calls on the reader to also pay attention to the artistic tradition of the church.

A further addition to these sermons that becomes possible because of their publication in written form is the deliberate use of capitalization for the purpose of emphasis—for example Sin, Death—to underscore their independent status as Powers (capitalized), separate from the human being and not susceptible to human choice. In other words, Rutledge's theology is emphasized by her use of typography. The published form of the sermon also allows for the use of epigraphs, most frequently brief quotations from John Donne's sermon "Death's Duel."

I want to look just for a moment at some of the themes Rutledge picks up in her sermons, and the way she works at them. Rutledge does commendable work in giving witness to the historic, Nicene, biblical faith that she thinks is necessary for the revivification of Protestantism. She simply refuses to allow the gospel message to be reduced or to be taken over by anything resembling platitudes. She confronts her listeners and readers with a robust account of sin and judgment. Further, her repeated insistence on the reality of the events of Holy Week must also be noted. Not for her some notion of the seasons changing, of the coming of spring, of papering over the desolation of death. To make any of those kinds of interpretive moves is for Rutledge to drain the gospel of its power. She sees this reductionist dynamic at work when she goes shopping for greeting cards—this mushiness, this humanistic reduction of the gospel—and she will simply have none of it (206–7).

As mentioned above, Rutledge includes a sermon in this collection, delivered on two separate occasions, to respond to the events of September 11, 2001, in New York City, a sermon I have described as "homeless." As with the rest of the book, I want to continue to ask what she is doing, and how she works. First, we notice immediately that this sermon is out of sync with the rest of the book—it's not part of Holy Week liturgy, certainly, and it gets stuck awkwardly at the end of the Good Friday section, when in fact it is nothing like the rest of those sermons. The connection, if there is one, is the cross. However, just because the cross is central to a talk does not mean that it is in fact cruciform in a biblical way. In fact, Rutledge takes pains to warn us exactly of that dynamic, alerting us of the kinds of misunderstandings of the cross that lead to Ku Klux Klan burnings of the cross, or to the placing of the cross over ruined Muslim homes by Serbian Orthodox Christians, and she repeats that warning one more time in this speech (xx, 226, 227). Here she does not follow the liturgical calendar, but describes how the text "spoke to me as I was searching the Scriptures with 'hunger for certainty, [that] precious commodity'" (227). And uniquely, in this book at least, she begins her public address in a church with the greeting "My fellow Americans" (225)—in church![11]

Rutledge proceeds to paint a stark picture of black and white, good and evil, based on that single event. In the wreckage we see a cross-shaped steel girder, of which much was made as it became an iconic image of the

---

11. Denny Smith, a member of the Take and Read group (and author of the foreword to this book), grew up in the southern United States. His comment (sent to me in personal correspondence) regarding the phrase used by Rutledge here: "the 'My fellow Americans . . .' phrase has long been the claim and call to true oneness with each other that we Americans seem to hold passionately in the abstract, but jettison at the first intrusive step of pragmatic reality in our relationships. I wish to make to no effort to justify the use of the term . . . it is warm and emotionally powerful to most American hearers (I still feel a little something about it) but it is simply without substance in this text, and elsewhere."

event. To this she says, "The Cross of Christ is the only symbol that matches the devastation at Ground Zero." She goes on to speak about "Cross-shaped acts of Christian courage," making what for me is an incomprehensible connection to Bonhoeffer, Martin Luther King Jr., Oscar Romero, and so on. She also remarks on the sending of American troops to Afghanistan: "Even pacifistically inclined people like myself are solidly united behind our armed forces in this hour." At one point in her description of September 11, she states that "the fires of hell have tried their best to extinguish the good" (225–32). I am simply not sure what Rutledge is doing here, but what makes this essay so jarring to me (I have no doubt that across the United States in those days this would have been a fairly mild rhetoric) is precisely because of how strange it is according to her own lights, according to the way she has done her theology to that point.

But I don't want to end there—to do so would be patently unfair to Rutledge and to the body of work that she has produced so far. Indeed, I think it is more accurate to say that Fleming Rutledge is often at great pains to do the opposite of what she does in that address. She lets the Bible have its way with her, so that it will have its way with us—in part because a sermon is a unique thing. That is, as she puts it, a sermon is a "language event" (291).[12] But even that description doesn't quite do justice to her work; the sermon isn't just a language event or a speech act, it is an attempt to witness to the power of Jesus Christ, an attempt to preach Christ crucified. "Preachers pray a lot about their sermons. We don't pray that the sermon will be good; we pray that Jesus Christ will make himself known" (66).

---

12. Rutledge is drawing here on Amos Wilder; see Rutledge, *Undoing of Death*, 357n41.

19

Migrations of the Holy

William Cavanaugh. *Migrations of the Holy: God, State, and the Political Meaning of the Church*. Grand Rapids: Eerdmans, 2011.

> *What do we mean when we use words such as "politics" and "religion?" Cavanaugh would have us consider very carefully how we frame our understanding and speech concerning these matters, since all too often what passes as religious fervor has migrated toward a new object of worship—the nation-state—and we don't even recognize what has happened. Here's our chance to talk religion and politics—very carefully.*

We now turn our attention to the writing of Roman Catholic political theologian William Cavanaugh, referenced briefly in Stanley Hauerwas's book where he asserts that "politics is speech."[1] Cavanaugh's book takes up issues of religion and politics, and described in that way, is one of many. So what might he be doing that is any different than any other book that addresses these issues? It is important to look carefully at *what* he's doing and especially at *how* he proceeds. My first observation is that Cavanaugh takes his title from the final chapter of a John Bossy book.[2] Bossy's piece is brief and dense, in which he shows that the sense of holy migrates not only from the Christian faith to the nation-state (his first cat-

---

1. Hauerwas, *Working with Words*, 90, 121.
2. Bossy, *Christianity in the West*.

egory); Bossy also shows the same pattern in music, wherein sacredness moves from the church to the concert hall, a section on which I am unqualified to comment. The same migration is seen in the use of words such as "religion," and "state." "The whole, for better or worse, was 'Christianity,' a word which until the seventeenth century meant a body of people, and has since then, as most European languages testify, meant an 'ism' or body of beliefs."[3] Cavanaugh acknowledges his debt to Bossy early in the book.

By Cavanaugh's own account, his book "[points] to practices that resist the colonization of the Christian imagination by a nation-state that wants to subordinate all other attachments to itself" (5). According to Micah Weedman, "This has been the heart of Cavanaugh's work from the beginning, and nearly all of his work follows a predictable but important pattern of dealing, both historically and theologically, with the rise and function of our convictions about the nation-state, followed by deep theological scholarship and constructive work about the 'complex space' the church must necessarily inhabit."[4] One might say that Cavanaugh works genealogically, looking to see where things come from, for the history of a concept, a word, a way of thinking, a way of imagining, taking care to bring to view the fact that ideas, beliefs, and practices do not just appear fully formed, out of nowhere.

The way that Cavanaugh proceeds for the most part is through writing essays, which then are shaped into books. That is, he acknowledges that he wrote these essays between 2004 and 2007, but here, by some process he does not quite explain, the essays become chapters of this book; he treats the project as a whole, arguing that it has a singular purpose, "to help Christians and others to be realistic about what we can expect from the 'powers and principalities' of our own age, and to urge them not to invest the entirety of political presence in those powers" (3).

Notable is his emphasis on language right from the start; Cavanaugh insists on using the language of salvation to discuss the state, because the state cannot be understood without theology. He speaks of "unthinking" the way we have been thinking; he wants to complexify things, to challenge our metaphors and re-narrate matters. That is, he examines assumptions and refuses to accept things the way they are and persuade us that the Christian role in politics is to have a voice in what is basically already a given. His stated intention is "to give Christians and others critical tools with which to turn the despair of modern politics toward real hope" (6). One clue to the way he works, all of this complexifying, re-narrating, re-conceptualizing,

3. Cavanaugh, *Migrations of the Holy*, 171. Subsequent references to the book will be included in the body of the essay.

4. Weedman, "Practices That Resist the Colonization of the Christian Imagination," Review of *Migrations of the Holy*.

re-describing, is the number of times he uses scare quotes, signaling that he wants us to pay attention to those words, that he will not be held to the conventional definitions and understandings of those words. To offer just a few such examples: "resurgence," "original sin," "secular age," "too big to fail," "secularized," "covert," "powers and principalities," "society," "political," "religion," "politics," and "spiritual." Cavanaugh's point is that much of the vocabulary of politics and religion, the language with which we think and act in realms of what we think is political, ought to be called into question. One of the ways to read this book might be simply to keep a running tab of all of the words, concepts, and ideas that he takes up, examines, and then redefines in order to prevent the colonization of the Christian imagination, to resist being controlled by the state, and ultimately to resist idolatry, to resist the migration of the holy from the church to the state and perhaps begin a return migration.

The reader of Cavanaugh's book would do well to identify some of the words, concepts, and ideas that Cavanaugh tries to re-describe, complexify, re-narrate, or re-conceptualize, and ask whether this way of talking about the issues of politics and religion is anything more than an esoteric head game. I will not take up every one of the terms to which he turns his attention, or attempt to see then how these discussions fit into his larger argument, but I want to take a solid sampling so that we can see how he works, and then seek to determine if there's merit to this approach, to this way of watching our language.

Cavanaugh signals very early in the book that the term "religion" is not to be understood in any straightforward way; it is not some special, non-empirical realm of which Christianity is just one instantiation among many others (4). That notion itself is an invention of the early modern era that facilitated the expansion of civil over ecclesiastical power. The term "religious" is problematic because it tends to identify certain kinds of belief (Christianity, Islam, Hinduism) as inherently different and less rational than other kinds of beliefs, such as faith in the market or the nation (171).[5]

Likewise, the term "politics" comes under Cavanaugh's scrutiny. Politics is *not*, as commonly understood, an "essentially distinct realm of human behavior" (4). Put another way, "there is no realm of life called 'politics' that is only indirectly under God's providential care" (4, 5). Cavanaugh attacks such an understanding by trying to change our imaginations, by seeking to move us from thinking about or conceiving of politics as that which happens only in one city to that which occurs in two cities. This is of course

---

5. Cavanaugh directs the reader to another of his books which deals with the development and use of religion in some detail. See his *Myth of Religious Violence*, especially chapter 2.

an extended and complex discussion of Augustine's thought, but at a basic level, Cavanaugh shows us that most people "share an imagination of one earthly city with which the political life of a people takes place" (56). That is, we live in a nation-state, and within that given, the church and state must maneuver for space. Says Cavanaugh: "What is important for my present purpose is the way that Augustine's image of the two cities breaks the modern monolithic conception of a single space, bounded by the nation-state, in which the church must somehow find a place" (63).

It is important to realize that "there is no sense that there is a single given public square in which the church must find its place" (57). Instead, the church too is a kind of public, the city of God makes use of the temporal goods as does the earthly city and the city of God is a public in its own right. Once the imagination of "space" changes from one city to two cities, we have to resist a lot of conventionally held notions about political space (59); we have to say "no" to many conceptions to which we cling, often without much thought. And so Cavanaugh spends a lot of time saying what politics is *not*. In fact, the negative term is used innumerable times in this chapter. Upon embrace of a two-cities understanding, upon rejection of the notion that there is one given public space and it is secular, there follows a call for the resistance to any number of related ideas, ideas such as the church as ideal or separated community, the church identifying with the state, and so on (see pp. 66–67 for an intensified negative argument).

The burden of Cavanaugh's second chapter is to show us that the nation-state is not the keeper of the common good, that being convinced of the necessity to kill or die on behalf of the state is like being convinced to kill for the telephone company. Cavanaugh's purpose is to examine the assumptions that bring people to those conclusions. He does so by investigating the history of the term "state," including a fascinating discussion of the etymology of the term, showing that large etymological shifts follow profound changes in social organization (10). He also explores the history of origins of the state and shows that once the state is a "something," then it becomes possible to create society, a gathering of people into a unitary space, and the state begins to tell the church where it belongs, by either absorbing the church or privatizing it. The creation of the state, which in turn creates society, is followed by the creation of the nation-state in the West (33), a creation that elides existing internal differences at the very same time as it accentuates external differences. If it is true that the "nation-state is neither community writ large nor the protector of smaller communal spaces," then it becomes the task of the church to "demystify the nation-state and treat it like the telephone company. At best, the nation-state may provide goods and services that contribute to a certain limited order" (41, 42).

The fourth term scrutinized by Cavanaugh is "providence," the acknowledgment and recognition of God's work in history, central to his argument in chapter four. While it is true that the chapter is focused on the notion of "American Exceptionalism," a form of this kind of thinking is also readily visible in other countries, including Canada, wherein the tendency is to think that the locus of God's work in this nation-state or that. Cavanaugh's burden is to help us reframe our understanding of God's work in the world. We are to read providence from the point of view of the cross. That is, "reading history for signs of God's providential activity is an exercise that Christians must undertake as independently as possible from ideologies of both the right and the left . . . the church is itself, as the body of Christ, a significant locus of God's activity in history" (100). Interestingly, this reframing of an understanding of providence is then closely tied to a new understanding of citizenship.[6]

Cavanaugh's constructive section is theologically demanding. This content is very important, but even before that is considered, it is also important to notice that the way to help us think about "politics" is to do good theology. So we are faced with the question of what a chapter addressing ecclesial monophysitism and ecclesial nestorianism has to do with politics. In brief, the discussion has to do with the invisibility and visibility of the church, which has everything to do with the way of the church in the world. Often the discussion seems to proceed along lines of visibility—the church shows the world how things should be. But that is problematic, because the church is obviously sinful. This then moves people to be "realistic," to "make the best of it," as it were, since the church is sinful anyway, as is the world. Cavanaugh is trying here to move beyond this impasse, and does so Christologically (168). In Micah Weedman's view, "it's this turn to unity and Christology that will and should get the most attention. Cavanaugh's essays about sinfulness and vulnerability (the latter of which is Cavanaugh directly reading Hauerwas) offer a vision of the church that accounts for both the presence of sin while still taking seriously the biblical notion that this

---

6. This description of samples that bring to view the way Cavanaugh works could go on, but I will just mention a few more here without developing them at all: a) his brief but fascinating chapter regarding the Inquisition asks us to consider that what is at stake is the way we narrate the Enlightenment; b) a discussion in which he tries to complexify our understanding of liturgy, of what is sacred and what is secular. National liturgy is not sacred, Christian liturgy is not sacred; in his chapter on the church as political, he examines the Christian notion that it is only the church that is the "people of God," forcing us to resist leaving Israel behind—before he's done the discussion of the church as political he also asks us to reconsider our understanding of Christendom and what it means to be considered sectarian.

church—sin and all—can and must be understood as the body of Christ, broken for the world."[7]

Throughout the book, Cavanaugh shows that he is an able reader of a variety of texts, moving in and out of the works of secular theorists, contemporary political theology, and key figures from the patristic age.[8] He embraces some, resists others, criticizes some, pushes others in new directions, and the pattern of who gets which response is not directly along lines of Christian or non-Christian, Catholic or Protestant. And his purpose in all of this is captured nicely on the back cover of the book: "Cavanaugh urges Christians to resist this form of idolatry, to unthink the inevitability of the nation-state and its dreary party politics, to embrace radical forms of political pluralism that privilege local communities—and to cling to an incarnational theology that weaves itself seamlessly and tangibly into all aspects of daily life and culture."

While it may be the case that Cavanaugh's vision of the church might allow room for us to think about the government/state as more than just the telephone service and mail delivery, especially in Canada,[9] nonetheless, the reader is challenged to imagine God, state, and the meaning of the church in ways that resist conventional accounts, both "secular" and "religious."

---

7. Weedman, "Practices That Resist the Colonization of the Christian Imagination."

8. Ibid.

9. I am indebted to Paul Heidebrecht, director of the MSCU Centre for Peace Advancement at Conrad Grebel University College, Waterloo, Ontario, for a helpful discussion here.

20

The Cross and the Lynching Tree

James Cone. *The Cross and the Lynching Tree*. New York: Orbis Books, 2012.

> *In this provocative book, black liberation theologian James Cone turns his attention to the intertwined cross and lynching tree, both symbols of death. In this refusal-to-look-away theology, Cone places the cross (the universal symbol of the Christian faith) alongside the lynching tree (the quintessential symbol of black oppression) in order to explore their symbolic connections, but even more importantly, to help us see Jesus in a new light. Cone draws on poetry, proclamation, song, and sermon to compel us to consider these matters as part of his own lifelong project of relentless truth-telling with considerable courage.*

This reflection on James Cone's book falls within a group of discussions under the rubric of "The Shape of God: Divine Presence in Human Space," an investigation of different ways that the Christian faith is framed and understood. A discussion of Cone's book necessitates a brief mention of various categories of theological forms, approaches, emphases, and approaches, although the classification of these matters is not my primary concern. However, it is important to situate the categorization of Cone's book, because his approach is so central to this book as well as to his larger theological project, which falls within the broad category of liberation theology, and more specifically the stream described as "black liberation theology."

Liberation theology, defined somewhat generally, "is a call to justice, to action, and even, in some cases, to armed struggle. It is a marriage of Marxism and biblical study. Central to its concern is the premise that state socialism is the last best hope of raising up the downtrodden masses of humanity. In the analysis of the Liberation Theologian, capitalism is responsible for poverty, war, misery and human degradation . . . this movement has numerous, quite independent streams, beneath a commonality of language and theme."[1] James Cone is considered a pioneer in black liberation theology, the task of which he describes as "to analyze the nature of the gospel of Jesus Christ in the light of oppressed blacks so they will see the gospel as inseparable from their humiliated condition, and as bestowing on them the necessary power to break the chains of oppression. This means that it is a theology of and for the black community, seeking to interpret the religious dimensions of the forces of liberation in that community."[2]

Cone describes *The Cross and the Lynching Tree* as "a continuation and culmination of all my previous books, each of them in different ways, motivated by a central question: how to reconcile the gospel message of liberation with the reality of black oppression."[3] It is a continuation in the following way: "What distinguishes this book and makes it a fitting capstone to his career is the way [Cone] uses the creativity of African-American theological and cultural sources to transform a central category of the Christian faith so that it resists the co-option of the faith by the forces of lethal iniquity."[4]

The theological methodology at work in black liberation theology gives primacy to black experience of the divine as well as to black pain and suffering.[5] This experience includes Cone's own life: "This black religious experience, with all its tragedy and hope, was the reality in which I was born and raised . . . If I have anything to say to the Christian community in America and around the world, it is rooted in the tragic and hopeful reality that sustains and empowers black people to resist the forces that seem designed to destroy every ounce of dignity in their souls and bodies" (xv). Further, "in *Black Theology and Black Power* and all the texts that followed, including this one, I begin and end my theological reflections in the social context of black people's struggle for justice" (151).

1. Yoder, "Biblical Roots of Liberation Theology," 55, 56.
2. Cone, *Black Theology of Liberation*, 5.
3. Cone, *Cross and the Lynching Tree*, xv–xvi. Subsequent references to the book will be included in the body of the essay.
4. Ray, Review of *Cross and the Lynching Tree*, 40.
5. Ibid.

This methodology is extended further in the womanist branch of liberation theology. Here it is the experience of the poor black woman that is given primacy within theological reflection. This is not to say that the Bible is ignored. In fact, these various approaches embedded in particular experiences have produced some very interesting biblical scholarship. We can begin to see what kinds of differences in interpreting the Bible might emerge, depending on the experience of the reader—a rich white guy reads a parable, and the same parable is read by a black woman who is downtrodden, oppressed, poor, uneducated—who knows what variations might emerge among these readings?

Closely related here is the observation that one of the most important dimensions of the black experience in America is that of being subjugated to white supremacy, which is so obvious in slavery, then in segregation, embodied in Jim Crow laws and practices, and continuing even after the formal rejection of segregation. According to Cone, white supremacy continues apace, with the ritual of lynching being the public celebration of ongoing white supremacy in America. Cone refers to this assumption of supremacy as a "defect in the white conscience" (32), both in terms of its existence and white blindness to it, a defect that is obvious in the work of white theologians, which in turn exacerbates the ongoing possibility of white supremacy.

A prominent example of this defective conscience of white supremacy is the work of white American theologian Reinhold Niebuhr, according to Cone, who admires much of Niebuhr's work, including his theological imagination and his sensitivity to problems of Jewish-Christian relations. And yet this highly competent and sensitive theologian somehow ignored the connection of the Christian faith to racism; he did not connect the cross to the lynching tree, and this despite Niebuhr's focus on sinfulness of the human and on the cross. To Cone, Niebuhr was a hypocrite, avoiding the controversy that taking a strong stand on race would have caused, refusing to cultivate relationships with people like Malcolm X or Martin Luther King Jr. Cone claims that Niebuhr did not "engage the race issue—the greatest moral problem in American history—in any practical way. During most of Niebuhr's life, lynching was the brutal manifestation of white supremacy, and he said and did very little about it. Should we be surprised, then, that other white theologians, ministers, and churches followed suit?" (45) In Niebuhr there was no prophetic outrage (56), merely the "limited perspective as a white man on the race crisis in America" (60).

However, says Cone, there are those who did and do recognize the problem of white supremacy, including Martin Luther King Jr., womanist theologians, black poets, and musicians. King understood the problem, since he did not just teach theology in a classroom but lived his faith in environs that entailed the risk of his life. His faith derived from the black church; he believed that the cross was the defining heart of the Christian faith, but unlike Niebuhr, King's understanding was shaped by his awareness of the lynching tree. While there are some similarities between the Niebuhr and King, Cone emphasizes the differences such as Niebuhr's notion of the relevance of an impossible ideal leading to proximate justice, versus King's focus on and achievement of what Niebuhr would have considered impossible. In other words, whereas Niebuhr analyzed the cross, King lived it (70ff.).

Black artists, musicians and poets especially, have also recognized the significance of the lynching tree. Static white theology draws on the imagination in ways that simply do not bring to view the parallels between the cross and the lynching tree, or has been simply too afraid of the consequences to make the connection. That is, white theologians have "lacked imagination of the most crucial and moral kind" (94). What is necessary, argues Cone, is "a powerful imagination, grounded in historical experience, to uncover the great mysteries of black life" (94–95). In a chapter on theological aesthetics, Cone presents sample after sample of the work of creative black artists to show the connection wrought there between cross and lynching tree. "Artists force us to see things we do not want to look at because they make us feel uncomfortable with ourselves and the world we have created . . . black artists are prophetic voices whose calling requires them to speak truth to power. Their expressions are not controlled by the institutions of the church. More than anyone, artists demonstrate our understanding of the need to represent the beauty and the terror of our people's experience" (118ff.).

Further, the womanist stream of liberation theology, starting from the experience of poor black women, helps us to make sense out of senseless situations. "On the one hand, faith spoke to their suffering, making it bearable, while, on the other hand, suffering contradicted their faith, making it unbearable. That is the profound paradox inherent in black faith, the dialectic of doubt and trust in the search for meaning, as blacks 'walk[ed] through the valley of the shadow of death'" (124–25). So, where white theology failed to shed white supremacy and failed miserably in recognizing the connection between the cross and the lynching tree (as seen most clearly in the work of Reinhold Niebuhr), Martin Luther King, black artists, and womanist theologians have exposed white supremacy and made explicit the connection between cross and lynching tree.[6]

---

6. Beginning on the first page of his introduction (xix), Cone asserts that there are obvious similarities between the cross and the lynching. See also pp. xiii, 2–3, 21–22, 25, 31, 75, 104, 158, 160–61, 166 for explicit comparisons.

But what exactly is that connection? Cone asserts early on (in the first page of his introduction) that there are obvious similarities between the cross and lynching. But have the symbolic connections been explored?

The profound heart of this book, as I understand it, is Cone's stated desire to "start a conversation so we can explore the many ways to heal the deep wounds lynching has inflicted upon us" (xix). In starting this conversation, Cone holds up a mirror to the kind of theology done by white people. That is, in his treatment of Reinhold Niebuhr, his aim is to make us ask ourselves: Do I see myself in this portrayal, and if so what will I do? Cone's work is a vivid reminder of the necessity of solidarity with the poor, the oppressed, and the disadvantaged. The heightening of the connection between Jesus's death on the cross and the suffering experienced by people at our front doors is a perpetual necessity, reminding us that the death of Christ on the cross is not only a solution to my personal need for the salvation of my soul. Linking the cross to the lynching tree reminds me that it is very easy to domesticate the cross and tame it specifically for my purposes, to coopt it in a way that puts me in a position of power, as a dispenser of truth, in a way that simply allows me to paper over a luxurious life with a spiritual veneer. In other words, it's hard to read Cone and continue to feel self-satisfied.

Reading this kind of theology reminds me again how powerful contextualized theology can be. It also reminds me that my own context can easily blind me—this is in fact a double-edged sword, it seems. To focus only on my own experience limits me, and yet the answer to those limitations is not to pretend that it is possible to do theology as if I'm doing from anywhere or nowhere. This latter approach is apparently a deep temptation for white theology, a tendency toward totalizing, toward pursuing theology with a disinterested, objective posture—as if that were possible—or to do theology in a way that tries to come up with universal application. The tendency is then to arrive at notions that favor the one who is doing the theology.

Further, Cone's work reminds me again just how much there is to learn from artists inside and outside of the church community. If theology is at least in part a shaping of our imaginations, then our theological imaginations have much to learn from people who are highly imaginative. The church needs to consider such sources, take them seriously, interact with and learn from them in vulnerable ways, subjecting theology to artistic questions and vice versa.

There's a lot to learn from Cone. The problem of racism is far from being solved; white theology has embraced and no doubt continues to embrace blind spots that hurt people, including ourselves. Who knows what white American theology has lost because of its failure of conscience in racial issues? Who knows what else is being missed or misconstrued as we speak? And by analogy, what does Canadian white theology have to learn from this kind of work, especially as it concerns Indigenous populations?

I also find myself asking a number of questions about Cone's work. For example, I would like to see reconciliation play a much more prominent role. I also wonder if Cone is self-critical enough, despite his own cautions on this point (28, 29). I have long been haunted by the work of Will Campbell, who after working for civil rights as a good white liberal, had a conversion of sorts and realized that he was preaching a very truncated gospel that allowed him to treat many of the people who were central to the problem of racism in the United States in what he came to see as a very non-Christian way. That is, Campbell realized that the racist whites needed to be converted, needed to know the gospel, needed to be ministered to, and invited to embrace truth, justice, and so on. Campbell then expanded his work to minister to blacks and whites, and as part of all of this he began to realize that there was no innocent party in the problem. He infamously suggested that the black community needed to recognize its own capacity for sin and abuse of power. Cone does some of this,[7] but it is not much in view in this fiery book. In addition, Cone's interlocutors are largely mainstream liberal theologians; he does not engage much with other, more grassroots Christian streams that may well be the basis of a very different account. I think too that there ought to be more emphasis on the resurrection of Christ, on the role of the church, especially as a worshipping community, and on Cone's treatment of martyrdom. Regarding the question of violence, it is not quite clear to me what role Cone is willing to grant to the use of violence in setting things right.

To conclude, I want to acknowledge the question of whether this book transcends the black American experience. Mel White, a well-known American evangelical Christian and now a very high-profile gay activist, claims that it does. He sees parallels with the ways gay people have been treated (lynched?) and sees blindness within Christian theology regarding the issues surrounding homosexuality, faith, suffering, and oppression.[8] I wonder, too, as mentioned briefly above, if it is possible for Cone's book to help us in Canada think about relations with Indigenous people. Perhaps we should follow Cone's method and encourage Indigenous theologians to do contextual theology from within, from which white folk can then learn, instead of presuming to do theology on someone else's behalf.

---

7. See Cone's introduction in his *Black Theology of Liberation*.
8. White, "Jesus Was Lynched," Review of *The Cross and the Lynching Tree*.

21

Spirit and Trauma

Shelly Rambo. *Spirit and Trauma: A Theology of Remaining*. Louisville: Westminster John Knox Press, 2010.

Shelly Rambo, an American theologian, draws on trauma theory to rethink the central claim of the Christian faith: that new life arises from death. She is "seeking a picture of redemption that adequately accounts for traumatic suffering, that speaks to divine presence and power in light of what we know about trauma." Rambo's approach is fascinating, as she proceeds by "reexamining the narrative of the death and resurrection of Jesus from the middle day—liturgically named as Holy Saturday—she seeks a theology that addresses the experience of living in the aftermath of trauma." Especially interesting is Rambo's notion of living a life configured as "remaining," a way of being, a form of life that is not first and foremost triumphant.

The consideration of Shelly Rambo's book continues a series of discussions I have entitled "The Shape of God: Divine Presence in Human Space," whereby we look at how to understand God's "intervention" in this world that is, after all, God's world. In the theology of James Cone, that presence is given shape by black American experience, as understood and put to use by black liberation theology, forging a way to understand the cross and to redeem it from the white appropriation and distortion.

A number of years ago, I was assigned to preach a sermon on Palm Sunday in my home church. In the process of my preparation, I learned a lot about Palm Sunday, Holy Week, and about myself and the ways in which we so easily misconstrue matters. I came to see that far too often, we are in a big hurry to get to Easter Sunday, and in so doing, we miss much of the possible depth and reality of our spiritual lives. Drawing on sources such as Fleming Rutledge's sermons, it became clear to me that we had to take the time between Palm Sunday and Easter Sunday absolutely seriously as a descent during which we take on the difficulties of the journey to the cross, and even then, to not take up the Hallelujahs of Easter a moment too soon. Put another way, I learned that it is essential to get off of the donkey of Palm Sunday, to see the false celebration of that crowd for what it was, and resist with all our might the premature triumphalism that so often marks our understanding and practice of Holy Week rituals. Shelly Rambo's book *Spirit and Trauma*[1] implores us to pay close attention to Holy Saturday—that day between the days that has been largely ignored by the Christian church in our embrace of a certain understanding of the story of redemption.

Rambo's project draws heavily on trauma theory, deconstruction, the work of Adrienne van Speyr and Hans Urs von Balthasar, the Gospel of John, and feminist theology (especially that of Catherine Keller), seeking to interrogate the linear sequence of cross and resurrection that is found at the heart of the Christian understanding of redemption. Her constructive theology, as I understand it, seeks to address and challenge a number of issues. Overall, she is seeking to provide "a way of interpreting Christian discourse itself and the continued search for new language and forms to speak about God's movement in the world" (14).

Some of the specific dimensions of Rambo's constructive theology include challenging a linear understanding of Christ's work in the world, especially the movement from death to resurrection, constructing alternative understandings for many of the traditional theological concepts such as the cross, resurrection, hope, comfort, and sacrifice, and challenging any and all notions of supersessionism and triumphalism. Further, Rambo's project includes the reframing of Christian pneumatology, focusing on what she calls "middle spirit," finding ways to get beyond the cross as the site from which to address suffering and violence, resisting the temptation to construct yet another theodicy, but instead seeking a picture of redemption that adequately accounts for traumatic suffering. Rambo is seeking to move the site of our theological considerations to the "middle," to "the figurative site in which death and life are no longer bounded—this middle is overshadowed by the two events of death and resurrection, but it must not be elided." In sum, "the work of this book is to uncover the middle discourse . . . looking from the

---

1. Specific references to the book will be included in the body of the essay.

middle, we are oriented to suffering in a different way—always in its dislocation, its distance, and its fragmentation" (8). This will be a theology of witness that remains, which requires a reworking of our maps, the pressing into use of a new lens of trauma through which we can do our interpretive work. All of this complexifies things so that we are forced to read through a shattered lens, which allows us to discover things we haven't seen before. So, Rambo pushes us to read from the middle, trying to envision life in the Spirit, birthed from the middle and not from the resurrection event, which results in a theology that is fragile; what remains bears the seeds of witness.

Rambo's constructive theology in this book begins not with the scripture or tradition but with trauma theory, in the chapter entitled "Witnessing Trauma." This field of inquiry forces us to confront that which remains after the traumatic event itself has occurred. This is not a search for closure, as if such a thing were even possible; it's not a search for a new beginning, as if *that* were possible. Rather, it looks at disruption, gaps, and experiences that are unregistered and invisible, and for which theology has been inadequate. What we need is what Rambo calls a "thick" witness to trauma, but this is no easy thing to find, since the nature of witness itself has changed so much since the Holocaust. Theology is faced with the question of how it can witness to the reality of the aftermath of trauma, since the very categories that we employ to make sense of things are shattered, and so we are faced with the task of reshaping theological concepts, not just pressing them into use as if the kind of trauma that is marked by overwhelming violence, the shutdown of adaptive processes, and the lack of integration has not happened.

To find our way theologically in light of trauma, Rambo suggests that we look for resonances between the two languages of trauma and theology, but to do so, we have to unmask, unearth, and track that which escapes interpretation. In other words, we have to participate in deconstruction, we must defamiliarize texts, ideas, assumptions, and assertions as we seek to find a way for theology to bear witness in light of trauma. To pursue this possibility means that we need to resist traditional models of Christian witness, namely those of proclamation and imitation, and instead learn to witness from the middle, to learn to gaze into the territory of remaining.

Having set out her project and the generative role of trauma theory within it, Rambo then turns to a theology of Holy Saturday, that day between the days, that second day of a three-day event that often is ignored in Christian churches, in Easter celebrations, and in our theology. Rambo wants to resist or at least interrogate a picture of triumphant life arising out of death. She turns to Hans Urs von Balthasar and Adrienne von Speyr, the latter who annually experienced mystical participation in Christ's descent into hell. That series of experiences became the generative material for von

Balthasar's theology of Holy Saturday, which for Rambo begins to do some of the work she thinks should be done—that is, the theology of Holy Saturday contains the seeds of the kind of witness needed by Christians, but also elides it to some extent.

Holy Saturday opens up a gap, hiatus, or abyss, which becomes the site of the witness between life and death, where love descends into the world. This is the place from which von Balthasar struggles to attest theologically to redemption—from the middle. He notably resists the more traditional understanding, which is known as the harrowing of hell. Instead, he calls for patience, because we have to confront absence, emptiness, and profound loneliness. God, after all, on von Balthasar's reading of it, descends to hell, and there is no way out. Any reading that refuses to take this seriously elides far too much; we must be prepared to embrace a very fragile picture of God. There's something like a bridge that allows for God not to remain trapped, as it were, in hell. But even here, the bridge should not be thought of as something that is too solid. Rather, it is more like a thread, which is where the presence and work of the Spirit becomes central as that movement that keeps things barely alive on Holy Saturday. Notice the picture here: things are very fragile indeed; there can be no thought of an assured, guaranteed victory, where we know exactly how the story ends. Even the resurrection is given a very different conceptual presentation, where instead of triumphalism, we are offered the picture of a rope that is "too short to span the distance from death to life . . . thread, a rope emerges out of the alienation of the abyss (the alienation within God, and the alienation of the world's sin), and God reaches down, clasps the end of the thread, and pulls upward" (78). It is to this theology, which finds itself in the fragile middle, that the disciple must bear witness—it is the "weary love of Holy Saturday that seeks expression" (80).

In the third chapter Rambo turns to the biblical witness in the Gospel of John. She is trying to bring together the notion of witness and the Spirit, a pneumatology of witness. But as we would expect, this is no straightforward task she sets for herself. Her sensitive reading of Mary Magdalene and the Beloved Disciple bring to our view just how ambiguous is the witness of these two followers. Their sight is uncertain and limited because they witness to absence; their vision is compromised by tears, by obstacles, and by indirectness as they confront a mixed terrain of absence and presence. While Peter, for example, is called to follow, the Beloved Disciple is called to remain and to witness as he remains, but here is "a witness without a clear referent" (97). He is called to persist, to enact presence, to bear with, and not to conquer (99). This remaining is connected to the middle space; the imperative is to remain and to love.

The fourth chapter seeks to think about God's presence in the abyss in terms of the "middle spirit." Rambo puts forward a number of orthodox assertions concerning the Spirit, but then reframes them or fills them with new content. Rambo's pneumatology highlights the "Spirit of Life," which nonetheless is also connected with death (114). Drawing on Catherine Keller, she resists the notion of creation *ex nihilo*, and instead wants to put forward a Spirit that oscillates in what she calls the abyss of creation—there is no pure beginning. This allows Rambo to make a move that sees the middle spirit oscillating in another abyss, that between recreation and redemption. She also highlights the Spirit as breath, not only connected to resurrection, which allows Rambo to focus not on the assurance of divine presence, but on the fragility of it. Further, Rambo asserts that the Spirit is love, but this is a love that remains as a middle term between life and death. After all, if love is expressed in terms of victory or sacrifice, this elides the truth of the love that simply remains; this kind of love opens up possibilities otherwise unrecognizable to us (141).

Rambo's fifth chapter, entitled "Remaining in Love," gives us her take on redemption and atonement. Traditionally, the story of redemption gives us hope and promise, but in so doing, Rambo claims, glosses over our realities of pain and loss, glorifies suffering, and in fact justifies violence. However, doing theology from the middle calls us to witness suffering in its persistence. Since trauma shatters all metaphors and models, all we have left to work with are dismantled models and metaphors. What remain are shards with which we try to do what is possible on those terms. Instead of shoring up this or that model of redemption and atonement, we work in the ruins. The problem we have had is that we have imposed a narrative and in so doing, we have in fact been guilty of enacting violence. Instead, by looking from the middle, we turn to see the movements of the Spirit that exceed the triumphant logic of cross and resurrection. We need to get beyond notions of restoring and renewing the dominant narrative that has been sealed and carried forward in the creedal tradition. We can't simply move from death to life, because in so doing, we are just exchanging one set of assertions for another. Both narratives elide what remains, asserts Rambo. Any effort that tries to call us to reconsider again the cross of Jesus Christ, to redeem our understanding of redemption, ultimately does not go nearly far enough. The movements of the middle spirit are much less discernable than all that, more inchoate and tenuous than visible or secure. Theology doesn't provide an answer, but theology testifies, and bears witness alongside.

Rambo's work has garnered significant attention and is gaining traction in fields where trauma is a central concern, such as the military. I think she's almost surely right to drag us to an almost full stop on Holy Saturday, an emphasis reminiscent of George Steiner's conclusion to his book *Real Presences*.

> But ours is the long day's journey of Saturday. Between suffering, aloneness, unutterable waste on the one hand and the dream of liberation, of rebirth on the other. In the face of the torture of a child, of the death of love which is Friday, even the greatest art and poetry are almost helpless. In the Utopia of Sunday, the aesthetic will, presumably, no longer have logic or necessity. The apprehensions and figurations in the play of metaphysical imagining, in the poem and in the music, which tell of pain and of hope, of the flesh which is said to taste of ash and of the spirit which is said to have the savour of fire, are always Sabbatarian. They have risen out of an immensity of waiting which is that of man. Without them, how could we be patient?[2]

I also raise several concerns in conclusion. Rambo's methodology raises serious questions for me. She seems more interested in applying the lens of trauma theory to theology than in developing a practical theology for trauma victims. Put another way, she lets trauma theory lead the way (her first chapter), which opens interesting avenues of investigation, but leaves the reader to wonder how differently things might proceed if her methodology began with theology and then turned to trauma.

---

2. Steiner, *Real Presences*, 232. I was alerted to this passage in Brueggemann, Review of *Between Cross and Resurrection*.

22

Ravished by Beauty

Belden Lane. *Ravished by Beauty: The Surprising Legacy of Reformed Spirituality*. New York: Oxford University Press, 2011.

Lane's book is a serious work of theology whose language celebrates and mediates the ravishing beauty of a world shot through with the glory of God. Lane celebrates a community of jubilant creatures of all languages and species, urging us to a sensuous enjoyment of God's beauty as the only real way of knowing God. Here theology becomes a way of reflecting on the arousal and relinquishment of desire, a spirituality of ravishment.

Our discussion of Lane's book follows consideration of James Cone's black liberation theology and Shelley Rambo's constructive theology, under the broader rubric of "The Shape of God: Divine Presence in Human Space." Lane's book was one of twelve books chosen by *Christianity Today*'s 2012 Book Awards, winning in the Spirituality category. This book is written explicitly from the Reformed point of view, with considerable emphasis on Puritans, a tradition not always closely associated with an emphasis on beauty. Founder John Calvin's reputation is that of a dour, uptight, control freak who was willing to burn a heretic, one who insisted on the following of many rules is the city of Geneva, where he exerted considerable influence. Puritans might not be the first people that come to mind when thinking positively and theologically about beauty and desire, given novels such as Nathaniel Hawthorne's *Scarlet Letter*. The popularized notion of 'puritanical" as being very strict in moral or religious matters, often excessively so, and even rigidly austere, brings to mind H.L. Mencken's famous dictum that Puritans harbor the haunting fear that someone, somewhere, might be happy.

Belden Lane, writing from within that Reformed tradition, feels it necessary to signal in his subtitle that his suggestion regarding Reformed spirituality as the source for thinking about God's beauty is a "surprising" legacy. However, Lane asserts that Reformed spirituality includes "an awakening of desire, the relinquishing of what initially may have seemed so important, a subsequent longing for God alone, and a discovery that what was sought had been there all along."[1] Lane admits that he has not always seen or experienced the Reformed tradition in this way, and so this book is a "journey into a retrievable past, allowing me to affirm a tradition I thought had failed me" (244).

Thus while Lane is at pains to locate his work within a theological tradition, this is also a deeply personal project (9). Overall, what he is trying to do, drawing on major Reformed figures from Calvin to Edwards, is emphasize "the beauty of the world as a way of contemplating the beauty of God" (13). That is, insofar as it is possible to identify the "shape of God," to recognize "divine presence in human space," it will have to do with coming to understand the world as the theater of God's glory. Timothy Hessel-Robinson summarizes Lane's project in the following way:

> Lane identifies the themes of beauty—nature's and God's—and desire running through the history of Reformed piety, and these themes hold the book together. As John Calvin, many Puritans, and Jonathan Edwards attest, the beauty of the earth mirrors the beauty and grandeur of God. Such beauty has the capacity to awaken desire in the human heart. When disciplined properly, desire mirrors the heart's deep longing for God, our true desire, and leads to enjoyment of God. God allures us through the radiant splendor of creation, stimulates our desires, draws us toward God, and "ravishes" the soul with beauty. For Lane, this aesthetic-spiritual logic is the foundation of a Reformed ecological ethic.[2]

Ravished by Beauty includes scholarly work that proceeds the way one would expect: reading of the sources, interpretation, bringing on of secondary sources and so on. In fact, a number of these chapters first saw the light

---

1. Lane, *Ravished by Beauty*, 4. Subsequent references to the book will be included in the body of the essay.

2. Hessel-Robinson, Review of *Ravished by Beauty*, 141.

of day as articles in scholarly journals or as oral lectures; as a result, the book sometimes feels more like a collection than it does a monograph. Further, Lane intersperses these scholarly chapters with personal essays that he entitles "Landscapes of Desire," the purpose of which is to express Lane's "own individual struggle to relate threads of the tradition to experiences of the natural world. These include pilgrimage narratives, stories of personal encounters with nature, and reflections on the interdependence of species—all related to the author's lived experience. They try to bridge the gap between the understanding and the practice of Reformed piety" (14).

Lane admits that his theme of "the awakening of desire for a God of ravishing beauty mirrored so generously (and flagrantly) in a world of nature" (18) is neglected in his tradition, but clearly he thinks that it is worthy of retrieval, in part because such a spirituality can act as the impetus, or better, the source of a faithful ecological theology, one that embraces this world in visceral, erotic ways without sliding into pantheism. The Reformed emphasis on God's sovereignty alongside an emphasis on God's beauty allows for the possibility of mutual self-correction and mutual stimulation (28). Lane is well aware of the dangers that lie near the surface of Reformed spirituality. The same tradition that passed early laws against animal cruelty, that goes on and on about the importance of trees, can also be downright dangerous when it is "transformed into an excuse for conquest and misuse" (37). Lane cautions us about the possibility of transforming a vision of the world as a theater of God's glory into a "subordinating or adversarial perception of nature as an object demanding possession . . . an excuse for conquest and misuse." "Women, Native Americans and land were increasingly colonized and turned into objects more readily controlled" (36, 37). Lane's argument here is that while the Reformed tradition recognizes desire as the starting point for theological reflection on creation and beauty, the attendant danger is always one of seeking to possess the object instead of standing in wonder in its presence (46).

Having set the stage by providing an apologetic of sorts for Reformed spirituality as generative of an ecologically faithful theology and practice, Lane explores various dimensions of desire and beauty, theologically shaped by Augustine, John Calvin, American Puritanism, and Jonathan Edwards. Several dimensions of this theological project are particularly engaging and constructive.

First, the theme of the generative power of worship can be identified as a thread throughout the entire book but is most explicitly taken up in the discussion of Calvin's notion of the world as a theater of God's glory. What I find fascinating here is the concept that worship is mimetic (58), that is, all of nature imitates God's beauty, and all parts of creation, including humans, mirror God in our beings and share in common praise as a performative act. The nature of praise, then, is not just reflective, but is in fact generative and constitutive (67–77). That is, praise is not just expressive, it is *magical*.

> To conceive of worship as an experience of "theater" is not to seek ways of "jazzing it up," enhancing its appeal as a matter of public entertainment. It is to recover, instead, the subversive character of worship, honoring its role in the making and unmaking of worlds. Like the best experience of theater, liturgy forces its participants into multiple levels of encounter. It pleases, but it also profoundly disturbs, prompting at times a complete reversal of things previously held certain. The performance demands deep participation. This was how Calvin understood the significance of the Sabbath. (82)

Second, Lane brings to view the role of Augustinian desire as displayed in Puritanism, leading to a positive embrace both of sexual love and celebration of nature in mystical forms. These kinds of mysticism, connected to our bodies and to nature, do not serve to take us out of the world but rather cash out in ethical guidance in areas such as equality, inclusivism, and creation care. However, desire and delight in themselves are not enough, and so the reader is warned that Reformed spirituality must combine delight in God's beauty with covenantal responsibility in the environment and in married life. "A Calvinist aesthetic remains restless until it expresses itself in moral action" (123).

A third important emphasis in Lane's book is the focus on nature as the purifier of desire. This material intuitively seems more like the stereotypical Calvin: "Hardships would come, but their ultimate function was to strengthen relationship, not question it. A covenant god utilized the threats of a disordered world to lead God's people beyond inordinate attachments and through adversity into deeper faith. Times of affliction served as a purification (or schooling) of desire, reorienting the faithful to the highest object of their longing" (135). The notion of threat and promise runs through this section of the book in very interesting ways, including a psycho-sexual mode, which brings to view the problem of pursuing the highest reaches of devotion while traversing the very edge of transgression and the breaking of taboos, which Lane sees in writers such as Teresa of Avila, Bernard of Clairvaux, and John Donne. Lane emphasizes the dimension of Reformed theology that embraces the keeping of desires in check by affliction, while the affliction can be managed by resources already possessed in Christ.

A fourth theme of note in Lane's book is that of aesthetic awareness, which seeks to resist any kind of dualism between our knowledge of the physical world by sensation and our knowledge of God by faith and/or reason. Drawing on Jonathan Edwards, Lane pushes hard for cultivating an awareness of the sensory world as a point of access in our search for God. The sensory world is a kind of secondary beauty that is available through our senses, a way of encountering the "super-sensory God of matchless glory" (179). The natural world understood in this way acts as a training ground for "discovering the affective receptivity that knowing God requires" (183). What is really interesting in this chapter is Lane's concluding concern, that is, his ethical concern. "Aesthetic sensitivity has to reach out to something beyond itself . . . To act ethically, then, is to act as if there truly are interrelated harmonies that exist among all beings as they cohere together in God . . .extraordinary attentiveness and moral passion are demanded of all lovers of God, as they bring the world to a consciousness of God's glorious presence with it . . . the work of recognizing and bestowing beauty has to be sustained ultimately by an eschatological hope . . . our longing for God's beauty is never finally satisfied, but presses from glory to glory" (194–95).

Lane's book takes us beyond anthropocentrism and idolatry. Not everything in the world is about us; this is God's world, in which we have a place, but neither the world nor its human inhabitants are enough to undergird and sustain a theology of ecology, of praise, and of beauty. Indeed, if one were to pull God out of Lane's vision for this earth and for human flourishing on this earth, his entire project would fall apart like a house of cards, which I think is exactly the way theological projects should work.

However, I fear that sometimes Lane's reach exceeds his grasp, as in his treatment of biodiversity and the Trinity. That is, Lane simply finds too much perspicacity in the Trinity for use in his understanding of biodiversity. Kathryn Tanner, in a fine essay about the role of Trinitarian theology in political theology, notes that all manner of claims are being made that argue from the Trinity to some conclusion, and she worries about that trend, because too many contemporary theologians overestimate the potential of such claims and thus make inflated statements. The problem has to do with just how one can or should make the move from God to human relationships. What the Trinity says about human relationships is not entirely clear, as much of what is said about the Trinity does not even apply to humans. Therefore, any "direct translation of the Trinity into a social program is problematic."[3]

At times throughout my reading of this book, I wondered about Lane's "mining" of Reformed spirituality. A recovering fundamentalist (a status he describes at numerous points throughout the book), he seeks to

---

3. Tanner, "Trinity," 326.

compensate for the harshness of his boyhood Calvinism by construing his tradition in a much more liberal way. He mines it for things he finds retrievable, discarding and even attempting to destroy what he dislikes (not an eco-friendly method). He is honest and open about this. In the end, though, his approach yields a rather attenuated Calvinism pruned for present purposes more than a panoramic picture of the Reformed spiritual landscape (in all its biodiversity).[4] On a related note of concern, I also found myself wondering about the role of Jesus Christ as a generative dimension to Lane's project. Christ is mentioned, but in a formal, theological way, and this not primarily as someone to follow. Therefore, while ethics play a prominent role in the book, the genesis of those ethics is not found in the Incarnation, life, teachings, death, and resurrection of Jesus Christ.

---

4. Fulkerson, "Jonathan Edwards and Reformed Spirituality," Review of *Ravished by Beauty*.

23

Scripture, Culture, and Agriculture

Ellen Davis. *Scripture, Culture, and Agriculture: An Agrarian Reading of the Bible*. Cambridge: Cambridge University Press, 2009.

Reflection on God's role as Creator and on the created world is a central dimension of understanding divine presence in human space. In this unique book, Ellen Davis creates a conversation between ancient Old Testament texts and contemporary agrarian writers. Doing so opens up the possibility of examining the theology and ethics of land use, especially the practices of modern industrialized agriculture, in light of critical biblical exegesis.

Davis's book develops the theme of God's shape, his presence in human space, in fairly direct, explicit ways. In discussing her theory of reading, she points out that her approach, which uses agrarian reading as a way of viewing our world and the text's representation of it, requires us to ask a particular question: "How do these texts view the relationship between humans (or Israelites in particular) and the material sources of life as an essential aspect of living in the presence of God?"[1] This matrix of realities—human relationship with the divine, divine presence in the world, and material sources of life—calls for careful and perpetual navigation and negotiation that does not just flow in one direction. While Davis's matrix of reality includes a focus on material processes, it does so in very different

1. Davis, *Scripture, Culture, and Agriculture*, 3. Subsequent references to the book will be included in the body of the essay.

ways than Marxist thinking, which focuses influentially on production and material processes as an analytic tool.

Davis is explicit about the connection of food and land to the presence of God in human space. For example, she uses the subtitle "Food as Revelation" as an occasion to analyze the contrast between the Egyptian harvest and the manna collection of Israel in the wilderness (72). She concludes that "in complete contrast to agribusiness in both ancient and contemporary cultures, the first story of Israel out of Egypt shows that food is, more than anything else, *an expression of God's sovereignty over creation and generosity toward humankind*" (73). Further, Davis claims that in the economy set up by God, "eating is worshipful, even revelatory; it engenders a healthful knowledge of God" (74). If I understand Davis correctly, she wants to bring to our attention the fact that God is present in the world within his creation, not just in the original act of creation but in the sustaining work necessary for creation to flourish. God is present and also active in self-revelation, not just through "spiritual" experiences but also through material processes, and all of this without degenerating into some sophisticated version of pantheism or even panentheism. So, Davis acts as an interesting and useful source for thinking about the question of God's shape in this world, God's presence in human space.

Davis's primary burden in *Scripture, Culture, and Agriculture* seems to be the fostering of a "tenacious but severely chastened hope" (180). She refers to this dynamic as a "finely balanced disposition [which] rests on faith in God . . . a character of hopefulness tempered by sad experience" (180). That dynamic is replicated, she argues, both in the Bible and in contemporary agrarian conversation. So, we have the biblical text that expresses a tenacious but severely chastened hope being read in conversation with and enriching agrarian sources, which themselves display that same kind of hope. This book is richly informed by biblical sources, although drawn almost exclusively from the Old Testament. The other main category of sources is agrarian writers, most notably Wendell Berry, who writes the foreword.[2] It's important that we identify agrarianism correctly as "a way of thinking and ordering life in community that is based on the health of the land and of living creatures . . . a comprehensive way of viewing the world and the human place in it" (1), and a "culture of preservation" (66). Agrarianism is not necessarily rural, but rather offers a "sober yet not hopeless reckoning with the present widespread destruction of the material sources of life, and therefore, a reckoning with the real possibility of disaster on a

---

2. Other agrarian or food writers discussed by the Take and Read group and included in this book are Wendell Berry, Norman Wirzba, and Michael Pollan.

massive scale" (6). Davis thinks that reading agrarian texts in conversation with biblical texts can bear exegetical fruit, a project that is very important because it may help us to delineate a responsible vision of what participation in the renewal of creation might mean, which she thinks is the most essential theological task of this generation (7). Davis's understanding of an essential theological task seems to have at least some traction in the church. For example, pastor Stan Wilson poses this reflection on Davis's work: "As a pastor, I am wondering what this movement means for the Church. Are there agricultural dimensions to the Church's calling to serve and celebrate the kingdom of God? I wonder if this surprising movement of young people into farming could be a movement of the Spirit. Do these fields, white with harvest, have anything to do with the mission field?"[3]

Davis's book is not quite a collection of discreet essays nor a monograph. She describes her first two chapters as foundational, with the rest of the chapters functioning as a series of "samples" that need not be read in sequence, as they do not form a singular argument by way of their particular organization in this book.

The first chapter, entitled "Rupture and Re-membering," alerts us to the moral crisis in which we find ourselves. We are in the midst of an ecological crisis, but this is not principally a technological crisis but a moral and theological one, which is not necessarily self-evident, or self-interpreting for that matter. Even if we are able to see the rupture that she describes, Davis is also clear that any kind of response to the crisis must be a moral and theological matter before it is a technological one. To simply apply more technology to what has been wrought technologically in the first place would be to multiply the ruptures already in front of us. But in order for us to be able to see, we will have to be brought to the point of remembering the way things ought to be, and to be reminded of where we have gone and continue to go wrong. Put more directly, Davis in this first chapter tries "to demonstrate that the biblical writers give us language, verbal images, to see what we are doing and the likely consequences" (20).

Davis's claim in chapter 2 is that agrarian writers can help us with the need she has brought to view in the first chapter, that of remembering. Reading the work of contemporary agrarians can make us better readers of scripture; she is putting on display a reading of the Bible through agrarian eyes.[4]

3. Wilson, "Of Mules and Mission," Review of *Scripture, Culture, and Agriculture*.

4. Davis's work is an example of contextual theology along the lines of the liberation theology done by James Cone, and reminiscent of the methodological move made by Shelly Rambo when she uses trauma theory to read the Bible. What is different methodologically is that Davis does not do the kind of so-called constructive theology

The agrarian approach Davis uses includes four aspects, the first of which addresses the primacy of the land, the notion that we have to "meet the expectations of the land." The soil is worthy of our service; there is potential for both doing good and inflicting harm. Therefore, we have to be aware of a relationship between humans, God, and the soil. We would do well to learn that the land is something that is a given; it has limits, and we encounter it as a creature to be respected or even revered (31).

Second, Davis promotes a mind-set she describes as "the forthright embrace of ignorance" (33). We need God's wisdom, broadly speaking, but also specifically in the realm of agriculture and our relationship to the land. To be clear, this is not a plea for or defense of scientific ignorance or stupidity, but rather a recognition and embrace of humility, since moral failure is undergirded by sin—specifically a culpable pride, a destructive lack of humility (34).

Third, Davis calls for modest materialism: no claim that what humans touch or see is exhaustive of what *is*. "We owe a certain courtesy to Reality, and that this courtesy can be enacted only by humility, reverence, propriety of scale, and good workmanship" (37, quoting Wendell Berry).

Fourth, Davis promotes the notion of value beyond price. Land is important, not primarily because of its real estate value or because possession of it is some kind of political exertion of power, but rather because "the claims of family, community, land, and human decency are treated as the ordinary and, therefore essentials of God's claim in human life; this . . . indissoluble web of relationships" (40).

Having established the importance of her initiative, the way she is proceeding and the kinds of sources she will be marshaling to shape her task, Davis then engages the Old Testament, drawing on all manner of texts, genres, and authors—the artists, the politicians, the scientists of the Old Testament, bringing them into conversation with poets, soil scientists, economists, and political theorists. It is not my intention here to rehearse each of the subsequent chapters; rather, I want to make a series of observations about the book and its arguments in a non-systematic way.

First, I learned a lot about food. We are shown that food ought to be understood as a gift; Davis also alerts us to the idea that food is revelation, that restraint and limit is an important dimension of thinking about and enjoying food, and that food is one of the ways in which covenant is communicated. After reading the book, I found myself still trying to come to grips with these and other ways of thinking about and experiencing food,

---

that Rambo attempts.

centering on the question of what it might mean for me to understand food as an important dimension of a vital faith in God.

Overall, the attempt to use agrarian readings as a perspective on Old Testament texts, read closely by a scholar like Davis who writes so elegantly, carries the potential to open up both the biblical text as well as the agrarian writers (these latter are not emphasized as much as the former). For example, reading chapter 3 on "Seeing with God: Israel's Poem of Creation" is a wonderful exercise, especially as it relates to an understanding of the early chapters of Genesis. Her sensitive reading of this text as a liturgical poem takes the creation accounts far more seriously than many of the commentators I have read on this. Davis is able to avoid the flatfooted, tone-deaf readings of those who see here only a science textbook rendering of facticity regarding the mechanistic maneuverings of creation, without regard for genre, poetic sensibilities, or theological nuance. Further, her readings also push me beyond my own smug, pseudo-sophisticated attempts to understand these passages as "theological," as though they only have to do with the relationship of God to humanity. Rather, her readings, shaped as they are by agrarian sensibilities, bring to view dimensions of this liturgical poem that are, appropriately, potentially fruitful. That is, she adds land to the theological treatment of the relationship of God and humans in a way that goes beyond understanding work as part of the curse or some such reading. Instead, she describes a vision of self-perpetuating fruitfulness of the land. Her discussion of dominion and the notion of what it means to conquer the land push us to take both God and the land more seriously than those who see some version of exploitation as intrinsic to the human responsibility toward the land. Here we are encouraged to see land as a gift, to perpetuate the productivity that is inherent in the land, to join our work to God's gift. It is this approach of Davis's that I find fascinating—she enables new readings of what I think are familiar passages such as Genesis 1 or the account of God's supplying of manna in the wilderness. She also provides a way in to parts of the Old Testament that I find nearly impenetrable—Leviticus, for example. Anna Peterson's discussion of Davis is relevant here:

> One of Davis's most important and provocative themes is materiality. Focusing on Leviticus, she argues for "a theologically profound vision of the complexity and interdependence of the created order," and of the ways that human beings can and should participate in that order (p. 83). This vision begins with the centrality of the land in God's covenant with the Israelites. The fact that God names the land as an active agent, according to Davis, shatters efforts to divide the material world from spiritual concerns. "The land is a semi-autonomous moral agent,"

she explains, which "retains a capacity to act for God, even when humans have forfeited their high yet humble calling to work with God" (p. 100). Humans, who depend upon the land, are likewise both material and spiritual beings, enacting religious values in their bodily comportment.[5]

Another area that I want to highlight is Davis's treatment of the city as part of the discussion of agrarian themes that inform her reading of the Scriptures. Jeremiah 29:7 (Seek the *shalom* of the city . . .) serves as one of the epigraphs for chapter 9, entitled "The Faithful City." This verse is noteworthy to those who are in some way or another students of John Howard Yoder, who makes a lot of political/theological/ethical mileage out of that verse, having to do with living as exiles and finding a way to live faithfully without being in control. This so-called Jeremian turn is one of the key interpretive moves in Yoder's work, and I would argue that he cannot really be understood without recognizing the importance of this concept within his larger body of work.

Davis opens up a theology of the city in new directions here, although not in ways that negate Yoder's work. Cities can stand for all manner of things, often for colonial power, even the demonic (Babylon), or for good. What interests Davis here is the relationship of the city to its hinterland. She is keen to help us imagine anew our cities and our metropolitan lives, so she turns to a discussion of the iconic possibilities of the city as found in Scripture. The city can be a place of blessing, understood as a creation of God (not just so-called nature). She emphasizes the possibility of reciprocal flow of blessing to and from the city, and she believes that it is possible to be able to live faithfully in the city (167-68).

A further strength of this book is Davis's provocative work in the area of integration. That is, she pushes us hard to see connections between God, the land, and humans; she encourages extending those relationships, or better put, trying to understand those relationships as potentially manifested in sexuality, economics, our understanding of community, food security, and housing. Here her dependence on someone like Wendell Berry comes through very clearly.

I also venture several cautions about *Scripture, Culture, and Agriculture*. In her introduction, Davis addresses the valuable question of connection of an ancient text to the contemporary world (4). She turns to the work

---

5. Peterson, Review of *Scripture, Culture, and Agriculture*, 428. Rowan Williams also develops a very appreciative appropriation of Davis's reading of Leviticus. Her reading helps him see that this often-ignored book is seeking to save people and property from being alienated from their "primary and defining relation to God." Williams, *Faith in the Public Square*, 186.

of Norm Gottwald for guidance in retrieving the notion that what the Bible has to offer us is "vision and principle." The dimension of vision—the idea that the Bible provides a vision of the world, humanity's place in that world, and God's relationship to the world and to humanity—seems like a legitimate way of reading the Bible, of bridging the gap, as it were. Davis is less convincing when, following Gottwald, she puts forward the notion that we should try to make the connection by way of principle. Any approach that endeavors to read the Bible in order to distill it into "principles" is a debatable move, since this carries in its train the possibility of being reductionist instead of constructive, of mining the text for my preconceived purposes, of being fundamentally utilitarian, and finally of thinning out the richness of the text in order to make it useable.

Further, I raise the same question regarding Davis's work as I might ask concerning James Cone or Shelley Rambo. That is, when we pursue contextual theology, calling on some context such as black American experience, trauma theory, or agrarian concerns to read the Bible, much insight is forthcoming, but I always long for more flow in the other direction than is often the case. What happens if agrarian understandings, concerns, topics, poetry, fiction, and philosophy are in turn subjected to biblical scrutiny in an explicit way? I am not at all sure what might happen; if anything, I sometimes have the impression that the agrarian body of work is not up for scrutiny by Davis in this book.

24

Christianity after Religion

Diana Butler Bass. *Christianity after Religion: The End of Church and the Birth of a New Spiritual Awakening*. New York: HarperOne, 2013.

Diana Butler Bass is convinced that our current ways of seeing the world and expressing faith are being "born again." This kind of "exponential change creates exponential fear along with exponential hope." What this means for the Christian faith, says Bass, is that Christianity is not a religion anymore—it's more of a spiritual thing. Can such a thing as "religionless Christianity" be embraced and still be considered authentic Christian faith?

By engaging this book by Diana Butler Bass, we are joining a widespread, influential conversation. On a recent Saturday morning, while trying to avoid work by reading the newspaper, I ran across an article by John Longhurst about the topic labeled as Spiritual but Not Religious (SBNR). Longhurst refers to a book by Lillian Daniel, entitled *When "Spiritual but Not Religious" Is Not Enough: Seeing God in Surprising Places, Even the Church*. Long, unwieldy, multi-clausal title aside, Daniel is reacting against precisely the kind of book being discussed in this essay. When someone tells her that they are spiritual but not religious, she wants to tell them this: "Thank you for sharing, spiritual-but-not-religious person. You are now comfortably in the norm for self-centered American culture, right smack in the bland majority of people who find ancient religions dull but find themselves uniquely fascinating."[1] Daniel offers a further description of SBNR in an interview:

> Often some shallow combination of exercise and caffeine, coffee shops as spiritual community, hikes as pilgrimages, *The New York Times* as sacred text, and sunsets—don't ever forget the sunsets. These people are always informing you that they find God in the sunsets. Well, excuse me, as if people who go to church don't see God in a sunset. You know, my take is that any idiot can find God in a sunset. What is remarkable is finding God in the context of flawed human community and a tradition bigger than you are with people who may not reflect God back to you in your own image.[2]

The heart of *Christianity after Religion* has to do with this shift from religion to spirituality, "a world of Christianity after religion, a spiritual space beyond institutions, buildings, and organizations, a different sort of faith."[3] At least part of the difference between religion and spirituality is novelty, a recognition of "new paths of meaning, exploring new ways to live their lives, experiencing a new sense of authenticity and wonder, and practicing new forms of community . . . new "Age of the Spirit," new patterns of faith, new pathways to the future" (4–6). The book is concerned with religion and change, arguing that "where Christianity is now vital, it is not really seen as a 'religion' anymore. It is more of a spiritual thing" (7).

The book proceeds in three parts, beginning with a section that details the "End of Religion," based on lots of survey reporting about a momentous historical change that is ostensibly in full swing; old gods are being questioned, old ways of pursuing religion are failing or have failed. The second section describes "A New Vision of Believing, Behaving and Belonging," wherein these practices are not only given new meanings but are reordered. The change is significant enough be labeled "The Great Reversal." Third, Bass describes an "Awakening," which she counts as the Fourth Great Awakening (241). The book ends with a call to "performing awakening,'" a call to prepare, practice, play, and participate.

While I will not rehearse the argument of the book nor respond to it systematically, I want to make a series of observations, ask some questions,

---

1. Quoted in Longhurst, "Spiritual but Not Religious? Path May Still Lead to Church."
2. Abernethy, "Rev. Lillian Daniel on 'Spiritual but Not Religious.'"
3. Bass, *Christianity after Religion*, 3. Subsequent references to the book will be included in the body of the essay.

and record a number of reactions, intending that all of these will be constructive, but not all will be positive.

To begin, it is clear that Bass has her finger on the pulse of American Christian practice, especially of the Protestant variety. However, her account of broad declension is not nuanced enough, her analysis is based too much on the summing up of social scientific surveys, and she sometimes almost unconsciously assumes that American Christianity is Western Christianity more broadly. Despite those cautions on my part, I think this section of the book is a good survey of surveys, enhanced from time to time with anecdotes. While there is virtually nothing approaching original work in this part of the book, nonetheless Bass does a fine job of capturing the 'holy discontent' and longing that she sees across America (88).

I find a number of dimensions of the book compelling, and I hope they find wide acceptance. I am thinking, for example, of the discussion of the nature of belief. Without getting lost in technical jargon or complicated material, Bass convincingly shows that belief is better understood not as intellectual assent to propositions but as a matter of trust (120–35). Her section on the experiential dimension of believing and embracing the creeds is interesting, refreshing, and I think extremely useful for the church, and acts as a foil to those who would accuse people like Bass of ignoring any kind of content.

On a related note, her focus on the practice of faith, with important connections to apprenticeship as a way of understanding what it means to be shaped and formed in a certain way by people who already practice the faith shows that Bass does not ignore the church. Her eschatological vision (157ff.), framed here in terms of the art of anticipation, is constructive, and she provides the basis for an explicit connection between practices and expectation that is very helpful (159).

I also find myself compelled by the way Bass messes with the formation of questions, in particular the way she often changes the conventional form of questions in ways that make a great deal of difference. I find myself paying attention when she changes "What do I believe?" to "Whom do I believe?"; from "How do I do that?" to "What do I do?" and "Why do I do it?"; from "Who am I?" to "Where am I?" and "Whose am I?" (190ff).

While I am compelled by these changed questions, which I think do a lot of work for Bass, I am less convinced by the reversed sequence she wants to put in place: believing, behaving, and belonging inverted to belonging, behaving, and believing. I simply do not buy the sequential argument as much as she does. I think this so-called reversal is far messier than she allows, and changing the sequence cannot carry the weight she needs it to carry for her argument. Nonetheless, her treatment of the reversal concludes with a clarion call to faith that is very compelling. "The Great Reversal is the Great Returning of Christianity back toward what Jesus preached: a beloved and beloving community, a way of life practiced in the world, a profound trust in God that eagerly anticipates God's reign of mercy and justice" (214).

Further, in my view Bass often describes issues in a limited binary fashion. Too often an issue is framed as either this or that: spiritual/religious, institution/individual, head/heart, Old Lights/New Lights. This way of working encourages the dumping of things into one or the other category and discourages paying attention to contingencies and thoughtful discernment of particularities. For example, setting up the antithetical categories of religion and spirituality truncates possible probing into where opposition to religious institutions and practice has been truly emancipatory, or where that kind of opposition is really just self-indulgence and self-absorption.[4] And, could it be that Christianity after organized religion will be the kind of self-satisfied, self-regarding, all-too-American faith . . . which conceives of God as part divine butler, part cosmic therapist, and which jettisons the more challenging aspects of Christianity that the traditional churches and denominations, for all their many sins and follies, as least tried to hand down to us intact?[5] Drawing on the many online discussions of *Christianity after Religion*, I want to observe that the book overlooks the interaction between religious subjectivity and practice and the broader social, political, and economic forces that are also at work in any given situation. In other words, in what ways are the Fourth Great Awakening a reflection of capitalist sensibilities? of conservative political ideologies? of Enlightenment liberalism? or all of the above all at the same time? Further, how would Bass's depiction of spiritual and religious matters change if she took into account African American churches, Anabaptist churches, and Orthodox churches?

I confess that there are a number of places where I find her just too facile. One reviewer, Kyle Childress, while complimenting Bass on her accessibility asserts that "none of this is all that original, nor does Bass work at it in deeply theological ways."[6] She tends toward the facile when she uses biblical references to shore up a point made on other grounds (42, 124, 125, 154, 203, 210, 211), and, it must be said, her treatment of *metanoia* (220ff.) is almost entirely devoid of the notion of repentance, and her vision President Obama's reference to the American flag as a display of the Great Awakening is at best unconvincing.

---

4. Lough, "Christianity after Religion: A Review."
5. Douthat, "Is Liberal Christianity Actually the Future?"
6. Childress, "Church as Problem and Solution," Review of *Christianity after Religion*.

Bass carries on conversation with usual suspects such as Rob Bell, Harvey Cox, and Brian McLaren, but she also explicitly draws on the work of Dietrich Bonhoeffer, using quotations from *Letters and Papers from Prison* as epigraphs for various sections of the book, especially his enigmatic statements regarding the so-called religionless Christianity with which Bonhoeffer was struggling as he languished in a Nazi prison. But Bass does precious little with this fascinating material, not wrestling with what it was that Bonhoeffer might have been trying to articulate in those dark days. She tries to give us the impression that she is dealing with the same kinds of issues as was Bonhoeffer. She is right in the sense that the calling into question of "religion" is part of theological discourse in the twentieth century. But that conversation, which is still ongoing, was of a very different ilk in Bonhoeffer's context, as a relatively brief discussion will now show.

The basic outline of Bonhoeffer's biography is fairly well known.[7] The central focus for my purposes here is the collection of letters, poems, and sermons edited by his brother-in-law Eberhard Bethge, and published as *Letters and Papers from Prison*.[8] Bonhoeffer, after rejecting an opportunity to wait out the war in America as a visiting scholar, led an illegal seminary and eventually was prevented by the Gestapo from preaching, publishing, and teaching. Bonhoeffer then joined the *Abwehr*, a German military intelligence agency. His ecumenical work was to provide him with a cover for gathering intelligence information for the Germans. However, this position was a cover for Bonhoeffer's work as a double agent: he joined the *Abwehr* in order to be part of a resistance movement, intent, among other things, on the assassination of Adolph Hitler. The plot was uncovered by the Gestapo, and Bonhoeffer was imprisoned along with many others who were implicated as part of the resistance movement. When an assassination attempt on Hitler went wrong, the fate of the conspirators was basically sealed. Bonhoeffer spent from April 1943 until April 1945 in various prisons, and then was executed on April 9, 1945, at Flossenberg Prison, only two days before the Allied liberation. His brother-in-law, Eberhard Bethge, also a former student of Bonhoeffer's, is largely responsible for collecting, editing, and publishing Bonhoeffer's prison writings.

While Bonhoeffer was already widely known through his earlier writings, especially *The Cost of Discipleship* and *Life Together*, as well as his more academic theology, the phrase "religionless Christianity," which appears only a few times in *LPP*, would give Bonhoeffer international influence. The

---

7. The best full-length treatment is the massive work by Bethge, *Dietrich Bonhoeffer*. A shorter essay is by Nelson, "The Life of Dietrich Bonhoeffer."

8. I will refer to this book as *LPP* in the rest of the chapter.

phrase is inherently ambiguous, largely undeveloped by Bonhoeffer, and appears within writings never intended for publication. By his own admission, many of the concepts associated with religionless Christianity were embryonic in nature—the job of explaining, clarifying, and changing was too big for him to finish under the circumstances.[9]

LPP begins with a deep concern for responsibility. In a Christmas 1942 communication written to several friends, entitled "After Ten Years," Bonhoeffer reflects on life in Nazi Germany and what it might mean to be responsible people in such circumstances.

> One may ask whether there have ever before in human history been people with so little ground under their feet—people to whom every available alternative seemed equally intolerable, repugnant, and futile. . . . Or perhaps one should rather ask whether the responsible thinking people of any generation that stood at a turning-point in history did not feel much as we do, simply because something new was emerging that could not be seen in the existing alternative . . . Are we still of any use?[10]

Bonhoeffer's writings over the next several years, produced amidst great stress, boredom, and fear often return to similar kinds of questions, presumably with a view to life after the war. The notion of religionless Christianity surfaces in this context.[11]

> What is bothering me incessantly is the question of what Christianity really is, or indeed who Christ really is, for us today. The time when people could be told everything by means of words, whether theological or pious, is over, and so is the time of

---

9. *LPP*, 359.

10. Ibid., 3, 4, 16.

11. A number of related terms used by Bonhoeffer, such as "unconscious Christianity," "non-religious interpretation of Christianity," "Christianity in a world come of age," and "religionless Christianity," form a cluster that is difficult to disentangle with certainty. For example, the Anabaptist theologian, A. James Reimer makes the following distinctions: "I think 'non-religious interpretation of the Bible' and 'Christianity in a world come of age' are related and concerned with more or less the same problem but not interchangeable. The first (non-religious interpretation of the Bible) Barth could have agreed to: that is, Christian Faith is not a religion—religion is a human enterprise, humans trying to climb up to God. The biblical message is ultimately not that. The latter ('Christianity in a world come of age') is a concept that Barth would, in my view, have had serious problems with because Bonhoeffer makes positive 'liberal' assumptions about the modern age (he was still to some degree enamored by what the Enlightenment had achieved in the West). He rejected for instance Barth's 'positivism of revelation' forced upon the secular world. So I think one should not confuse these two concepts." Personal correspondence with A. James Reimer, October 31, 2002.

inward and conscience—and that means the time of religion in general. We are moving towards a completely religionless time; people as they are now cannot honestly describe themselves as religious any more . . . "Christianity" has always been a form—perhaps the true form of "religion." But if one day it becomes clear that this a priori does not exist at all, but was a historically-conditioned and transient form of self-expression, and if therefore mankind becomes radically religionless—and I think that is already more or less the case (how else, for example, that this war, in contrast to all previous ones, is not calling forth any religious reaction?)—what does that mean for Christianity?[12]

The necessity of a religionless Christianity came directly from Bonhoeffer's critique of the practice of Christian religion in the post-Enlightenment West, as well as from his assessment of secular culture. The world had "come of age," a term that was in effect a reference to the double movement of human autonomy on the one hand and the decay of religion on the other.[13]

But what of Christianity in this world come of age? Bonhoeffer had begun to notice in himself that religiosity was beginning to bother him. For example, while he had begun to make the sign of the cross (following Luther), at the same time he confesses that "my fear and mistrust of 'religiosity' have become greater than ever here."[14]

> I often ask myself why a "Christian instinct" often leads me more to the religionless people than to the religious, by which I don't in the least mean with any evangelizing intention, but, I might almost say, 'in brotherhood.' While I'm often reluctant to mention God by name to religious people—because that name somehow seems to me here not to ring true, and I feel myself to be slightly dishonest (it's particularly bad when others start to talk in religious jargon; I then dry up almost completely and feel awkward and uncomfortable)—to people with no religion I can on occasion mention him by name quite calmly and as a matter of course.[15]

Bonhoeffer's analysis led him to believe that religion had become an obstacle to genuine faith in Jesus Christ.[16]

12. *LPP*, 279, 280.
13. Rasmussen, *Dietrich Bonhoeffer*, 83.
14. *LPP*, 135.
15. Ibid., 281.
16. DeGruchy, "Development of Bonhoeffer's Theology," 39. Ralf Wüstenberg

In his very personal and moving "Thoughts on the Day of Baptism of Dietrich Wilhelm Rüdiger Bethge," Bonhoeffer insists that Christianity will be driven right back to the beginnings of understanding, since things such as reconciliation, redemption, regeneration, life in Christ, discipleship, and so on have become so remote that it has become virtually impossible to speak of them. The church has been occupied with self-preservation as though that were an end in itself, and thus the church "is incapable of taking the word of reconciliation and redemption to mankind and the world."[17]

Bonhoeffer is clear that repentance is an essential component of Christian faith. Since there is no way back from the adulthood of the world, the way forward is based on Matthew 18:3, "Unless you turn and become like children, you will never enter the kingdom of heaven." Bonhoeffer adds, "i.e. through repentance, through *ultimate* honesty."[18] He connects this to "participation in the sufferings of God in the secular life. That is *metanoia*: not in the first place thinking about one's own needs, problems, sins, and fears, but allowing oneself to be caught up into the way of Jesus Christ, into the messianic event."[19] In other words, Bonhoeffer does not want even this theological notion of repentance to be turned into yet another instance of a religious error, that of turning something properly theological into something psychological. So the concept of *metanoia* is extended to refer not only to something subjective, but also to this sharing of God's suffering in this world.[20]

Bonhoeffer clearly did not consider abandoning the connection with traditional words and customs of the church, such as prayer, meditation, worship, and coming together. Rather, the practice of these things as an arcane discipline would protect the world from violation by religion, and also prevent the church from collapsing back into mere religion. This does not entail the creation of a new privilege or a retreat from the world, but rather provides a way to face others and the world. "Arcane discipline without worldliness is a ghetto, and worldliness without arcane discipline is no more than the streets . . . arcane discipline in isolation becomes liturgical mockery, and non-religious interpretation an intellectual game."[21]

---

notes that Bonhoeffer's understanding of the term "religion" goes through three distinct phases: a) positive, liberal; b) critical; and c) non-religious. Wüstenberg, "Religionless Christianity," 59.

17. *LPP*, 299–300.
18. Ibid., 360.
19. Ibid., 362–63.
20. Woelfel, *Bonhoeffer's Theology*, 258–65.
21. Bethge, *Dietrich Bonhoeffer*, 788. I take the ideas of this entire paragraph from a very informative section in Bethge's book (784–90). John DeGruchy also includes an

Bonhoeffer has thus begun to redescribe Christianity, rejecting especially those instantiations whereby Christianity fights only for self-preservation, only uses God as a stop-gap measure, or where Christianity only undergirds individualistic piety or comfortable bourgeois existence. Practices of *metanoia*, a clear view of our penultimate place in history, arcane disciplines such as worship and prayer, and the centrality of the mystery of Christ have been identified as the heart of the Christian faith.

Bonhoeffer's religionless Christianity can be seen as counsel to Christianity to live "out of control." Instead of assuming that faith demands having and uttering the final word, and exerting control on an institutional and societal basis; instead of making primary the self-preservation of the church; rather than using God to answer questions until we can find the answers for ourselves, Bonhoeffer begins to show that the people of faith who continue to practice prayer and worship can live in terms of a determinate Christianity without false religion.

In what may by now seem like an unnecessarily long excursus concerning Bonhoeffer, I simply want to observe that the kind of analysis and reflection in which Bonhoeffer engaged in times of change and turmoil is in fact a potentially fruitful resource for our day. Bass is right to invoke his work, but it seems to me that it cannot be done simply through inclusion of pithy sayings drawn from Bonhoeffer's writings.

---

excellent discussion of arcane discipline in his essay "The Reception of Bonhoeffer in South Africa," 364, 365.

25

Dementia

John Swinton. *Dementia: Living in the Memories of God*. Grand Rapids: Eerdmans, 2012.

> *This unique book addresses the issue of the nature of Christian faith beyond memory. The book can be described as a constructive theology written about the important place of the deeply forgetful in our communities. Swinton pushes us to think theologically, not just medically, about the complicated and often excruciating experience of dealing with dementia, asking gently but rigorously about the nature of faith and personhood in people who suffer and those who surround them.*

Not all books that I read have an immediate connection to my current experience, which is the way I like it. In fact, that's one of the reasons I read: to enter other worlds, to think thoughts that are not generated by my limited experience and/or creativity, or as C.S. Lewis said so nicely, to know that I am not alone. So, much of my reading acts eschatologically, you might say. While it occurs today, it may only have a direct role to play at some future date. Nonetheless, just because a book doesn't have something to say to my immediate situation does not render it irrelevant, abstract, or obscure. I resist strongly any understanding of relevance that is somehow synonymous with "immediately pragmatic," a view that I think has important implications for education, for preaching, for scholarly activity, and for parenting, among other things.

But then, once in a while I read a book that addresses an issue that coincides with my life and experience is very direct ways. *Dementia* is such a book; that is, it is a book, that, as I read it, is interpreted through the lens of my personal experience with my mom. Unfortunately, the world of sickness and death has been a companion in our family for the last number of years, as my brother's thirty-plus years as a quadriplegic were followed by a difficult three-year hospitalization, ending sadly in his death in February 2013, and as we try to walk alongside my mom, whose life since 2002 could be described in terms of declension as she has endured a stroke, diabetes, broken arm, broken hip, osteoporosis, Parkinson's disease, and two broken legs sustained in a fall in her nursing home, where she continues to struggle with confusion and forgetfulness (although having read this book, I know that's not the only way to describe all of this). I hasten to add here that this is *not* about me and how difficult this is for *me*, but just to say that when I read a book about dementia, about care of people, understanding of disease, and so on, I simply cannot do so with any kind of detachment, objectivity, or cool rationality. As I read this book, I thought about Mom all the time, about the way she acts, the way I act when I'm with her, the way the church has responded to her, the way she is treated, the way I talk about her, and the way our children respond to her.

I want to begin our reflections on John Swinton's book by looking at the cover artwork designed by Willem Mineur.[1] The cover picture of what appears to be an autumn scene elicits upon examination a number of questions, causing the viewer to wonder if the picture is right side up or not, what time of day is being depicted, the source of the darkness, and whether the picture evokes hopefulness or sadness and melancholy. Author John Swinton, who did not choose the design, comments, "I would want to add the idea that still waters run deep. The picture is a mixture of reversal, beauty, and mystery. But underneath the obvious beauty is the suggestion that the waters are much deeper than the surface appearance may allow us to see."[2]

Swinton offers readers a very different kind of book than Diana Butler Bass does with *Christianity after Religion* (discussed in the previous chapter). Swinton describes his book as "self-consciously theological," and then on the next page distances his work from the kind that embraces broad forms of "spirituality," which he considers to be generic, thin, and vague.[3] The

---

1. My discussion of the cover art owes much to a discussion with Dr. Denny Smith.

2. Email correspondence with John Swinton.

3. Swinton, *Dementia*, 5. Subsequent references to the book will be included in the body of the essay.

seriousness with which he makes this claim about being self-consciously theological is manifested in his further claim that theological reflection on dementia is not to be done within a medical, psychological, or neurobiological framework; rather, theology provides the basic context into which the medical sciences speak (8).

> In giving voice to certain key questions that arise in the context of the experience of dementia, particularly advanced dementia, the intention of this book is to provide a practical and theological re-orientation that moves beyond current tendencies to perceive the subjective, self-aware, cognitive self as the necessary qualification for humanness and theological construction, and to open up the possibility that knowing *about* God may not be as important as *knowing God*, and that knowing God involves more than memory, intellect, and cognition. (15)

I will engage the content of this book by thinking about it in three discreet but interrelated sections, beginning with the task of redescription, or "retaking territory"(methodological), moving to a discussion of the retaking of the territory of the self/personhood (manifestation of the methodological), and concluding with a charge to the church.

The task of redescription is one that echoes H. Richard Niebuhr's insightful observation concerning the work of Christian ethics, namely, that "responsibility proceeds in every moment of decision and choice to inquire—'What is going on?'"[4] For Swinton, the task of asking what is going on is a theological one, courage for which comes from Romans 12:1, the theology of Karl Barth, and the example of Walter Brueggemann. Another way of labeling Swinton's enterprise would be to call it the telling of counterstories. For Swinton's project, what needs to be redescribed is dementia, what he presents as a "revised map of the territory of dementia" (27). Running across this notion of a map was especially interesting for me, as I was coincidentally reading James Scott's book *Seeing Like a State*, in which he shows how government initiatives in measuring of various kinds, including maps, function as instruments of control—they are not "mere tools of observation."[5] In the specific cases Scott describes, he shows that mapping can serve the interests of the centralized state by providing information that is useful to some, but detrimental to others, thus illustrating the power of a map, which we tend to see as neutrally descriptive. Scott's work shows that maps are anything but neutral; some things are highlighted, some ignored

---

4. Niebuhr, *The Responsible Self*, 60–61.
5. Scott, *Seeing Like a State*, 47.

or omitted, others categorized in a number of different ways, none of which are merely descriptive.

Drawing on Michael Ignatieff's wonderful novel *Scar Tissue* as a way of showing how differently dementia can be understood (medical vs. lived experience), Swinton brings to view the problem of accepting certain kinds of descriptions of dementia, primarily those that can be categorized as "defectology accounts," which tend to focus primarily on pathologies (41). Swinton argues that "the language we choose to describe dementia matters" (46). Therefore, it is important for Christians to use language that does not exclude important dimensions of the human condition such as God, faithfulness, discipleship, and love (47).

In chapter 3 Swinton begins the task of retaking territory, of resisting certain understandings of what it means to be a person, of what it means to describe people only in terms of impaired thinking or define them only in neurobiological terms: "The subtle work carried out by definitions and diagnoses in creating worldviews often has latent malignant functions that are easily hidden beneath manifest beneficence" (53). To provide just one example, to describe someone has having impaired thinking goes well beyond neutral description, argues Swinton, since to make such a judgment assumes we are competent to do so, that the mind resides only in the head, and that the mind is the essence of the person. Each of these assumptions carries unnecessarily negative weight that affects treatment of the person (63). Another way of putting the matter might be to say that definitions do not simply define but are "value-forming" (65).

If the standard neurobiological paradigm is not up to the task, then we need to move beyond it, which is the burden of chapter 4. Here Swinton considers the possibility of replacing the straightforward "pathology plus brain damage equals dementia" understanding to see if there is something to embrace in a relational paradigm. Swinton finds that social experiences are indeed part of the picture, but these social processes can be negative, resulting in malignant social psychology, which becomes possible when someone is "positioned" in ways that are negative and misinformed. There is no stable self that simply erodes with the onset of neurological developments.

However, even a move to thinking about the person rather than a cluster of symptoms is not without its shortcomings, according to Swinton. If the focus is on personhood, then depending on that understanding of personhood, it might become possible to believe that the person is disappearing, that only a shell remains, that the real person is gone. So, for example, if by "person" we understand something like a cluster of capacities, then the erosion or even disappearance of those capacities means a diminishing of personhood, a situation that makes it possible to think that someone with dementia might be "better off dead," or a candidate for divorce as Pat Robertson notoriously suggested.

A move from some notion of capacity as the basis of personhood to a relational understanding of personhood might be positive here, but Swinton is concerned that if personhood is described primarily in relational terms, then the self can vanish as relations disappear. To address that shortcoming, Swinton turns to explicitly theological material, that is, to theology and church practices. So, in chapter 7, he makes a very important theological move to situate this discussion within the Christian doctrine of creation. He tries to situate an understanding and description of dementia within the counter-story told within the strange new world of the Bible—creation, sin, and redemption. The basic theological premise is "that it is impossible to understand the full meaning of being a human person without first understanding who God is and where human beings stand in relation to God" (160). Drawing on the work of Robert Spaemann, Swinton asserts that personhood precedes capacities and properties (158ff.).[6] In fact, "to be human is to be (1) dependent and contingent, (2) embodied, (3) relational, (4) broken and deeply lost, and (5) loved and profoundly purposeful" (161).

Having addressed methodology and the retaking of territory, Swinton turns his attention to what will become his charge to the church: beginning to think about memory and the embrace of God, the material to which the book's subtitle (*Living in the Memories of God*) refers. He is wary of any account of memory that is somehow constitutive of the self, since to understand it in such a way would mean that the loss of memory associated with dementia would be, as he puts it (drawing on David Keck), "deconstruction incarnate" (190). Further, he cautions against framing being remembered by God as something that is primarily prospective and eschatological. Rather, he focuses on what it might mean to be remembered by God now. "God is mindful of human beings. To be human is to be held in the memory of God. God watches over human beings, knows them intimately, and remembers them" (211). Swinton's inclusion of the church, especially in chapter 9, challenges us to consider what it might mean for us to be friends of time, to learn to live in the present moment, framed as the sacrament of the present moment. This is not some kind of *carpe diem* notion but a rich, theological discussion that encourages Christians to reorient our understanding and marking of time. Central to the cultivation of all of this is the church's corporate worship and development of the practice of hospitality among strangers, to become Christian communities as places of belonging.

6. Swinton bases his argument here in large part on a theological understanding of *perichoresis*, the dynamically interrelated Trinitarian God (154–60), the exposition of which is beyond the scope of this essay.

Swinton's methodological and theological moves, whereby he refuses to accept the map of the territory of dementia provided in many conventional accounts that seem to rely primarily on neurological descriptions changes the very nature of the discussion around dementia. We find theologians also beginning in the wrong place, as they add to the conventional account a theological dimension, which nonetheless just won't do, according to Swinton. I'm reminded of Shelley Rambo's book *Spirit and Trauma* (discussed in an earlier chapter), where it seemed as though trauma theory set most of the terms of the discussion, inviting theology to then join a discussion already in progress, as it were. Rambo seemed more interested in applying the lens of trauma theory to theology than in developing a practical theology for trauma victims—or, she lets trauma theory lead the way. Here, Swinton's recognition of the power of description and of language leads him to pay close attention to how this investigation ought to be pursued. That recognition is itself a hard-won theological insight, a recognition that then leads to the reclaiming of territory, which, once reclaimed, forces us to take seriously the person who has fallen ill, the neurophysical realities and social dimensions, but especially it makes us work at this matrix of issues as though God actually matters, as though the church is real. In other words, as a Christian writer, as a "practical/pastoral theologian," Swinton works in such a way that if God doesn't exist, then his project falls apart for all intents and purposes.

On a related note, here is a practical/pastoral theologian for whom the distinctions of that kind (i.e., between practical and other kinds of theology) simply do not apply. The theological discussion of *perichoresis*, for example, is important not only because it has an "application" but because our understanding of God is important. Swinton defies false dualism between theology and ethics and between belief and practice.

To conclude, I wonder about the translatability of this material into something like a public health system, but then I wonder about my wondering. I think it's entirely possible that a Christian could take what is to be learned from this book and embody much of the material in either a personal situation or as part of a job in the field. However, what happens in the case of someone who does *not* believe and practice all of this, for whom God does not matter in the same way—how much traction can this vision of Swinton's have then?

A final (and personal) comment: several of my siblings have read Swinton's book and have agreed that his theological work has been of tremendous practical help in training us to engage with our beloved mom, and we are grateful for that guidance.

26

When I Was a Child I Read Books

Marilynne Robinson. *When I Was a Child I Read Books*. New York: Farrar, Straus, and Giroux, 2012.

Over the past thirty years Pulitzer Prize–winning author Marilynne Robinson has achieved an outstanding reputation in fiction and nonfiction for her careful, delicate prose, her penetrating wit, and her deeply lucid, willing Christian faith. When I Was a Child I Read Books *is a collection of essays, each of which displays all these traits to great advantage. From the American debt crisis, to truthfulness in fiction, to manners of dialogue between religious faith and modern science, this book offers a view of Robinson at the height of her craft in a variety of arenas. It also opens for the reader a vista of passions and interests in both historic and truly contemporary ways.*

I think it's revealing and important for understanding Robinson's work to take a quick look at her career to this point, and consider several key turning points for her. One of the first happened while she was studying in university, and it has to do with a footnote.[1] In an interview published in *The Paris Review*, Robinson explains the impact of reading this footnote, in Jonathan Edwards's "The Great Christian Doctrine of Original Sin Defended," on her thought and life:

---

1. Robinson, *When I Was a Child I Read Books*, 5. Subsequent references to the book will be included in the body of the essay.

> [Edwards] talks about the arbitrariness of "being" itself. He uses the metaphor of the reflected light of the moon, which we see as continuous light. Yet it is not intrinsic; it is continuously renewed as light. No physicist can tell you why things persist as they are, why one moment follows another. The reality we inhabit and treat like an old shoe is amazingly arbitrary.[2]

Robinson went on to earn her PhD in literature, writing about Shakespeare, and then published *Housekeeping* in 1980,[3] which she claims came about as the result of a long-term collection of metaphors, which she then turned into a novel. *Housekeeping* received considerable attention in part because of the review written by Anatole Broyard. As Robinson puts it, "Anatole Broyard—God love him—reviewed it early because he thought no one would review it and he wanted to make sure it got attention."[4]

This novel, which has garnered the reputation as a kind of flagship American feminist novel, takes its cue from the biblical book of Ruth but famously features a transient woman, Sylvie, whose ideas and practices of housekeeping are unconventional. I have to limit myself here to the comment that the stereotypical American male hero, that rugged self-sufficient individual who goes where he wants and when he wants, is replaced here by a female hero for whom family is important, but as I say, in an unconventional way. "At a certain level housekeeping is a regime of small kindnesses, which, taken together, make the world salubrious, savory, and warm. I think the small acts of comfort offered and received within a household as precisely sacramental. It is a sad tendency of domesticity—as of piety—to contract and of grace to decay onto rigor and peace into tedium" (93). *Housekeeping* provided a great start to the career of a novelist, but Robinson did not publish another novel for twenty-four years. She explains her reasons for turning to essay writing:

> To change my own mind. I try to create a new vocabulary or terrain for myself, so that I open out—I always think of the Dutch claiming land from the sea—or open up something that would have been closed to me before. That's the point and the pleasure of it. I continuously scrutinize my own thinking. I write something and think, How do I know that's true? If I wrote what I thought I knew from the outset, then I wouldn't be learning anything new.

2. Robinson, Interview by Sarah Fay.
3. Robinson, *Housekeeping*.
4. Robinson, Interview by Sarah Fay.

> In this culture, essays are often written for the sake of writing the essay. Someone finds a quibble of potential interest and quibbles about it. This doesn't mean the writer isn't capable of doing something of greater interest, but we generate a lot of prose that's not vital. The best essays come from the moment in which people really need to work something out.[5]

Instead of fiction, what followed from Robinson's pen is a significant body of nonfiction writing, including a highly polemical article and book dealing with the dumping of nuclear waste by Britain.[6] Robinson's own description of *Mother Country* is instructive:

> If I could only have written one book, that would have been the book. It was a real education for me. It did as much as anything to undermine the education I brought with me when I started the project. It was as if I was writing a dissertation over again in my mind, trying to establish what would be the relevant thing to know and where to look next. Also, if I had not written that book, I would not have been able to live with myself. I would have felt that I was doing what we are all doing, which dooms the world....
>
> ... We know that plastic bags are killing animals in Africa at a terrific rate, but everybody still uses these things as if they just float away. We know that these new lightbulbs cut down on electricity, but where do they come from? China? Hungary? They have to be dealt with as toxic waste because they have mercury in them. So who's being exposed to these chemicals when they're manufactured and what are the environmental consequences in China or Hungary? What is the tradeoff in terms of shipping them long distances to save a little bit of electricity?
>
> I'm also partial to the Sellafield book [*Mother Country*] because I think it exposes the ways in which we're racist. We assume that Europeans are white and therefore more rational than other populations and to find something weird and unaccountable and inhumane we must go to a darker continent....
>
> It was largely as a consequence of the experience of writing *Mother Country* that I began what amounted to an effort to reeducate myself. After all those years of school, I felt there was little I knew that I could trust, and I did not want my books to be one more tributary to the sea of nonsense that really is what most conventional wisdom amounts to. I am not so naive as to imagine that I have escaped that fate except in isolated cases and

---

5. Ibid.
6. Marilynne Robinson, "Bad News for Britain"; and Robinson, *Mother Country*.

small particulars. But the research and criticism I have done have helped me to be of my own mind in some degree, and that was a feeling I had to achieve before I could enjoy writing fiction.[7]

After *Mother Country*, Robinson published *The Death of Adam* (1998), various other essays, the novel *Gilead* (2004), then *Home* (2008), then two more nonfiction books, *Absence of Mind* (2010) and *When I Was a Child I Read Books* (2012), and then *Lila* (2014), wherein she returns to the same location as the two previous novels, now taking a woman as a central character again. Her essays address a wide range of issues—the relationship of science and religion, environmentalism, cosmology, the nature of the good, championing John Calvin and rehabilitating his reputation, the relationship of faith and fiction—and more.

Given that context, the book before us should be understood as Robinson working something or other out, by her own self-description, seeking to make sure, or at least as sure as may be possible, that she is not being duped by conventional wisdom. Her purview is far-reaching; the dust jacket claims that "Robinson returns to and expands upon the themes that have preoccupied her work with renewed vigor."

Dealing with a collection of essays that are expansive and deal with a variety of issues is a difficult task. Clearly we can't take up all of these rich essays and give them the attention they deserve. So, my plan is to focus more specifically on three elements, which in each case have several dimensions to them: faith and fiction, a strong yet chastened American patriotism, and Robinson's Christian humanism.

But before we get to those specifics, we want to ask what Robinson thinks she is doing. There is a sense in which it might be fair to say that Robinson is trying to do what she realizes cannot be done. That is, along with many other writers across the ages, she is joining in working out "demonstrations of the failures of language, which are, paradoxically, demonstrations of the extraordinary power of language to evoke a reality beyond its grasp, to evoke a sense of what cannot be said . . . as a writer, I continuously attempt to make inroads on the vast terrain of what cannot be said—or said by me, at least . . . We live on a little island of the inarticulable, which we tend to mistake for reality itself" (19–21). She is trying to expand that little island of the articulable, so that we can expand our perception of reality.

As a Christian writer of both fiction and nonfiction, Robinson is interested in the relationship between faith and fiction. As a writer, she wants to free herself from constraints, and it's her Christian religion that

---

7. Robinson, Interview by Sarah Fay.

will allow her to do so. Early in her educational pursuits, Robinson found herself looking for a "real love for human life" (3), but found her thought and experience constrained in significant ways, none more prominent than the problem of reductionism peddled in the form of Freudianism, behaviorism, and economic analysis, and all of it in ways that she experienced as a diminishment of the human condition (3–5). What she read did not encourage systematic doubt, it retreated from beauty, and did not square with her sense of things—concerns that did not necessarily let religion off the hook, since it too can take forms that are distorting to the nature of reality. Writing fiction therefore is very important for Robinson, since it consists largely of *exploring* reality. That is, fiction is central to her concern to inhabit a reality for which explanation, especially in any reductionistic form, is far too small. In her explorations of reality, Robinson is keen to keep on board notions such as the soul, which for the most part, is either ignored (secular) or reduced ("saved" or "lost"). In her view, there is no dispute between the reality of fiction and religious reality. For Robinson, faith frees us from unnecessary constraints; fiction is a way of expressing and exploring reality (3–18). Further, fiction acts as an exercise in the capacity for imaginative love, or sympathy or identification, thus contributing constructively to the life of the community, the pursuit of the common good (20–23).

A second element of Robinson's work is its fairly robust embodiment of American patriotism; indeed, her preface to *When I Was a Child* is largely a meditation on American heritage, describing her fear of losing the important value of loyalty to democracy (xvi). To be sure, Robinson sees clearly many of the problems besetting American civilization, offering her diagnosis regarding concerns such as the culture of organized fear, declarations of the necessity of austerity, and distorted economics that function as ideology (46–49). If I understand her correctly, she is keen to identify ways in which American society is seduced by various habits of mind and ideologies that distort America at its very best. While Robinson disclaims any notion that God loves one nation more than another, she firmly believes that "the United States of America has done many things right" (137). Robinson's patriotism might be described as a kind of wistfulness for just how good America was and could be if it lived up to its own best impulses.

The third element of Robinson's thought I want to focus on is her Christian humanism; she labels herself "a humanist, profoundly impressed with civilization" (199), and "an unregenerate liberal" (138). The kind of "liberal" Robinson purports to be is shaped by her reading of the Bible, especially the Old Testament, and the work of John Calvin; this is liberality, the most important dimension of which is generosity (64–69), a vision which she also sees in the thought of Jonathan Edwards (81, 82).

I have singled out several of the themes in Robinson's book: the relationship of faith and fiction; her version of patriotism, which embraces a "good society" of which America at its best is a good example, although it flounders too much in its self-understanding, too often ignoring or forgetting its own best impulse as a society; and finally, her version of Christian humanism (connected to liberalism), a robust anthropology that finds its generative force in the Christian faith. I have not addressed her treatment of the relationship of faith and science, her enthusiastic promotion of Calvin, or her ventures into economic issues that are to be understood primarily as moral. But before I turn to some critical comments, I want to also point out that many of the issues that she deals with in her essays are also addressed in her fiction, where she does not only assert arguments. Rather, as a good novelist, she explores, she shows rather than tells, and her characters press at the same kinds of questions while not necessarily reaching her own conclusions. But having said that, her fiction brilliantly offers the reader faithful possibilities for being human, for embracing "fragments of the quotidian"[8] as being luminescent with a sacramental quality without which many of us would not be able to navigate in this world. My own experience of teaching a course primarily based on Robinson's writing has helped me to see these kinds of connections, and as my students and I made our way through her work, we increasingly observed how her nonfiction helps us understand her fiction, and vice versa.

I conclude with several questions concerning Robinson's work. While I think I like her idea of "human exceptionalism," especially when kept in concert with a sense that human capacity cuts both ways (89), I worry that she takes the notion of exceptionalism too far as it relates to America. Her patriotism isn't blind by any means, it isn't jingoistic as far as I can see, but I fear that it's just too triumphalist (I readily admit that this may say more about me than it does about her, since I am allergic to almost all forms of nationalism).

Further, I wonder if Robinson succumbs in part to the danger that haunts all those who somehow take or are given the mantle of public intellectual—that is, the temptation to pontificate about a wide variety of topics, often brilliantly, but sometimes treading where one ought to fear to do so. For example, while we don't see much of it here, Robinson's forays into science and religion, as well as her entry into the fray that is environmentalism, have earned her vociferous criticism that she's overreaching or even being arrogant. Even Rowan Williams, former Archbishop of Canterbury, in an otherwise glowing review of this book claims that "she is a bit hard on some

---

8. Robinson, *Housekeeping*, 73.

serious interpreters such as Regina Schwarz, who in fact allow far more nuance to their criticisms than the more familiar and journalistic authors she castigates."[9]

Criticisms aside, I'm a fan of Robinson's work. To quote Rowan Williams again, "These essays are pure gold. Written with all her usual elegance, economy, and intellectual ruthlessness . . . The book is a breath of fresh air, the testimony of one of the world's most compelling English-speaking novelists to her debt both to American communitarian ethics and an orthodox Reformed theology remarkably free from obsessive moralism, while remaining toughly and subtly moral in all sorts of ways."[10] Williams goes on to say that her voice is needed in British church and society, and I would add, also in North America.

---

9. Williams, Review of *When I Was a Child I Read Books*.
10. Ibid.

27

David and Goliath

Malcolm Gladwell. *David and Goliath: Underdogs, Misfits, and the Art of Battling Giants*. New York: Little, Brown and Company, 2013.

Malcolm Gladwell's trade is in taking the assumed, the obvious, the conventional, and turning it all on its head in public perception. Interpreting established research in new ways, Gladwell challenges his readers to consider what they think they know in all-new lights. David and Goliath: Underdogs, Misfits, and the Art of Battling Giants includes what has been for Gladwell a rare foray into the realm of faith; it challenges us to rethink what it means to be disadvantaged or victimized, what constitutes a weakness, and what makes an obstacle. It also suggests how many of the things we feel are holding us back could be our greatest assets. This book, written by one of the 100 most influential people in the world as rated by Time *magazine, also features a full chapter on Winnipeg's Wilma Derksen and her struggle to overcome after her daughter's tragic abduction and murder.*

This chapter continues a series on "Public Prophets: Thinking Theologically about the Opinion-Shapers." Our first discussion centered on *When I Was a Child I Read Books* by Marilynne Robinson, who exerts significant public influence through her teaching, public lectures, popular novels, as well fiction primarily in essay form. If Robinson can be described as a "public intellectual," then Malcolm Gladwell is that in spades; he embodies that term in many ways. He was raised in Elmira, Ontario, and wrote for the *Washington Post* before being recruited by Tina Brown to become a staff writer for the *New Yorker*. Gladwell's public profile and influence took an exponential leap when he began publishing books that caught the public's attention, beginning with *Tipping Point* (2002), the title of which has become a part of the public lexicon. He went on to publish *Blink* (2005), *Outliers* (2008), *What the Dog Saw* (2009), and most recently, *David and Goliath* (2013). Not only does Gladwell write wildly popular books, he also carries on with his writing at the *New Yorker*, he delivers speeches, grants interviews, writes blog entries; he's ubiquitous. He has won all manner of accolades and prizes: in 2005, *Time* magazine named Gladwell one of its 100 most influential people, he has been awarded honorary degrees, and his books have spent a lot of time atop the *New York Times* bestseller lists.

Gladwell has turned several of his essays into book-length projects. His writing is compelling, accessible (some say breezy), fluid, and draws on an impossibly wide range of material. His approach might be characterized as anecdotal storytelling shored up by academic source material. His work is marked by a counterintuitive dimension, including novel perspectives on things with which we all thought we were familiar, new takes on conventional wisdom, with a significantly pragmatic dimension as well, showing us how to make things happen in ways that are useful in business, decision-making, and even in signing up your kid for hockey.

David and Goliath gives us more of the same in many ways, but now with a significant difference—he uses a biblical framing story, beginning each section with an excerpt from the Bible. This overtly religious, specifically Christian dimension is part of Gladwell's "return to faith," a process that apparently happened during the writing of this book.[1] Gladwell means to give us, as the dust jacket tells us, the *real* story of David and Goliath.[2] At its heart, the book is "about what happens when ordinary people confront giants" (5). So, Gladwell marshals a large number of stories to explore only two ideas: that lopsided conflicts often produce what we consider valuable, because greatness and beauty comes from the act of facing overwhelming odds, and that we often misread and misinterpret conflicts (6). The powerful are not always what they seem, and this book is about getting things *right* (15). This stance acts as a kind of two-edged sword. Pointing out conventional interpretations and showing how those views might be wrong is part of what makes Gladwell so interesting, but if a reader is unconvinced, Gladwell can come off as a bit pompous, as the only one who finally gets

---

1. Bailey, "Interview: Malcolm Gladwell on His Return to Faith."

2. To suggest that people have understood some topic in a certain way, which will now be turned on its head, is a move often made by Gladwell. See for example *David and Goliath*, 9. Subsequent references will be included in the body of the essay.

things right. An example of the latter response can be found in Joe Nocera's reaction to *David and Goliath*:

> As Gladwell puts it: "We have a definition in our heads of what an advantage is — and the definition isn't right. And what happens as a result? It means that we make mistakes. It means that we misread battles between underdogs and giants. It means that we underestimate how much freedom there can be in what looks like a disadvantage."
>
> The "we" of course does not include Gladwell. That's the whole point of a Malcolm Gladwell book. He has delved into the literature; he has interviewed lots of people—scientists, economists, deep thinkers and others who wind up in the book—and he has divined meaning and found counterintuitive connections that would otherwise elude the rest of us . . . As always, Gladwell's sweep is breathtaking, and thought-provoking. What it is not, however, is entirely convincing.
>
> You don't have to be a knee-jerk contrarian to realize that there is a good deal of common sense in Gladwell's thesis. It's just that it's not always as counterintuitive as he makes it out to be. When he writes about the actual example of David and Goliath, he makes the point that David—quick and accurate with the slingshot—was in fact the one with the advantage over Goliath, who was "too big and slow and blurry-eyed to comprehend the way the tables had been turned." "All these years," he adds, "we've been telling these kinds of stories wrong." But have we really? It strikes me that many Americans already understand the advantages of the seeming underdog, thanks in part to an example that Gladwell does not include: the way America's immense military power could not win the Vietnam War, or tame Iraq and Afghanistan.[3]

Both Gladwell's work and Nocera's reaction deserve our further attention. I will not work through the argument of the book in any kind of careful detail here. The book is organized around three sections. Part 1 is entitled "The Advantages of Disadvantages (and the Disadvantages of Advantages)." The three chapters deal with a relatively unskilled basketball team that challenges its disadvantages by playing in an unorthodox way, thus turning that disadvantage into an advantage; we read of the advantage (or not) of smaller class sizes, and the apparent advantage of growing up poor and the disadvantage of growing up rich; along the way we are introduced to the science of the inverted U curve. The reader encounters a mixture of

---

3. Nocera, "Killing Giants."

anecdotes supported by various studies, with connections between parenting, Impressionist painters, economics, and pedagogy made in ways that force us to reconsider whether it's better to be a big fish in a small pond or a small fish in a big pond, the benefits (or not) of relative deprivation. Gladwell concludes that "there is a point where money and resources stop making our lives better and start making them worse," and "we strive for the best and attach great importance to getting into the finest institutions we can. But rarely do we stop and consider . . . whether the most prestigious of institutions is always in our best interest" (68).

The second section deals with "The Theory of Desirable Difficulty." Here we find chapters dealing with the difficulty of dealing with dyslexia, the effect of trauma, especially near-miss trauma, and the lesson from Brer Rabbit, that great trickster, a lesson also on display in the work of Wyatt Walker in the Civil Rights Movement, namely, that being in a position with nothing left to lose produces unexpected freedom to break the rules—in other words, difficulties can sometimes bring positive results.

The third section addresses the "Limits of Power," where Gladwell treads on complicated and troubling ground to investigate the limitation of exerting power, exposing the ironic truth that sometimes too much power imposed too aggressively turns in on itself and loses its influence. Unbowed by historical complexities of incredibly messy scenarios, Gladwell tackles the Troubles in Northern Ireland, the genesis of the Three Strikes legislation in the aftermath of a young woman's horrific murder in Fresno, California, the all-too-close-to-home murder of Candace Derksen, along with her mother Wilma's excruciating experience, and the work of Andre Trocmé and his fellow French villagers and church members in hiding Jews in the face of Nazi occupation.

> It was not the privileged and the fortunate who took in the Jews in France. It was the marginal and the damaged, which should remind us that there are real limits to what evil and misfortune can accomplish. If you take away the gift of reading, you create the gift of listening. If you bomb a city, you leave behind death and destruction. But you create a community of remote misses. If you take away a mother or a father, you cause suffering and despair. But one time in ten, out of that despair rises an indomitable force. You see the giant and the shepherd in the Valley of Elah and your eye is drawn to the man with the sword and shield and glittering armor. But much of what is beautiful and valuable in the world comes from the shepherd, who has more strength and purpose than we ever imagine. (274–75)

Let me turn to a few comments of reaction and analysis of Gladwell's book. Gladwell has taken his lumps. For example, Christopher Chabris attempts to show "Why MG Matters, (and Why That's Unfortunate)."[4] It is probably sufficient to observe that Gladwell, while wildly popular, is not a critic's darling.

I want to add several comments shaped by theological concerns. I begin by confessing that I like Gladwell's essays far better than his books, primarily because his books feel like essays that have been turned into books, but with only enough of an argument for a really good essay. What is sharply argued, succinctly expressed, and provocatively stated in essay format is expanded at length without changing the argument to any great extent, if at all, so that after reading a few anecdotes supported by academic studies, his point has been made. One of Gladwell's great strengths, in my view, is clarity, but after a while it feels like piling on.

I fear that by now, what with the astounding sales record, it must be tough for any editor to push as hard as Gladwell needs to be pushed. His books sell in part because they sell; they are a commodity treated in a certain way by the publishing industry, whose first concern is sales, not coherence of argument, tightness of logic, judicious use of sources, peer review, and so on. Christopher Chabris suggests that it is precisely because of Gladwell's popularity and the fact that (influential) people take his theories seriously that the propagation of wrong beliefs among a vast audience is itself a serious matter; when Gladwell speaks, people listen.[5]

But what about the content? Is it good, reliable, convincing, theologically sound? Regarding the story that generates his argument, I suggest that, unlike Gladwell's strong assertion (9), we have not all gotten this story wrong over the centuries, but that *he* is missing a very important dimension because of a problem that is endemic to his work. That is, Gladwell's work is reductionistic (he boils down complex matters to some kind of basic premise). This is problematic on several levels, including the moral level—a complaint of mine that goes back to *The Tipping Point*. It's one thing to analyze trends, learn how to make things happen, how to make things "tip," and so on, but such analysis does not necessarily take into account the moral dimension of matters at hand—just because you *can* make something happen does not mean you should. Here, Gladwell reduces the David and Goliath

---

4. Chabris, "Why Malcolm Gladwell Matters." Gladwell is accused of "Pseudo-profundity, the nonfiction equivalent of Dan Brown, author of *Da Vinci Code*" in Poole, "Pseudo-Profundity of Malcolm Gladwell." John Gray describes Gladwell as "America's Best-Paid Fairy-tale writer"; see Gray, "Malcolm Gladwell Is America's Best-Paid Fairy-Tale Writer."

5. Chabris, "Why Malcolm Gladwell Matters."

story to a study in battle techniques, arguing among other things that Goliath has some kind of disease that causes double vision. By the time Gladwell is done with story, it is all understandable on a scientific, material basis. To be fair, in an interview published subsequent to the publication of the book, Gladwell acknowledges the power of the spirit of God, but that is not part of the chapter here at all. In fact, in that same interview, Gladwell, when asked about Jesus, describes Jesus as having accomplished an unfathomable amount of good; "He is almost the perfect illustration of the idea that you have to look in the heart to know what someone's capable of."[6] While that understanding of Jesus deserves considerable attenuation, in this interview Gladwell gestures toward a dimension of the biblical account of David and Goliath that is missing from his book, a dimension that would have (rightly) complexified his treatment of this well-known story considerably.

It seems to me that the David and Goliath story actually depends on David being an actual, palpable underdog replacing King Saul, who really ought to be stepping up. David has no plan or technique to beat Goliath. The risk taken by David is made possible only by faith in God. There is no law of human nature, there are no rules of engagement to be learned here that can be applied in situations in which we find ourselves the seeming underdogs, only to realize that such status may in fact be advantageous. David and Goliath needs to be read as a story that only makes any kind of sense within the history of God's chosen people Israel, a story that blows open the usual possibilities within this world to the possibilities brought on by God's sustaining intervention in this world. If that dimension of the story is missing, if the living God of Israel is taken out of the inner logic of the account, then all we have is a story of clever technique applied by a nimble young man against what only *appears* to be a much superior foe, a technique that can be applied anywhere, whether God exists or not. When you do that to the story, you have distorted it beyond recognition.

This search for technique in any story or anecdote, which is then supported by academic research, this uncovering of human laws, of causal rules that explain how the world works should we manage to understand these rules the way he does, reveals what I consider to be a serious flaw in Gladwell's work. He presents as proven laws that may be intriguing possibilities, supports them with academic studies that support the principle of human nature a given story points to, resulting in stories supported by social science that are convertible to actionable insights.[7] So, Gladwell's approach of identifying one or two big ideas that then govern a huge amount

---

6. Bailey, "Interview: Malcolm Gladwell on His Return to Faith."
7. Chabris, "Why Malcolm Gladwell Matters."

of heterogeneous material,[8] combined with his penchant for identifying causal rules of human behavior that generate actionable practices is a potentially distorting, misleading, or even toxic method that often upon close examination cannot be sustained. Can a lawyer who is a good reader also be a good listener? Does dyslexia help to create success (as understood by Gladwell), or does it fill our jails? Gladwell is close to asserting that a rule holds true except for when it does not hold true.[9]

> Is it really advantageous to have severe dyslexia? *Yes, and certainly not.* Are children better off without their parents? *Don't be silly, but it could be so.* These non-answers rub the dazzle from Gladwell's clever thesis statements, until they all begin to look like dullish intuition. We don't need another book to tell us that adversity can lead to greatness (see: memoirs by CEOs, episodes of *The Moth*, every college essay ever written), just as we don't need another book to say that adversity really, really sucks (see: the world outside your window). But couched in the golden armor of anecdote, Gladwell's overgrown ideas seem powerful and new.
>
> It's impossible to read *David and Goliath* with the care and skepticism it deserves, since the subject matter ranges so outrageously from one page to the next. That's what makes Gladwell's readers into underdogs: In nine chapters, his book delves into the fields of sports, oncology, education, psychology, military history, law, finance, civil rights, fine arts, and criminal justice. It draws case studies from the London Blitz, the civil rights protests in Birmingham, the Troubles in Northern Ireland, and resistance to the Nazis in southern France. Also, there's a girls' basketball team in California, and a family of Mennonites. How can anyone keep pace with Gladwell's superhuman breadth of knowledge and ambition? We're doomed to glimpse the world the way he does, through the eyes of a giant.[10]

A related problem is Gladwell's source of authority for his work, namely science. As John Gray points out, there seems to be an uncritical reverence on display here. The problem is not that Gladwell does not exercise discernment among sources, but that the sources he uses as authoritative are scientific studies. In doing so, Gladwell is part of a large club that is very popular in social scientific circles, in which people, relationships, and trends are studied in an ostensibly neutral way and the results then reported

---

8. Poole, "Pseudo-Profundity of Malcolm Gladwell."
9. Engber, "Gladwell Is Goliath."
10. Ibid.

in a manner that professes to be merely descriptive, yet exerts an enormous amount of prescriptive influence. Says Gray, "It is not simply that Gladwell appeals to psychology and sociology as sources of intellectual authority. Along with many of those who promote them today, he believes these disciplines can provide practical guidance—not just policy proposals, but wisdom for living." Gray suggests that one of the problems with such an approach is "a refusal to accept that intractable difficulty is normal in human affairs." In the end, says Gray, Gladwell is in the self-help racket, in which "comforting tales of self-improvement and overcoming evil are given a thin gloss of scientific authority. It is this combination, together with the conceit of presenting counterintuitive truths, that makes his work so popular."[11]

My fundamental issue with Gladwell has to do with an incipient instrumentalism, trying to find a handle on some story or topic, and once having identified that handle, you now have a mechanism to make things turn out the way you want them to. Instrumentalism is not without its usefulness and pragmatic quality, but it carries in its train all kinds of possibilities, some negative, some toxic, some murderous (for example, modern efficiency employed in factories can produce a relatively cheap car, but it can also help you "process" humans efficiently).[12] But even if not employed to nefarious ends, instrumentalism also is essentially incapable of taking seriously those dimensions of human life that cannot be "used" for our own ends, as is often the case with spiritual realities. For example, I think of the Christian practice of self-emptying, exemplified by Jesus, discussed at length by St. Paul in Philippians 2. This is not a way to get things done, it's not a rule of life or a law of human nature; it is a spiritual truth we are asked to consider in light of Jesus Christ's incarnation and sacrifice. To follow in obedience will have some effect, but we may not like that effect, and it may make our lives more difficult and more complicated. The Christian gospel is not a self-help message, and insofar as Gladwell's work is in the self-help business, it needs to be treated carefully. It remains to be seen if and how his own return to faith will change his writing, in terms of method, in reliance on certain kinds of authority, and in the ends toward which he does his very influential work.

---

11. Gray, "Malcolm Gladwell Is America's Best-Paid Fairy-Tale Writer."
12. See for example Bauman, *Modernity and the Holocaust*.

28

My Bright Abyss

Christian Wiman. *My Bright Abyss: Meditation of a Modern Believer*. New York: Farrar, Straus, and Giroux, 2013.

> *In 2006, poet Christian Wiman published a short essay entitled "Love Bade Me Welcome," reflecting on despair and hope: "losing the ability to write, falling in love, receiving a diagnosis of an incurable cancer, having my heart ripped apart by what, slowly and in spite of all my modern secular instincts, I learned to call God."[1] The unprecedented public response to this essay prompted Wiman to expand on those words.* My Bright Abyss *is Wiman's pursuit of a dialogue between the poetry he loves and the prose he has come to need, in the hope of articulating the nature of faith as he has rediscovered it: a faith more terrifying than cancer and more hopeful than a cure, blooming amidst the wreckage of everything that once was certain.*

After growing up on the barren plains of West Texas, Christian Wiman set out to become a poet. This apprenticeship included four years bouncing around Europe, followed by a variety of teaching positions and two well-received books of poetry. Things changed when *Poetry*, America's most prestigious poetry magazine, received a $200 million bequest from Ruth Lilly in 2002, resulting in Wiman's being chosen as *Poetry*'s new editor and making him one of the leading voices in American poetry. In 2005,

---

1. The essay appeared as the final chapter in Wiman, *Ambition and Survival*.

Wiman learned that he has a mysterious, incurable cancer of the blood, which has meant frequent hospitalizations and a bone marrow transplant. He then discovered—or rediscovered—his Christian faith.[2] He also fell in love and got married. Wiman now teaches literature and religion at Yale Divinity School and the Yale Institute of Sacred Music; all in all, a truly public voice.

We know at least some of Wiman's experience along these lines because of his essay "Love Bade Me Welcome," which I think should have been republished as the opening chapter of *My Bright Abyss*. "Love" is a sparkling gem of an essay, moving, personal, poignant, and brilliant; it acts as the orienting focus of this book in many ways, as we see in Wiman's own preface. It is in that essay where we see him draw on the Nietzschean notion that "when you gaze long into the abyss, the abyss also gazes into you." The abyss reappears in Wiman's poem that brackets this book, but now transfigured as a "bright" abyss. The thing to notice is that the opening poem ends with a colon, the final version with a period. In between we find eleven chapters, with titles that send the reader searching for the source of the titular phrase, which almost always plays a significant role in understanding the thrust of the given chapter.

It's hard to talk about this book, since it's the sort that risks being distorted in the act of talking about it. The writing has the feel of a parable to me, in that the reduction of a parable to some kind of moral lesson or some such thing is reduction indeed, as well as distortion. A parable teaches in the telling of it, and so I find with *My Bright Abyss*. If someone asks me what it means, the only truly respectful response, to both book and reader, is to hand over the book.

Nonetheless, something can be said about the book. Wiman refers to it as a "mosaic, not a continuous argument or narrative," in which he attempts to "help someone who is at once as confused and certain about the source of life and consciousness as I am."[3] It's been variously described as a "kaleidoscope," an "aphoristic rumination," a "tenebrous call of dereliction." Whatever the label others give the book, Wiman himself calls it a meditation; perhaps it's accurate to call it a meditation "on the cost of experience."[4] Wiman uses the term "modern believer" in the subtitle to describe himself—which is interesting, given that he describes one of his own poems, written as a young man in Prague, in the following way: "It is . . . I've come

---

2. I take this basic biographical information from Skeel, "Edge of All We Know."

3. Wiman, *My Bright Abyss*, x. Subsequent references to the book will be included in the body of the essay.

4. Stimpson, "Review of Christian Wiman's 'My Bright Abyss.'"

to think, in a peculiar and very modern sense, a devotional poem, or at least an early unconscious attempt at one, though God is nowhere in it. That's what makes it modern" (45). Understood in this way, "modern believer" is a paradoxical term, which fits nicely with many turns of phrase and concepts in the rest of the book.

The book treats readers like adults, offering both the intellectual and the mystical, as it tries to do what is nigh impossible to do well, that is, communicating non-ironically about faith to a secular audience, a task that Mary Karr (who has herself traded whiskey for Jesus) has described as "doing card tricks on the radio."[5] Whatever else it is, the book is a wide-ranging conversation with often disparate voices, ranging from the usual suspects to the obscure, from poets to theologians to novelists to philosophers and back again.

As with many writers who are skilled in the use of language, Wiman is very aware of what language can and cannot do, something that he signals very early in the book and returns to several times. For example, he admits that some forms of language are no longer accurate or helpful (4), that language sometimes displays inaccuracy and slippage (117), and that there are times when words begin to "leak" (127). This concern is coupled with a kind of hope regarding the role of language, but not in any straightforward way. Wiman relies on Fanny Howe to raise a significant question about the vocabulary of faith. "Can you build a vocabulary of faith out of the rhetoric made of dread and then stand behind this new language? Is faith created by a shift in rhetoric, one that can be consciously constructed, or must there be a shattering experience, one that trashes the old words for new things?" (54) Wiman's response is that there must be a shattering experience (54). In an interview, he claims that "everyone has shattering experiences. It may be falling in love or having a child. It may be the death of someone you love or thwarted ambition. It may be just some tiny crack in consciousness that deepens so slowly over the years that, by the time you notice it, it takes only a spilled drink or missed flight to tear it—and you—wide open. One way to look at this is: no one is spared. Another way—everyone is gifted."[6]

It is this "building up of a vocabulary of faith out of a rhetoric of dread" that Wiman is interested in; his contention is that we need a "poetics of belief," the kind of possibility found in the work of Marilynne Robinson. So we watch Wiman struggle to use language to "play card tricks on the radio," to wrestle with the possibilities of language even as he struggles with faith, love, suffering, and so on. These struggles are all inextricably linked in this

---

5. Garner, "Turning a Dark Place into a Beacon of Discovery."
6. Williams, "Jolts from Life."

book. You might think of it this way—the more Wiman is convinced that language isn't up to the task, the more careful, attentive, and precise he becomes (see pp. 146, 177 for his use of the phrase "grain of grammar"). Says Wiman, "We must be conscious of language as language, must call every word we use until we refine or remake a language that is fit for our particular religious doubts and despairs—and of course (and most of all!) our joys" (138).

I can't decide whether Wiman is frustrating or appropriately evocative in the way he makes assertions that range from paradoxical and ambiguous to definitive and decisive. In "Love Bade Me Welcome," Wiman signals the importance of Simone Weil's often-paradoxical thought for his own writing and reflection, and he returns to such paradoxical thinking early in this book (10), and specifically to Weil's thought (111, 112); he struggles to wrestle meaning from the absoluteness of meaninglessness (136, 137), arguing that those things that led us to God must be sacrificed (175).

But it's important to recognize that Wiman isn't putting forward some kind of soft notion that we cannot assert anything definite. In fact, Wiman frequently is quite definitive and even assertive in the claims he makes for his beliefs.[7]

> We do not need definite beliefs because their objects are necessarily true. We need them because they enable us to stand on steady spots form which the truth may be glimpsed . . . Definite beliefs are what make the radical mystery—those moments when we suddenly *know* there is a God, about whom we "know" absolutely nothing—accessible to us and our ordinary, unmysterious lives. And more crucially: definite beliefs enable us to withstand the storms of suffering that come into every life, and that tend to destroy any spiritual disposition that does not have deep roots. (123)

When an artist/poet/writer writes about faith, it is sometimes the case that art is seen as a replacement for faith, or poetry a substitute for prayer. The pursuit of art *becomes* the expression of faith, or the transgression of the same, leaving little room for creeds, theology, and certainly not anything smacking of dogma. Wiman is interesting here; as Kathleen Norris points out, he does not take up the elite status of the heroic artist,[8] although clearly the book prefers wonder and interpretation to dogma.[9] Wiman is

---

7. I acknowledge a helpful conversation with Julie Doerksen about this dimension of Wiman's book.

8. Norris, "Faith Healing," Review of *My Bright Abyss*.

9. Stimpson, "Review of Christian Wiman's 'My Bright Abyss.'"

perhaps a bit too predictable with his claim that art is better at theology than theology is (130).

Nonetheless, Wiman is relatively modest about the potential and possibilities of art—first, because, as he puts it, "Life is a hell of a lot more difficult—and important—than art"; and second, life forces the creation of art (152). And so, he goes about interrogating *both* faith and art in this book, with art sometimes being called onto the carpet, since it's not always an act of grace (4); art can compromise (41).

Another striking dimension of Wiman's work is his emphasis on the importance of earthly experience and existence *in* or *as* the life of faith. "I was brought up with the poisonous notion that you had to renounce love of earth in order to receive the love of God. My experience has been just the opposite: a love of the earth and existence so overflowing that it implied, or included, or even absolutely demanded, God. Love did not deliver me from the earth, but into it."[10] You might describe *My Bright Abyss* as a contemplation on existence. "God calls us at every moment, and God is life, *this* life (8)."[11] Despite all of this emphasis on personal experience, the nature of existence and so on, Wiman pauses nicely to warn of the danger of letting experience be the arbiter of our lives. In fact, he goes further than that—he warns against the danger of making of our experience an idol (162).

As I noted earlier, Wiman subjects faith to interrogation. As Kathleen Norris says, this book might be read as an "assault on complacent pieties."[12] His own coming to faith as an adult is different than the faith of his West Texan upbringing. After all, he asserts, if you believe at fifty what you believed at fifteen, then you have not lived or have denied the reality of your life (7). Nonetheless, he describes his conversion as "assenting to the faith that was latent within me" (12). But there's nothing straightforward about the faith that he embraces, as we have by now come to expect. Faith doesn't "work," it's mutable, messy and provisional (9, 17–18, 26). Therefore, it is not surprising that doubt creeps into the picture as well, but not merely as the opposite of faith (75–77). Part of Wiman's reflection on the nature of faith includes alerting us to the dangers of that mutable, messy, provisional treasure to which we cling. That is, the coming to life of the faith latent within us is not without its vagaries, if not downright dangers (108, 167). "We need to be shocked out of our easy acceptance of—our facile resistance to—propositional language about God. Besides being useless at any defini-

10. Wiman, "Love Bade Me Welcome," 244.

11. See also Wiman's discussion in a similar vein, focusing on the poetry of Gerard Manley Hopkins (35); other passages which extend these ideas can be found (84, 90, 97–98).

12. Norris, "Faith Healing," Review of *My Bright Abyss*.

tive description of God, such language is simply not adequate for the intense and sacred spiritual turmoil that so many contemporary people feel" (138).

Finally, I find Wiman's discussions of God and Jesus Christ really interesting. We have already noted his acknowledgment of the inadequacy of language for the task, and in this he might be described as being part of the apophatic tradition, something that he embraces explicitly (136–38). But Wiman really likes Jesus Christ, especially the doctrine of the Incarnation (11). It's Wiman's focus on Incarnation that is central to his oft-repeated assertion that Christ is contingency (16–17). "It was pure contingency that caught fire in our lives, and it was Christ whom we found—together, and his presence dependent on our being together—burning there. I can't speak for other people. I only know that I did not know what love was until I encountered one that kept opening and opening and opening. And until I acknowledged that what that love was opening onto, and into, was God" (22–23).

To conclude this discussion, I think that this book could be classified within the genre of spiritual writing in which we find Augustine's *Confessions*. That is, what we have here is an attempt to meditate on the work of God in the world, and more specifically in one's own life, but not in a maudlin, self-absorbed manner. It's an exercise in interpretation, in trying to understand what is going on here on a particular and universal scale, but not in a saccharine "spiritual but not religious" kind of way. I really like Wiman's perpetual dance between ambiguity and the definite, contra some "gauzy ontology" (123). That kind of constructive dance happens within a lifelong practice of engagement with art, theology, people, memory, suffering, going to church, exploration of the meaning and depth of human love, struggling with the simultaneous power and weakness of language, and a radical openness to the contingency of Christ.

29

The Good Funeral

Thomas Lynch and Thomas Long. *The Good Funeral: Death, Grief, and the Community of Care*. Louisville: Westminster John Knox Press, 2013.

Thomas Lynch, a poet, funeral director, and American Book Award winner, together with Thomas Long, a professor and theologian, explore what constitutes a "good funeral" under three basic convictions. First, they claim that the rituals and practices around death are a window into the soul of a culture. Second, they assert that "a society that is unsure about how to care for the dead and is confused about what to do with grief and loss is a society that is also uncertain about life." Last, they suggest that "[the West's] cultural soul is currently troubled on this very score." Lynch and Long move from the theology of the recent "bodiless memorial service" trend, through the good, the bad, and the ugly of the funeral industry. They also address the fundamental dimensions of grieving, care, and ceremony. Long and Lynch open this immensely relevant conversation to the public with tenderness, humor, wisdom, and humility.

Some writers/thinkers shape public opinion in unique and significant ways, thus garnering the title of "public intellectual." While clearly insiders to society in important ways, nonetheless such people also can be seen as outsiders of sorts, as they offer analyses and critiques of practices, trends, positions, and ideologies held by many of us, sometimes even unconsciously. The kind of influence wielded by such public figures isn't limited to one style or genre, connected with a specific institution, nor necessarily dependent upon formal academic credentials.

Within the public discourse about funerals, these two writers, "the thanatology Toms," as Will Willimon calls them, seem to be the most prominent. In fact, Willimon (of Duke Divinity School) claims that these are our two best writers on American ways of death, burial, and grieving who have now given us our best book on funerals. "No pastor can be said to be prepared to lead in the essential liturgies of death and dying without having read this book and having shared its truths with the congregation."[1]

As always, I come to the book with my own baggage, impressions, experiences, and background. In this case, I had read both of these authors before, and I had also watched a few seasons of *Six Feet Under*, quickly grew tired of it, and gave up watching after a while. Coincidently, however, I too was moved by the very first episode, which includes a scene where the funeral director's burial turns dramatic, as family members grab handfuls of dirt and fling them onto the exposed coffin. This scene that has stayed with me to this day, making my reading of Lynch's commentary on that program quite personal. More important than a television show are funerals that have marked me in important ways: my dad's funeral in 1975 when I was fifteen years old, my brother's funeral in 2013, and then very sadly, and not long after Levi's death, the funerals of two former students from the same high school class. It was at my brother's death and funeral that I had some part in shaping things, and Lynch's previously published book[2] and that first episode of *Six Feet Under* were part of my thought process. Our family, including my teenage children, was in the room when my brother died. As soon as he died, I asked the nurse to remove all of the medical paraphernalia from his body, and so we sat with him for hours, went to the airport to pick up a brother flying in from the West Coast, returned to the hospital room and sat some more. As I wrote the obituary, I resisted the funeral director's attempt to use the term "passed away" instead of "died" because, as he put it, the term he preferred was "softer." Our family rejected planning things in such a way as to invoke "closure," as if that is possible when someone you love dies. Further, we insisted that we fill the grave with dirt without the use of machinery. And, I wish I had read *The Good Funeral* as well, as it opens up further understanding and possibilities, bringing to view what is or ought to be happening at a funeral, what's at stake, and so forth.

The burden of this book is framed in theological language. A woman asks Lynch at some event "how we might 'redeem' the funeral . . . from

---

1. Willimon, "Body in Question," 36.
2. Lynch, *The Undertaking*.

its failed and fallen ways. Her question is at the heart of this book," says Lynch.[3] There are actually several assertions or questions that vie for our attention, such as "A society that is unsure about how to care for the dead and is confused about what to do with grief and loss is a society that is also uncertain about life" (xxiv). Another way of describing the burden of the book is found in Patrick Lynch's foreword, who in describing brother Thomas's work claims that funerals should not be anything less than an existential experience possessing certain basic elements: someone who has died, someone to whom that death matters, and someone to broker the message between them (xii). In Thomas Lynch's own words, it takes great courage to "stand between the living and the dead and broker a peace between them and God" (27). Lynch also provides focus to his work with his oft-repeated line: "A good funeral is one that gets the dead where they need to go and the living where they need to be" (xii).

The Good Funeral is the result of one of those happy coincidences of friendship: a theologian (Long) who writes about funerals meets an undertaker poet (Lynch) who writes about what he calls "the dismal trade."[4] While one is much more active in the church than the other, one is Catholic and the other Protestant, they forge a relationship and eventually publish this book. The book is not coauthored; rather, they write discreet essays, which are organized into five rather broad categories. Lynch's essay appears first in nearly every category, and each chapter opens with a reading of some kind. Lynch mostly uses poetry, with one exception which is an excerpt from a Shakespeare play. Long uses scripture, again with one exception, in this case a passage from John Donne. It must be said that Long does the theological heavy lifting, which is not to say that Lynch's work is not undergirded by his own theological concerns.

In response to my reading of these essays, I want to make a few idiosyncratic comments without rehearsing the content of the book, and then pose a few questions. First, the opening testimonials, under the rubric of "Why We Do This," are quite enjoyable, in part because the writing is so good, drawing on a wide range of sources, offering nice turns of phrase. They are funny, a bit self-deprecating, and just smart. But more important is the fact that these essays give us readers a sense of in whose hands we are placing ourselves, as we open ourselves to the possibility of change, of reshaping our views of what it means to be human, our understanding of death and life, and the practices that surround death and dying. Further,

---

3. Lynch and Long, *Good Funeral*, 28. Subsequent references to the book will be included in the body of the essay.

4. Lynch, *The Undertaking*.

these introductory essays bring to our attention some significant differences between the writers, alongside some obvious similarities. One (Lynch) does what he does because of deeply entrenched family tradition running to several generations now; the other (Long) because of a strong call from God. Lynch draws from poetry, literature in his field, on rare occasions from theology, but seldom from scripture; Long draws on theology, the Bible, and literature. Lynch does not attend church, at least not on Sundays, and describes things in the following way: "I arrived by the grace of Whomever is in Charge Here at a provisional article of faith, to wit: if there's a God, it's not me" (27), which is perhaps not the most robustly orthodox confession of faith I've run across, but charmingly stated. Whatever religious sensibilities he has find their source in the Roman Catholic tradition. Long attends church, is a member of the clergy, a well-respected professor of church ministry and author; his religious bona fides are all in order. But he too is charming about these matters, I find, declaring that he likes the relatively new situation in America in which Christianity finds itself, without bygone sureties, wherein culture does not give him and his faith "free passes" (35–36). All this to say that our authors share many similarities, but their differences are also real and obvious.

Second, these essays provide a compelling argument for the power and possibilities of a funeral. While much of the book is given over to critical analysis of funereal practices, both in the case of funeral directors and clergy, I'm struck by the kind of work paying attention to dying and the dead can do. Lynch poses the stark question of what must be done about a dead human, and he offers very helpful guidance in response to his own query. First, the presence of the dead is the essential, definitive element of a funeral. The second essential element is that there must be those to whom the death matters. Then, there must be some narrative about meaning, and lastly, the funeral must accomplish the disposition of the dead. Lynch has offered an important mechanism that can provide a way to separate the essential element from the accessories, the fundamental obligations from the fashionable options, the substance from the stuff, the necessary from the knick-knacks, and the core from the pulp (81).

Long offers some very fine guidance as well in his chapter entitled "A Sense of Movement, A Sense of Meaning, A Sense of Hope." He argues that a "good funeral, then, not only honors the body of the deceased, it also makes it clear, in an active sense, that the one who has died is moving from here to there and the rest of us are accompanying the deceased along the way" (206, see also 208–9). In a funeral, says Long, "we both enact and interrogate yet again what we believe about life and death, what are our practical and ethical responsibilities toward each other in life and death, and who we are called to be" (210). Another notable contribution Long makes is his re-narration of Elizabeth Kübler-Ross's stages of grief material, concluding that discussion with the assertion that

> we do not do this task of rebuilding out life narratives alone. In the wilderness of grief, God provides narrative manna—just enough shape and meaning to keep us walking—and sends the Comforter, who knits together the raveled soul and refuses to leave us orphaned. Sometimes the bereaves say they are looking for closure, but in the Christian faith we not seek closure so much as we pray that all of our lost loves will be gathered into that great unending story fashioned by God's grace. (225)

Third, Lynch and Long provide a valuable service by exposing the problematic dimensions of funerals on the part of both clergy and funeral homes/directors. In fact, the identification and exploration of failing and fallen funeral practices takes up much of the argumentative energy of the book. We are exposed to dubious retail practices, to an analysis of casket sales, harsh criticism of preneed funeral services, and the trend toward personalization of funerals (95, 142, 144, 168).

By far the biggest problem that besets funerals is the disappearance of the body; "the theological theme that runs through *The Good Funeral* is that bodies matter to Christians in life, in death, and in any life beyond death."[5] Here both Lynch and Long, as undertaker and preacher, offer interesting and constructive material. In Lynch's long and impassioned engagement with Jessica Mitford's influential *The American Way of Death Revisited* (1998) (Long also deals with the same book, but not as extensively), Lynch charges Mitford with wanting to banish bodies, which to him is anathema (76). This strong notion about the presence of the body is fundamental to Lynch's very helpful discussion of cremation. He is not opposed to cremation, but offers strong cautions, especially on the grounds that cremation lends itself too easily to proceeding without the body (187). Cremation may be an alternative to burial, but it should not be an alternative to bothering (189). So, if cremation is to take place, at least the body ought to be accompanied to the burning.

Long too is worried about the presence (or absence) of the body at the funeral, and offers a more theologically rich account of this in his wonderful chapter entitled "Habeas Corpus . . . Not." Broadly speaking, we know that bodies matter, but more specifically for Christians, bodies matter to God (88–89). His analysis of the Christian struggle to embrace materiality as spiritual is very compelling, revealing the problems with the "spiritual but

---

5. Willimon, "Body in Question," 36.

not religious" phenomenon, showing how our faith often feels trapped by solid things (104) and putting forward a constructive vision of the "materiality of our spirituality" (107).

I want to move from highlighting central dimensions of the book to offering some reactions and responses. To begin, the book is just too repetitive. The same material sometimes shows up in different essays by the same author, or is sometimes used by both authors, the most obvious example being the repeated discussions of Jessica Mitford. Further, some of Lynch's material is repeated from his book *The Undertaking*.

More substantively, however, I like the book a lot. Admittedly, I would find it less compelling without Long's theological heft. Nonetheless, the very fine writing, the literary quality of both authors' work, the drawing on sources ranging from poetry to fiction to theology to cultural commentary to personal narrative to biblical material allows for this kind of important public discourse—openly Christian without being unnecessarily exclusive, clearly exhortative without being pedantic. The writing could be described as humane. I find this especially the case with Thomas Lynch, who is very humane, and I confess, sometimes a little too humanistic for me. By this I mean that his chapter entitled "Humanity 101" is dangerously compelling; I really want to buy what he's offering there, but when I take a step back and think again, I realize that I want to ask, loudly, "Where's God?" In fact, were I to be a bit churlish, I would ask this more broadly of the book's authors, and more so of Lynch than Long. Here is how I would pose the question: You assert a strong argument for the importance, indeed the necessity of the "presence of the dead" in our funerals; where then is your strong sense of the importance, indeed the necessity of the presence of God in the funeral?

In part, my concern is shaped by the work of my colleague, Harry Huebner, who worries that funerals have much more to do with a celebration of the good works and character of the deceased, an understanding widely embraced in the Christian church that seems intuitively correct, even if only because that is the widespread practice within Christian churches. Huebner argues strongly for placing our faith in the God of creation and resurrection at the core of our thinking about life and death, and therefore such "God-language" should be at the center of Christian funerals.[6]

Here's what I want for my funeral (I hope in describing this I'm not succumbing to personalization). I want the funeral service not to have a PowerPoint presentation, I hope that the music will be well chosen, which means that someone else will have to choose it besides me; I want there to be an actual sermon that talks about hope, the resurrection, and God; and

---

6. Huebner, "Christian Ethics as Art?" 32–34.

then at a different event, I hope people gather to eat, drink if they want to, and play Lucinda Williams way too loudly, starting with her brilliant song "Fancy Funeral."

Sermons

30

And Grace, Too . . .[1]

At the heart of this morning's chapel time is the concept—the reality—of grace. We will allow what is perhaps the most well-known hymn in the world, "Amazing Grace," to be the center of our thoughts. You've already heard the modern melody played on the bagpipes. As many of you may know, John Newton wrote the words of this beloved hymn. Newton was a profligate slave trader of the eighteenth century, and for a time he owned and operated a slave ship. Partially as the result of a terrifying experience in a nasty storm, he converted to the Christian faith, but he kept slave trading for a time until giving it up to become a pastor in England—you can see it all in the movie titled *Amazing Grace* (2006). The hymn he wrote has taken on all kinds of forms. It is thought that the original tune may have come from the very slaves who had been bought and sold by Newton, but whatever the source, the hymn can be heard in many styles and genres, and throughout our chapel, we will hear some of these diverse forms and allow this great hymn of the Christian faith to be a point of orientation as we consider what grace is, and how the reality of God's grace might become part of our lives.

---

1. This sermon was delivered as a chapel address to students and staff at Mennonite Brethren Collegiate Institute (MBCI) in Winnipeg, Manitoba. The sermon was interspersed with the performance of various versions and settings of the great hymn "Amazing Grace": on bagpipes, as a jazz tune, a countrified song, and by an elite choral group.

GRACE IS AMAZING

Here's the starting point of our reflections and what the hymn communicates so clearly—grace *is* amazing. We need to proceed carefully, since that short phrase, "grace is amazing," seems easy enough to understand. But if you take just a moment to consider these words, it's perfectly obvious that this is a very difficult phrase, not grammatically but conceptually, because it's so easy to think that we know exactly what "amazing" means. It's a word that is used to describe everything, and when a word is ubiquitous like that, when it appears everywhere, it becomes almost plastic, stretched to describe so many things that it ceases to be useful. After all, if the same word is used to describe both God and my lunch, then maybe that word has stopped being very useful. So, in my own practice, when a word is overused in such a manner—"like," "awesome," "super," and "sweet," come to mind—I try to stop using it entirely.

But in *this* case, I refuse to stop using the word "amazing," since the song makes it impossible to separate "amazing" from "grace." But we need to understand what that word means in this context. "Amazing" here means that we are truly set back on our heels when we think about grace, overwhelmed with wonder and even great surprise. That is to say, it's something that amazes us in the sense that it's far beyond our expectation of what is usually the case. The thing that is amazing is beyond normal, beyond the ordinary, it stretches our credulity. Despite its overuse, "amazing" is a good word here, if we think of it in these terms and apply it to God's grace, which *is* amazing in the real sense of that word.

Then there's the word "grace," which is a word that gets up and walks around on you if you don't watch it (to use Richard Church's lovely phrase). That word "grace" itself appears everywhere. Listen to a list of words that are related to the word "grace," the Latin root of which is *gratia*: graceful, grace before a meal, grateful, coup de grâce, gratitude, gratuitous, gratuity, gratify, ingrate, congratulation. In Greek the word is *charis*, which finds its way into words such as charismatic, charity, Eucharist. Names that are based on some form of the word include Grace, Charis, Anna, Hannah, and Nina. So when we say the word "grace," we have a job in front of us—that is, what is it we're saying when we use that word?

Let me begin to define and describe this concept by saying what it is *not*—grace is *not* somebody being nice, grace is *not* letting you get away with whatever you have just done without any consequences, grace is *not* some kind of blanket statement that allows you to simply carry on living the way you're living without any call to change or transformation. Sometimes Christian writers come awfully close to making this kind of mistake in their zeal to communicate the amazing nature of grace. Philip Yancey, in his book, *What's So Amazing about Grace?*, makes me a bit uncomfortable here in his description of grace as "free of charge, no strings attached, on the house."[2]

Grace properly understood in our Christian context has to begin with God, which should not be surprising to us. However, I find that our tendency is to begin elsewhere. I think we should *begin* with God's grace in order to understand this amazing reality. This is an important move, this starting with God, because often we start with some concept that we think we know something about, and then we intensify that and imagine that's what God is like. When we talk about grace, we may think about somebody who's nice, or a nice thing that somebody did for us, and then we think something like, "If that person is nice, then God must be way nicer than that, and maybe that's what grace is, the nicest anyone could ever be." You see the problem we've raised. If that's how we proceed, we've managed to turn God into the kind of person we wish he would be. But if we turn that around and try to understand God's grace by looking first at God, and letting that shape our understanding of grace, then it seems to me we're on much firmer ground. Grace, according to the Bible's teaching, is a gift from God to us for the purpose of salvation, and by definition is something that cannot be earned. The central concept we need to keep in front of us is that of a gift; if you can earn it, grace is no longer grace. St. Paul, in Romans 5:5, refers to this as "the love of God that is poured forth into our hearts by the Holy Spirit." What a lovely picture that is—our empty and thirsty hearts being filled, as though an empty vessel is being filled with water—but here we are being filled with God's love, remembering that it is a gift and not an exchange. All of us are equal in this sense. Picture all of us standing in a line with open hearts, and then quite apart from our position, age, status, wealth, personality, or whatever else, God, with reckless abandon, pours out equal amounts of his love to all of us as pure gift. That's grace, that's amazing, and that grace is always greater than all our sin.

GRACE IS AMAZING . . . BUT IT'S NOT CHEAP

I want to repeat myself here, on purpose: grace, God's free gift of love *is* amazing. But I also am going to call into question the notion that because of God's grace, we are somehow free to do whatever we want, because after all, God will simply cover it, and the love that is freely poured out into our

2. Yancey, *What's So Amazing about Grace?*, 26.

hearts will magically take care of everything. Think for a moment of the relationship we've seen displayed in the drama *Suite 180*.[3] Luigi is a really nice guy, and you can't help but like him, and I for one am delighted that he is going to get married to the lovely Amber. But Luigi is missing something very important: he thinks that the love and grace extended to him within this relationship provides space for him to slack off, to shun his responsibilities, and in fact to be less than truthful to Amber, and his misunderstanding threatens the very love and grace that is the foundation of their blossoming relationship. He refuses to see, at least at first, how Amber's love has the potential to change him.

This drama brings to view a danger that has long been recognized. In fact, St. Paul wrote about this 2,000 years ago when he was addressing a new church in the city of Rome. Paul writes some moving and wonderful material about these matters in the book of Romans, and it's no coincidence that it is this book that has turned some very well-known people's lives around, Augustine and Luther to mention just a couple. In Romans 5 and 6, Paul writes about all the good things of grace, God's gift, but then something seems to strike him, namely the possibility that some folks will take his teachings and warp them. His immediate concern is that people will think that if grace covers sin, then more sin will result in more grace. Paul anticipates this so-called argument and responds to it: "What shall we say then? Shall we go on sinning that grace may increase? By no means" (Romans 6:1–2). This phrase that is tactfully translated as "By no means" is really far too polite. Paul had a bit of a salty tongue, and if you go back to the Greek text, the phrase is really something much stronger. He uses foul language here to make his point. More accurately translated, the verse reads, "What shall we say then? Shall we go on sinning that grace may increase? Hell, no!" Now, please understand, I'm just translating, but St. Paul's point is well-taken. Just because grace is a gift does not mean that you can just carry on as though the gift makes no real difference, as though nothing more than a pat on the back has just occurred. One of the more well-known twentieth-century writers about these matters was Dietrich Bonhoeffer, a German theologian who died at the hands of the Nazis in 1945. I've asked Kelly Binda, who has read some Bonhoeffer, to explain his treatment of the difference between cheap and costly grace.

> If we choose to believe that Christ will always forgive us no matter what we do, then we believe in grace. However, there is

---

3. The reference here is to a brief drama directed by a colleague at MBCI, Shane Cooney. While it's true that "you had to be there," the point I'm trying to make can still stand without the benefit of watching the drama.

another question lying underneath this broad concept that we call grace. Which kind of grace are we accepting? According to the German theologian Dietrich Bonhoeffer there are two types of grace, cheap grace and costly grace. And while they are both referred to in his writings as different types of grace the grace itself could not be any more different.

Cheap grace is an excuse, a way of passing off sins as a fact of life. As if they are always pardonable because Christ will always forgive us. This grace is temporary, a Band-Aid that covers up the sins we commit instead of initiating any sort of life change. It is a grace that needs to be asked for again and again, as it is obviously not good enough to last forever because we don't ask it to. It's the kind of grace we ask for when we do something wrong, say we are sorry and then continue to make the same mistakes, commit the same sins. This is not the grace of God, it is the grace we give ourselves to justify or explain away the mistakes we make.

The notion of costly grace, however, is best explained through an excerpt of Bonhoeffer's writing: "Such grace is costly because it calls us to follow, and it is grace because it calls us to follow Jesus Christ. It is costly because it calls a man to give his life, and it is grace because it gives a man the only true life. It is costly because it condemns sin, and it is grace because it justifies the sinner. Above all, it is costly because it cost God the life of his Son, and what has cost God so much cannot be cheap for us. Above all, it is grace because God did not reckon his son too dear a price to pay for our life, but delivered him up for us. Costly grace is the incarnation of God."[4] This grace that Bonhoeffer speaks of demands much of us. For while it is a free gift, the result of this costly grace is something so rare and irreversible. One cannot accept this costly grace and then go and live for oneself, because this costly grace demands everything of us. It is a grace that justifies the sinner, not the sin. Because if one receives costly grace knowingly, making the same mistakes over and over is not an option. Costly grace changes the person who receives it in such an irrevocable way that nothing can be done but respond to it. Costly grace really costs something, both for the One who gives it to us as well as for any who receive it.

Costly grace demands that like the disciples and like so many other people who throughout history have given up their lives to serve the Lord, we must give up our own life and follow at the call of Jesus. For this grace which is costly does cost something

---

4. Bonhoeffer, *Cost of Discipleship*, 45.

to those of us who receives it, it costs us our control and love of our own life. It calls us to follow the one who calls us, Christ. We should realize that following Christ is not an optional activity. If we confess to believe in God and yet refuse to obey his command then we must not really believe in the complete and awesome power of the Lord.[5]

GRACE IS AMAZING . . . BUT IT'S ALSO PAINFUL

> All human nature vigorously resists grace because grace changes us and the change is painful.
>
> FLANNERY O'CONNOR, *THE HABIT OF BEING*

If you ever have the chance to read Flannery O'Connor's writing, you should do so, or if your teacher forces you to read some of her work, enjoy it. Every one of her short stories includes a "moment of grace," but this is not some sucky, schlocky, saccharine-sweet, overblown, heartstring-tugging, violin-music-swelling, nausea-inducing, clichéd moment. Quite the opposite; often these moments come as total surprises or shocks in O'Connor's fiction. Her point is that grace calls for us to see things as they really are, and thus grace also calls for change. God's free gift is one that reveals to us the kind of people we are, and what needs to happen in order for us to change in right ways, and that kind of change is often painful. It's easier to stay as we are, but *costly* grace does not let us wallow in self-centered, self-satisfied solipsism; rather, grace calls for us to mature, and then provides a way forward. To be made aware of what I have done wrong is itself an act of grace; to be given a chance or a call to change so I can stop repeating my sins and mistakes is also an act of grace. It is no act of grace to be left wallowing in my abject ignorance and pathetic sin.

Let me try to illustrate from the life that we share, namely, life in the classroom, where words like grace and forgiveness are often used, and rightly so. But we don't all understand this in the same way. When I'm asked for grace, this is often code for letting a student get away with something, or lowering some standard, or allowing for late submission of an assignment

---

5. The material describing Bonhoeffer's view of cheap grace was presented by a senior student, Kelly Binda. I'm grateful for her permission to include her good work here.

and so on. Fair enough. But let me point out that to be given a failing grade on a paper or test can also be an act of grace. Grace does not mean giving everyone the equal mark of 100%. That's not grace, it's bullshit; and worse, it makes that mark completely meaningless and prevents every one of those students from learning anything about themselves, the subject at hand, or anything at all. It's an act of grace to be confronted with reality, and then to be granted opportunity, time, and space to change, to grow, to mature: that's an extension of grace. After all, on a much larger scale, isn't it the case that God himself grants all of us the grace of each new day, a day in which we have the time and space to obey him? The call is not to lurch around in self-indulgence, since we have been given a new day; rather, the call is to be what we are called to be in Christ, and that process of growth and change, made possible only by the free gift of God, is painful, even excruciating. My favorite story in the Gospels is found in John 8, where a woman caught in adultery is confronted by a crowd of self-righteous folks, and Jesus sends them on their way by showing them who they are—sinners—which is an act of grace. If they hadn't been confronted in this way they might well have committed some horrific act of violence, and the scene ends with Jesus pronouncing forgiveness on this woman. Make no mistake, she's guilty, and so he instructs her to change her ways. His message is not something like, "Go, it's all right, we all make mistakes, let's just forget this ever happened." No, his message is far more gracious than all that. Instead, he says, "Go—and sin no more." Grace calls for change, and change is painful.

GRACE IS AMAZING . . . AND IT CALLS US TO PRESS ON

> Forgetting what is behind and straining toward what is ahead, I press on toward the goal to win the prize for which God has called me heavenward in Christ Jesus.
>
> PHILIPPIANS 3:14

The letter of St. Paul to the Philippian church is short and interesting, including in chapter 2 one of the most sophisticated descriptions of what it means for God to become fully human. The same chapter shows how the birth, life, teachings, death, resurrection, and exaltation of Jesus Christ provide the way for us as humans to receive this gift of grace we've been talking about. Another way of putting all of this would be to say that Jesus has done everything that needs to be done. Our tendency, when we hear that the work has been done for us, is to want to relax and assume the job is finished. But St. Paul will have none of that. Right after arguing that everything should be counted as loss for the sake of Christ, his argument takes a surprising turn, and at the end of chapter 3 he asserts that the response to God's free gift of grace is not to sit back; rather, "Forgetting what is behind and straining toward what is ahead, I press on toward the goal to win the prize for which God has called me heavenward in Christ Jesus."

Here's the clarion call: as the humble recipients of God's free gift of grace, we are called to get down to the business of living as gifted people—and so, we just keep pressing on.[6]

---

6. The chapel ended with Bob Dylan's song "Pressin' On," performed by a band consisting of several teachers and students.

31

Called to Working with (the) Word(s) in the Light of Faith

I'm delighted, honored, and humbled to have been invited to participate in the ordination service for Kevin Derksen.[1] I'm grateful for the hospitality and warmth shown to me as a guest here. I've known Kevin and Pam for many years and with great interest have watched their lives unfold to this point. I want to begin simply by affirming publically this ordination of Kevin for the work of the ministry. I do so with some trepidation, not because of any hesitation about suitability or qualification or some such thing, but because of a note Kevin sent me as we wrote forth and back about these matters: "My hope is that an ordination service not finally be about the one ordained. I want the gospel to be preached." And so, that will be all you'll hear about Kevin, or our friendship, what I've learned from him and so on.

To be ordained is in some sense at least to be called to the ministry of the gospel in and to the body of Christ, the church. However, what this might entail is not immediately obvious or not self-evident. As Karl Barth describes the situation, when the preacher sits down to face the task of ministry, before him lies his Bible, full of mystery, and before him are seated his more or less numerous hearers, also full of mystery, and so the question emerges: Now what?[2]

---

1. This sermon was delivered in St. Jacob's Mennonite Church, St. Jacob's, Ontario, on February 17, 2013, the occasion of long-time friend Kevin Derksen's ordination service.

2. Barth, "The Need and Promise of Christian Preaching," in *Word of God and the Word of Man*, 104.

A TASK THAT DEFIES US

I want to contend that the shape or content of that ministry is, at least in part, a call to "working with words in the light of faith,"[3] a task that defies our capacity to complete it. Ministers must speak of God, but we quickly come to realize that we are human and we literally cannot (after all, only God can speak of God), but it is in the recognition of both our obligation and our inability that we can begin to come near to giving God the glory.[4] So, "the theological task requires that we speak of God, but the God to whom and about whom we must speak defies the words we use."[5] And yet we believe that those who worship God and those who minister in God's name, must be witnesses. Moreover, since the very character of the church is a missionary character, we know that insofar as the task of ministry entails working with words in the light of faith, "the testing of the words we use as well as their grammar can never be finished."[6] This kind of witness, this way of working with words is not a kind of desperate shouting, but rather what is crucial here is an essential relationship between what we say and how we live.

A DANGEROUS TASK

The necessary task of working with words in the light of faith is one that defies us—but not only that, it is also a dangerous task that requires us to simultaneously court serious danger. "Why do people in churches seem like cheerful brainless tourists on a packaged tour of the Absolute? . . . On the whole I do not find Christians, outside the catacombs, sufficiently sensible of conditions. Does anyone else have the foggiest idea what sort of power we so blithely evoke? . . . For the sleeping god may wake someday and take offense, or the waking god may draw us out to where we can never return."[7] Here then is the locus of a conundrum—the way we talk about God may lull us into blithely messing with power that we don't recognize or acknowledge, which in turn may lull those we work with into that same illusory state.

---

3. John Howard Yoder's formulation of what he considers to be the task of theology more broadly. Yoder, *Preface to Theology*, 41.

4. Barth, *Word of God and the Word of Man*, 186, 214.

5. Hauerwas, *Working with Words*, x.

6. Ibid., xi.

7. Dillard, *Teaching a Stone to Talk*, 40–41.

A TASK THAT EMBRACES AND PARTICIPATES IN GIFT

But we ought not to let certain defeat and danger deter us in the ministry of the gospel. After all, the ministry is not the application of a technique, some "vaguely spiritual response to free-floating, ill-defined omnivorous human desire."[8] Despite the warnings I am highlighting, the readings from the Psalms and the Prophets in today's service highlight the fact that the God of whom we haltingly try to speak is our sun and shield, that here is a God who bestows honor and favor, and who does not withhold good things from those who walk uprightly; here we have a God who invites us to abundant life, who cheerfully sends rain and sets in motion the process wherein we are fed with all manner of good things. I think it fair to say that while following the call to ministry is to embrace danger and failure, it is also to embrace a gift, to receive the word of God as a gift to the world, to the church, to the gospel ministry. This is not a gift to be received in isolation, or only as an ordained minister. Rather, accepting this gift is to join other recipients, to participate in something that is already happening, and on a scale that is truly global. This is a gift that is given to the whole earth, which in turn responds in an attempt to articulate praise to the One from whom every good and perfect gift proceeds—mountains, hills shall burst into song; trees will clap their hands. This joining with others in participation of joyful receiving of God's gifts is a giving over of oneself to the hope that the words with which we work, with which we join with all of creation will not return empty.

> For as the rain and the snow come down from heaven, and do not return there until they have watered the earth, making it bring forth and sprout, giving seed to the sower and bread to the eater, so shall my word be that goes out from my mouth; it shall not return to me empty, but it shall accomplish that which I purpose, and succeed in the thing for which I sent it. (Isaiah 55:10–11)

A TASK REQUIRING HEAVENLY WISDOM

It is this hope, this fundamentally eschatological posture that cannot be reduced to techniques, which places worldly and heavenly wisdom in stark contrast to one another, a point put forward with great clarity in Paul's epistle to the Corinthians. This difference between biblical and worldly wisdom

---

8. Willimon, "Making Ministry Difficult," 11.

is often highlighted in Christian literature—for example, in John Bunyan's *Pilgrim's Progress*.

Early in his pilgrimage, Christian, the hero of the tale, meets with The Worldly Wiseman. Christian has been through several obstacles such as the Slough of Despond when he runs into a gentleman, Mr. Worldly Wiseman, who upon seeing Christian bearing a heavy burden, offers him advice—counsel that, I have to admit, doesn't sound too bad. Mr. Worldly Wiseman says, "Hear me, I am older than thou; thou art like to meet with, in the way which thou goest, wearisomeness, painfulness, hunger, perils, nakedness, sword, lions, dragons, darkness, and, in a word, death, and what not." Christian is not quite convinced, since the burden he carries seems even worse than the things just listed. So Mr. Worldly Wiseman offers safety and friendship—he counsels Christian to go to the village of Morality, where he will meet a gentleman named Legality and his son Civility. If he listens to these people, he can rent a house at a reasonable rate, send for his wife and children, and lead a really comfortable life. But when Christian tries to climb the hill to the town of Morality, he finds that the hill is just too steep to climb and sees that he has taken bad advice, since the counsel of Mr. Worldly Wiseman has forced him to reject the counsel of God. Christian's advisor, Evangelist, points out that Mr. Worldly Wiseman's counsel is in fact something to be abhorred, because it turns people aside from the true path; it renders the cross odious, ridiculous (repulsive); and it leads to death. Thus he pronounces: "Mr. Worldly Wiseman is an alien, and Mr. Legality is a cheat; and for his son Civility, notwithstanding his simpering looks, he is but a hypocrite and cannot help thee. Believe me, there is nothing in all this noise, that thou hast heard of these sottish men, but a design to beguile thee of the salvation by turning thee from the way in which I had set thee."[9]

The apostle Paul is equally harsh regarding the wisdom of this world, and no doubt this is just on whom John Bunyan is drawing. In 1 Corinthians 1:18–25 Paul points out very clearly that human wisdom and divine wisdom are at odds with one another. The wisdom we seek is not just human wisdom topped up a bit by reading the Bible from time to time. Rather, Paul declares that human wisdom simply cannot carry the weight, as it were, of the Christian message—since the gospel of Christ has to give an account of the cross. "We preach Christ crucified . . . which is to both Greeks and Jews the power of God and the wisdom of God."

This is to say that the wisdom the Bible refers to is not some version of so-called "common sense" that is easily available to all no matter what or whether there is any connection to God. Karl Barth argues that human

---

9. Bunyan, *Pilgrim's Progress*, 11–19.

wisdom apart from God is simply capricious; it's random, since it cannot find any grounding, any orientation in the reality of God's world or in the community of faith that has been called together by God, which places its faith in the cross of Jesus Christ.

So it's abundantly clear that the wisdom we seek is not available through the process of education alone, and in fact it does not consist primarily in intellectual activity—rather, the pursuit of wisdom begins in the fear of the Lord. That is, wisdom cannot be separated from its divine source, or from the work of Jesus Christ on the cross.

A CROSS-SHAPED TASK

And it is exactly here that the shape of the call to the work of the gospel ministry is generated—in the cross of Christ—and the Gospel reading of this morning drags us right into the heart of darkness and death—which is the only way to any kind of flourishing, any kind of life.

> Now among those who went up to worship at the festival were some Greeks. They came to Philip, who was from Bethsaida in Galilee, and said to him, "Sir, we wish to see Jesus." Philip went and told Andrew; then Andrew and Philip went and told Jesus. Jesus answered them, "The hour has come for the Son of Man to be glorified. Very truly, I tell you, unless a grain of wheat falls into the earth and dies, it remains just a single grain; but if it dies, it bears much fruit. Those who love their life lose it, and those who hate their life in this world will keep it for eternal life. Whoever serves me must follow me, and where I am, there will my servant be also. Whoever serves me, the Father will honor. (John 12: 23–26)

It is here that we see on display the logic of cross and resurrection, "the gospel's pattern of death-to-self with its invitation to true life,"[10] seen so clearly in Jesus Christ, whereby we are shown a "profound display of the placement of one will into the other."[11] Such is the call to the gospel ministry, to embrace that logic of cross and resurrection which leads to abundant life. And all of this can never "be anything but the work of beginners . . . What Christians do becomes a self-contradiction when it takes the form of a trained and mastered routine, of a learned and practiced art. They may and

---

10. Kevin Derksen, email to me, January 15, 2013.
11. Harry Huebner, *An Introduction to Christian* Ethics, 641.

can be masters and even virtuosos in many things, but never in what makes them Christians, God's children."[12]

---

12. Karl Barth, as quoted in Eugene Peterson, *Practice Resurrection*, 191.

32

Simultaneously Satisfying and Insatiable

The Desire for God[1]

> My Lord God, I have no idea where I am going. I do not see the road ahead of me. I cannot know for certain where it will end. Nor do I really know myself, and the fact that I think that I am following your will does not mean that I am actually doing so. But I believe that the desire to please you does in fact please you. And I hope that I will never do anything apart from that desire. And I know that if I do this you will lead me by the right road though I may know nothing about it.
>
> Thomas Merton, *Thoughts in Solitude*

My personal approach to writing sermons is pretty simple—when I'm asked to preach, I always hope for an assigned passage of Scripture, which I then study. The point is that I always want the Scripture to generate the content, and not the other way round—that I have some personal agenda that I want to get out there, and then go to the Bible to kind of give

---

1. This sermon was originally preached at the Fort Garry Mennonite Brethren Church in Winnipeg, Manitoba, on Sunday, August 12, 2012. I gratefully acknowledge permission to reprint this sermon, which first was published in *Direction* 42 no 1 (Spring 2013) 82–91.

it a bit of a veneer. Far too often our talk about God is a thinly disguised discussion of ourselves, and we sometimes make God in our own image, I'm afraid. By this I mean that we are sometimes tempted to think about God in very human terms, and make him look like a more refined version of ourselves—which is very misleading.

So, I have to confess that today I'm running this risk. I'm beginning with a topic, and then moving to Scripture—and I do so with a bit of trepidation. But despite my own precautions, I want to focus on us as humans, and specifically I want to talk about a common experience: that of wanting, yearning, of desire—whether the object be things, people, or something else. I thought a lot about the nature of desire when I was asked to write a short piece for the Mennonite Brethren Board of Faith and Life about gambling. I tried to write the piece without using the word "gambling," because it seemed to me that the issue isn't at heart about trying to make fine distinctions between raffle tickets and slot machines, but rather that all of us need to confront what it is we are chasing in our endeavors. And so I didn't want to leave any of you off the hook, even if you don't spend your entire paycheck in front of video lottery terminals with a cigarette hanging from your lip and a cheap beer beside you. My argument was something like this: gambling isn't about gambling—it's about misplaced desires.

Paul Oppenheimer, in his book *Infinite Desire: A Guide to Modern Guilt*, says this:

> The only genuine human problem is the problem of desire. All other problems, and those in no mean or superficial way, are bound to it by steely or silken ligatures. All religions, in their moral and even spiritual aspects, confront the issue of desire, seeking to temper it, channel it, dam it, and often condemn it . . . [He goes on to describe it as an "exquisite aching, the fiery quest."] *In the modern Western world, infinite personal desire has replaced God* [italics added]. It possesses many of the same powers as the old and now mostly dead god of Christians, Jews and others—of omnipotence and omniscience, for instance, though it is not quite as good at miracles—plus a vastly and paradoxically greater capacity to inspire guilt. It is infinitely subtle, and has no trouble in assuming a Christian or Jewish or Islamic disguise for the sake of many of its believers, who for social and psychological reasons wish to continue calling themselves Christians, Jews, Moslems and other things. Its adaptability, its complete elasticity, is one of its most commendable and bewildering qualities. Nonetheless, one cannot escape the conclusion

that this widely worshipped and also despised god [of desire] is merely the divine incarnation of solipsism. [2]

That lengthy quotation is just a sample of how one writer, steeped in literature and poetry, recognizes the sheer power of desire. It's hard to describe—that deep yearning for something or someone; a yearning, a wanting that isn't always under control, that you can't quite understand and don't know from where it comes; you may not even want your desires, ironically. Think about what you really want, what you really, really want, so much that that feeling itself becomes dominant in your thoughts and emotions. These kinds of feelings are often depicted in poetry and song lyrics as being like a fire—something hot, something that is warming, and cozy, and yet is also always on the verge of being dangerous. Bob Dylan's song "Caribbean Wind" includes one recurring line in the chorus which is at the heart of this song, "fanning the flames in the furnace of desire." Isn't that a great line? I don't want to kill it by explaining it, but you'll easily recognize that a furnace, which is after all just a controlled fire that warms all those inside a house, can quickly become a danger if its flame is fanned too much. And so Dylan signals to us that desire is like a furnace that is being fanned—and who knows what can happen if the flames of desire are fanned? What happens if you fly too close to the sun, like poor old Icarus in that Greek myth?

THE INTENSITY OF DESIRE

Let's pay some more attention to the intensity of desire for a moment. When you really want something, or desire to have a relationship with someone, say, the intensity of desire can be overwhelming. And when it develops like that, you find yourself open and vulnerable, even embracing the possibility that if this goes wrong, you might be facing a world of pain. But still, you say: I want that thing, that experience—I want you.

Say what you want, do what you want, when you love someone, when you want someone, something, it's that feeling that takes over. Whatever else you do, whatever assignments are due, whatever pressures you face, it's the overwhelming feeling of desire that takes over, and believe me, it's not easily distracted, not even by the things that accompany that relationship—it's not that you just want all of a person—but *all* you want is him, her. And so you say over and over again, "All I want is you." This song is just one sample of the attempt to capture just how powerful desire can be:

---

2. Oppenheimer, *Infinite Desire*, 89.

> You say you want
> Diamonds on a ring of gold
> You say you want
> Your story to remain untold
>
> But all the promises we make
> From the cradle to the grave
> When all I want is you.[3]

Songs are far more powerful ways of communicating this truth than some speech, no matter how well organized.

But to simply identify and celebrate the existence of raw desire isn't the end of the discussion, at least in my view. Sometimes I fear, however, that this is seen as the essence of the discussion—in other words, desires exist, and since they do, we feel obliged to act on them, to pursue them no matter what the cost. It's many a novel or movie that exposes the power of desire, but then also presents the strong message that because those desires exist they should be followed, acted upon.

But it's not quite that simple. Desires are not simple things that call for only one response—that is, desires are not the same thing as appetites.[4] And so if we pause to reflect just a little, we'll see that the issues around desire are not straightforward. For example, we might want to ask where desires come from. Are they simply natural? Can it be that sometimes we need to set aside one desire in order to pursue another? Or, that we might have to do something we absolutely hate doing so that we can then pursue a strong desire? Put another way, are desires natural? Instrumental? Terminal?

I really don't want to get caught up in this kind of more technical discussion, so let me simply register the fact that desires are not simple things. But it's also *not* the case that just because you experience some kind of desire for something or someone that you will, just by pursuing it, necessarily come to fulfill that desire. Sometimes, we are disappointed, our dreams die, and bitterly so. And then it becomes clear: you can't always get what you want. Put another way, sometimes, no matter how hard I try, and I try, and I try . . . I can't get no satisfaction.

As the Rolling Stones taught us many years ago, sometimes the very thing you want is what you can't get. But worse, perhaps, is when you get what you think you want, and it turns out that very thing does *not* provide the satisfaction you thought it might; it's not all it's cracked up to be. And so now we realize that the things that we want, the desire for which may be overwhelming, intense, even mesmerizing, may not only be the occasion

---

3. U2, "All I Want Is You." http://www.u2.com/lyrics/13.
4. Oppenheimer, *Infinite Desire*, 89.

for desire but also for the equally overwhelming experience of frustration. What's worse than getting what you want, only to find that that wasn't at all what you really wanted? Perhaps you just thought you wanted it; maybe you only wanted that thing because someone else showed interest (mimetic desire), and once that person stopped showing interest, your own desire dissipated. And so the fulfillment of desire presents itself as a moving target—always in front of us and yet never realizable, or if realizable, then frustrating after all.

DESIRE IN THE GOSPEL OF MARK

There's a chilling story in the Gospel of Mark that brings to view some of the complex dimensions of the nature of desire. In chapter 6 we find the account of a deadly confrontation between Herod, the local Roman ruler of Galilee, and John the Baptist. John was in prison because he had the audacity to point out that Herod's marriage to his brother's wife, whose name was Herodias, was immoral. And the text tells us "she had a grudge against him [John], and wanted to kill him." But Herod refused. He was kind of afraid of John, didn't really like John, but he found him fascinating to listen to—very complex dynamics. So Herod protected John. There follows the account of a party in which a toxic matrix of the dynamics of power, desire, bloodlust, and envy all come together. Herod celebrates his birthday, and present are all kinds of officials—courtiers, officers, and leaders of Galilee—and all no doubt wanting to ingratiate themselves further with Herod. All of this comes to a climax when Herod's daughter Salome is asked to dance. And the Bible claims that her dance "pleased Herod and his guests." Because the dance was so fine, Herod tells his daughter that she can ask for whatever she wishes and he will give it. No doubt he's a bit drunk. Everyone there is mesmerized by the spectacle. And Herod then solemnly swears: "Whatever you ask me, I will give you, even half of my kingdom."

Well now there's an offer that's hard to resist. But notice that Salome doesn't know what to ask for. She's old enough to incite desire and pleasure, but when she's asked what she wants, she heads off to talk to her mom, Herodias, to ask her what she should ask for. Well, you can't blame her too much. Which one of us really knows what we want? But her mom knows what she herself wants—"I want you to give me at once the head of John the Baptist on a platter." Herod doesn't like this (he was deeply grieved), but his brazen promise to his daughter in front of his guests makes him feel as though he has no options. And so the deed is done. A soldier goes to the prison, decapitates John the Baptist, and the head is delivered—not to

Herod, not to any of the guests, but to Salome, the dancing daughter, who didn't want this in the first place. And the text tells us cryptically that "the girl gave it to her mother."[5]

Now *that* was a party. You young people think you know how to party; you middle-aged folks think you can still party with your gourmet food and birthday parties to mark someone's new decade; you senior citizens think you can party because no one is gonna tell you what to do anymore. But have you ever been to a party like this one? It's absolutely terrifying. Chills me to the bone. Here we see various desires: to take advantage of a brother; to exert dominion, power; to do away with someone who tells the uncomfortable truth; to please people in various ways. And as we watch the interplay of these desires, we see that, here at least, shocking violence results.

We often don't even know what we really want, what we'd do to get what we want, do we? That is to say, sometimes our own desires work to camouflage the things we really want. And so we chase this, we pursue that. We become obsessed with him, focused on her. But when we lie awake at night, staring at the ceiling, surrounded by what we were pretty sure we wanted, it turns out we still haven't found what we're looking for.

It's not as though we don't find anything at all. It's just that what we find turns out not to be what we're really looking for, because frankly, how often do we really know what we're looking for?

Well, it's not my goal to convince you that because of the complexity of our desires we should now suppress them all, and offer some lame suggestion that our desires, our longings are sinful, and all we need is God. Rather, I want to say that despite all the vagaries, the difficulties of trying to figure out what I want, and what to do with what I want, and what to do when I find out that what I want isn't really what I want—despite all of that, desire is a very important dimension of being a Christian, or of thinking about being a Christian. After all, the ability to love, to want, to desire is itself a gift from God. So all of us need to pay close attention to these matters.

HOLY DESIRE

It's been interesting to me that in much of Christian writing, there is often a very close relationship between human desire and our relationship to God. As Augustine put it, "The whole life of the good Christian is a holy desire." [6]

---

5. See P. Travis Kroeker's fine paper on this passage in "Making Strange: Harry Huebner's Church–World Distinction"; or René Girard's "The Beheading of Saint John the Baptist."

6. Augustine, Fourth Homily of the First Episle of John, 4.6.

Indeed, it is sometimes the case that when we read Christian thinkers or listen to Christian hymns and choruses, or read or listen to a religious poem, we are witness to writers pouring out their emotions to God in such a way that sometimes it's difficult to tell if this is religious or romantic. The twelfth-century monk St. Bernard of Clairvaux wrote many sermons on the Old Testament book Song of Songs (a.k.a., Song of Solomon). I've often read a piece entitled "The Three Kisses" with my students. Here Bernard describes his relationship with Christ in terms of evermore intimate contact with Christ—first kissing his feet, then his hands (once he has raised you), and then there's the ecstasy of the face-to-face kiss—he's so descriptive that it sometimes gets just a bit awkward. (You'll see it also in the vision of Teresa of Avila and the Holy Sonnets of John Donne). Notice what's happened here: there has been a welding of the intensity and intimacy of romantic desire to the pursuit of God, a move that has sometimes been seen as controversial.

Desire is a funny thing. It's overwhelming. It has the power to mislead us. After all, four of the seven deadly sins directly involve desire that has gone astray—envy, gluttony, lust, and greed. It has the power to control us, it has the power to utterly frustrate us, but at the same time it can provide the impetus necessary to cultivate passions, to order and invigorate relationships, and to energize our lives. So as a Christian, I want to identify and embrace desire and yearning. I want also to learn about the intensity that can lead to danger. But one thing I don't want to do is to extinguish desire or to assume that to follow Jesus Christ requires the extinction of all of our passions or the detachment from all of our loves. However, it is also true that, as a Christian, I will no doubt find it necessary to detach myself from some desires and to cling to others, and to cultivate still others that should be overwhelming and provide focus for my life. In other words, it's not the case that I have to abandon all of my desires if I want to be a Christian, if I want to be a follower of Jesus Christ, which is sometimes the way things are put to us—that is, just give it all up and follow Jesus and then your real needs will be met. Rather than thinking about the abandonment of desires, I believe we should think in terms of the ordering of our desires. This means that we will want to abandon our sinful desires, we will try to detach ourselves from others, we will surely want to cling to some, and we will also want to cultivate some desires that currently aren't part of our lives, but should be.

To be as clear as I can here, as a Christian I believe that the ordering of our desires can only find its way in relation to God. The Christian life is one that at its best is one both of detachment from sin and an intense desire for God.[7] True desire is patient, able to grow with time in ways that can be sustained.

Augustine, that great church leader of the fifth century, has much to teach us about the nature of desire in his book *Confessions*. Augustine himself was a man of passions. As a young man, his pursuit of passion led him to a number of somewhat predictable, tawdry, illicit sexual relationships, but when he became a Christian, he seemed to realize that the intensity of those passions was not simply to be abandoned. Listen to what he says in one of his sermons: "Give me a man in love: he understands what I mean. Give me a man who yearns: give me a man who is hungry; give me a man traveling in the desert, who is thirsty and sighing for the spring of the eternal country. Give me that sort of man; he knows what I mean. But if I talk to a cold man, he does not know what I am talking about."[8]

Augustine returns often to these kinds of thoughts, and nowhere more poignantly than in book 10 of *Confessions*. In some of the most moving passages regarding spiritual desire that I've ever run across, Augustine tries to make sense of the kinds of things we've been discussing. He famously opens Book 1 with his assertion that the human heart is restless, and our hearts cannot find peace until they rest in God. But this isn't merely some kind of platitude, some bogus, cheesy "chicken soup for the soul" formulation. Rather, he struggles to understand and live with this interplay of physical, emotional, and spiritual realities.

> My love of you, O Lord, is not some vague feeling. . . . But what do I love when I love my God? *Not* material beauty or beauty of a temporal order; *not* the brilliance of earthly light, so welcome to our eyes; *not* the sweet melody of harmony and song; *not* the fragrance of flowers, perfumes, and spices; *not* manna or honey; *not* limbs such as the body delights to embrace. It is *not* these that I love when I love my God. *And yet*, when I love him, it is true that I love a light of a certain kind, a voice, a perfume, a food, an embrace; but they are the kind that I love in my inner self, when my soul is bathed in light that is not bound by space; when it listens to sound that never dies away; when it breathes fragrance that is not borne away on the wind; when it tastes food that is never consumed by eating; when it clings to an embrace from which it is not severed by fulfillment of desire. That is what I love when I love my God.

---

7. St. Gregory, known as the "Doctor of Desire." See Leclercq, *The Love of Learning and the Desire for God.*

8. Augustine, *On John's Gospel*, 26.4; quoted in Rist, *Augustine*, 157.

I really wish we had time to do a close reading of this remarkable passage. But please notice, at the very least, that Augustine wants us *not* to think that we can find satisfaction in the earthly pleasures of life, and yet, it is only in loving God that it becomes possible to truly find pleasure in the things of this world that are meant for us to enjoy. It is in loving God that our desires can be ordered, sorted out. Our embrace of God makes possible our embrace of his world. Augustine himself mourns the fact that he went too long without this ordering of his own desires.

> I have learnt to love you late, Beauty at once so ancient and so new! I have learnt to love you late! You were within me, and I was in the world outside myself. I searched for you outside myself and, disfigured as I was, I fell upon the lovely things of your creation. You were with me, but I was not with you. The beautiful things of this world kept me far from you and yet, if they had not been in you, they would have had no being at all. You called me; you cried aloud to me; you broke my barrier of deafness. You shone upon me; your radiance enveloped me; you put my blindness to flight. You shed your fragrance about me; I drew breath and now I gasp for your sweet odour. I tasted you, and now I hunger and thirst for you. You touched me, and I am inflamed with love of your peace.

This is Augustine talking about getting his life right—recognizing that his desire for God is simultaneously satisfying and insatiable. He is serious about getting right with God. Like Augustine, I wish I had come across this truth much earlier in life, and desire to embrace it ever more completely.

33

The Gospel as Prisoner *and* Liberator of Culture

The question that is being considered in this sermon is: How might we, how can we, how ought we to think about the relationship between Christ and Culture?[1] When I hear the term "Christ and Culture," I always think of at least two things. First, I'm reminded of a shocking statement that originates in a play written by Hanns Johst, a play that celebrated Hitler's rise to power in Nazi Germany. The play *Schlageter* (1933) is, among other things, an attempt to combat Jewish influence on German culture. One character says in the middle of a conversation, "Whenever I hear the word 'culture,' I reach for my revolver," indicating that he'd rather fight in order to dominate German culture than study or discuss these matters—a sentiment that became a practice and pursuit within Nazi Germany.

The second thing I am reminded of when I hear the term "Christ and Culture" is a book published originally in 1951, perhaps the most famous and influential attempt to work at the question we're trying to address here. *Christ and Culture* is the title of the book written by American theologian H. Richard Niebuhr, and we often frame discussions in this dualistic way precisely because of his enormously influential book.[2] Niebuhr's famous fivefold typology—Christ against Culture, the Christ of Culture, Christ above

---

1. This sermon was delivered at the Fort Garry Mennonite Brethren Church in Winnipeg, Manitoba, on April 12, 2015. It was part of a series entitled "Trending toward Faith: Christ and Culture," shaped by Carl Heppner, lead pastor of the church.

2. Niebuhr, *Christ and Culture*. Many of us wish we could write a book that's discussed for a week, never mind more than half a century.

Culture, Christ and Culture in Paradox, and Christ Transforming Culture—continues to set the terms of the debate, either by way of functioning as the framework of discussion, or by setting oneself in relation to that very typology.[3]

Niebuhr (in)famously places Mennonites in the first type—Christ against Culture: "The Mennonites have come to represent the attitude most purely, since they not only renounce all participation in politics and refuse to be drawn into military service, but follow their own distinctive customs and regulations in economics and education."[4] Niebuhr thinks that we're nice to have around—in fact, he calls Mennonites (and others) "necessary but inadequate" (which has a striking parallel to the way teenagers sometimes see their dads). Niebuhr draws a sharp distinction between withdrawal and renunciation on the one hand, and the necessary movement of responsible engagement in cultural tasks on the other.[5] If one accepts his typology, then it appears obvious that everyone who is in this necessary-but-inadequate category should become adequate, which is presumably done through more "responsible engagement," or "transformation," understood on his terms.

Quite aside from Niebuhr's condescending tone, his wrong-headed categorization whereby Leo Tolstoy, monastics, Quakers, and Mennonites are all lumped together, it seems to me that the two larger categories of "Christ" and "Culture" are themselves problematic. In a lengthy essay,[6] John Howard Yoder levels a series of criticisms of Niebuhr that range from an analysis of the use of types, the feigned objectivity of Niebuhr's work, which clearly favors the final type (Christ Transforming Culture), the particular (and misleading) portrayal of Christ, the doctrine of the Trinity that comes dangerously close to modalism, and so on. But the basic criticism is that both sides of this dualism are treated as monoliths, subjected to a process of reification that simply cannot stand close scrutiny.

In the case of Christ, it is true that every statement we make about Christ is already enculturated—no single statement can be reduced to enculturation only, but is surely in part at least a statement about ourselves and the times and cultures we inhabit. Therefore, any engagement of Christ and Culture cannot be separated from enquiry into that engagement itself; there can be no full distillation of Christ from cultures; there is no single access to Christ.[7]

3. Carter, *Rethinking Christ and Culture*, 13.
4. Niebuhr, *Christ and Culture*, 56.
5. Ibid., 68.
6. Yoder, "How H. Richard Niebuhr Reasoned."
7. See Ward, *Christ and Culture*, 2–21.

If Christ and our statements about him are enculturated and therefore constantly held before us for consideration and reconsideration, then we must hasten to add that all cultures are complexities that are in constant flux—all cultures are human and inhuman, graced and ungraced.[8] There is no notion of global culture that can be used to function the way Niebuhr wants it to, and therefore there is no strategy that can be applied uniformly either by rejecting or transforming culture (or anything in between).[9]

Whenever any term that is dualistic in structure and includes "Culture" (that is, some version of "——— and Culture") is used, a mistake has already been made, argues Stanley Hauerwas, signaling that the very way in which we structure the discussion, the categories we press into service, and the language we use must all be scrutinized and perhaps reformed, filled with new meaning, or even rejected. In other words, we must not begin with the presumption that the gospel is one thing, culture another, and that our task is to simply learn how to make one "relevant" to the other. To see things in such a dualistic or binary fashion opens us up to all manner of distortion.[10]

Put another way, culture isn't a static "thing," a solid entity, an autonomous realm; it doesn't have the status of "being." More formally, it doesn't have ontological status, and therefore shouldn't be reified. It might be more accurate to describe culture as a sort of metaphor for the process that happens to people—temporal, human activities that also include the possibility of divine activity. If that's true, if culture is better understood as process rather than thing, then we ought not to think that there's some neutral space from which we can observe or transform culture; rather, we participate in it already. So the question isn't primarily "Should we participate in culture?," but "How should we participate in culture in which we find ourselves?"

If I'm right to think of culture as activity, then it's also true that our understanding of Christ, our faith, our embrace and expression of the gospel is enculturated to a significant degree. We don't have a "pure faith" over against a "static culture," with the task of trying to get one thing to change the other thing. It's all much more fluid than that, suggesting that there is in fact no single mode of relating Christ to Culture.

So, now what? Here's where I want to take up the title of this sermon, which comes from the work of Andrew Walls, long-time Christian missionary and professor; in fact, I took the title of the sermon directly from the title

---

8. Kreider, "Christ, Culture, and Truth-Telling," 210.

9. Yoder, "How H. Richard Niebuhr Reasoned," 69.

10. Including the kinds of bizarre possibilities such as are described in Richtel, "Thou Shalt Not Kill, Except in a Popular Video Game at Church."

of one of his essays.[11] His work on the transmission of faith is wonderful, in my view. Walls argues that Christian history has always and always will be a battleground for two opposing tendencies, both of which originate in the gospel itself. On the one hand, we discover the homing or indigenizing principle. That is, we live as Christians and yet are members of the culture in which we find ourselves. In fact, the expression of Christian faith finds its shape from our culture to some extent. There is a positive sense in which all churches are culture churches. To use the language of the title, the gospel is a prisoner of whatever culture in which it finds itself, and not necessarily in a bad way. So, a Christian in some part of Winnipeg expresses the Christian faith the way she does at least in part because she's in that area of Winnipeg. A Christian in Istanbul, say, expresses the Christian faith the way he does in part because he's part of some cultural community in Istanbul. (Insert whatever person or place you want.) That is the indigenizing desire or impulse that is part of the gospel—it seeks to be incarnated within whatever setting it finds itself in a way that will be familiar to the people in that setting.

On the other hand, according to Walls, the gospel also has a pilgrim tendency. It is out of step, it is in tension, at an angle in important ways to the society in which it finds itself. No society or particular culture can ever absorb Christ painlessly into its system, because the gospel will recognize dimensions of cultural expressions that are in desperate need of transformation and liberation, precisely on the terms of the gospel itself. That is, the gospel is both a prisoner of culture and a liberator of culture.

It's very important to remember that both of these tendencies—the homing and pilgrim quality—are the direct result of the person and work of Jesus Christ. That is, the process whereby God redeems the world is through incarnation and translation of Jesus Christ into this world. The birth, life, teaching, death, resurrection, and ascension of Jesus are fully enculturated in a particular time and place. The gospel is indigenous, and that particularity is at the same time universalizable; the gospel is pilgrim, mobile, and able to find a home in whatever culture it finds itself. That particular gospel is infinitely translatable across time and space. And so these two tendencies—the homing and the pilgrim, prisoner and liberator—must *not* be balanced, but must be kept in tension at all times. There's a real sense in which you can never have too much of either or both of them.

The well-known account in Acts 15, describing what is often referred to as the Jerusalem Council, displays a clash of cultures in which the central question is: Does a Gentile have to become a Jew in order to be a follower

---

11. Walls, "The Gospel as Prisoner and Liberator of Culture." I draw extensively on this essay for shaping my own argument for much of the remainder of this sermon.

of Christ? The short answer is no, but as you might expect, this isn't easy, straightforward, or uncomplicated. The account of Acts 15 brings to view the possibility of being Christian in two distinct but related ways, namely within a Jewish setting or as a Gentile, and a person not having to become one or the other in order to follow Christ; what was called for in *both* cases was conversion to Christ. What we're watching here in Acts 15 is not mere proselytizing of the sort that Jews had always done in inviting others to become part of the Jewish faith. Rather, here we see the call to something else, to Christ, where both Jew and Gentile, while remaining Jew and Gentile respectively, are called to change their ways of thinking and doing things toward Christ, opening themselves up to his influence. In the first century church, we see Jews who follow Christ, and in so doing they confront what it is about their culturally embedded lives as Jews that needs to be changed in order to remain faithful to Christ. We also witness Gentiles who follow Christ, and in doing so confronting what it is about their culturally embedded lives as Gentiles that needs to be changed in order to remain faithful to Christ. We see the gospel simultaneously imprisoned by Jewish culture and liberating that culture in the direction of faithfulness to Jesus; we also see the gospel imprisoned by Gentile culture and liberating *that* culture in the direction of faithfulness to Jesus. This is an important turning point for the emerging early church, not in establishing that there are two ways to express the Christian faith, but establishing that it is the nature of the gospel to move across boundaries into new cultural expressions in order to be incarnated there, and that it is the nature of the gospel to keep doing that time and time again.

St. Paul's writing in Ephesians 2:13–22 functions as the theological expression of the truths that I've been trying to express here. St. Paul shows here in this moving passage how the fullness of Christ's humanity can take diverse cultural forms, in this case as Jewish and Gentile. Both of those groups can come together socially to experience Christ, with any kind of dividing wall effectively torn down by the work of Christ. Both groups are being reconciled to God, being brought near to God and to each other by Jesus Christ. Here then is a Christian vision of Christ and Culture, if you will, in which diverse groups embody the gospel in culturally specific ways and yet are brought near to each other because of the fact that each and both of them are experiencing the work and person of Christ, causing each specific cultural expression in turn to express its faith in terms of that culture while also having that cultural expression transformed by the gospel.

The implication of all of this is that the church needs to move by discrimination, being ready to reject some things, accept others within limits, offer motivation and coherence to some dimensions of the world, strip others of claims to autonomous truth and value, and in some cases, create new aspects of culture that are missing, as argued by Yoder.[12] He ends this argument with a call not to withdrawal, but to *authentic transformation*—transformation that is both procedural (how?) and substantial (what?). At every point, then, there is a call for the follower of Jesus to assume a stance of discernment. There is no simple, definitive, appropriate response to the question of Christ and Culture, but a series of questions such as: Shall we go with this? Shall we oppose this? Shall we opt out? Shall we subvert matters? Shall we encourage change and transformation?[13] We cannot possible know the answers to these questions before we ask them; we must refuse to embrace some mode of relating prior to the experience of relating.

We will always struggle with making the gospel "relevant" to culture precisely because gospel, Christ, Culture, and relevance itself are all contested realities. It is not simply taking a thing and repackaging it so that some other thing will accept it or be transformed by it. Rather, we are called to a stance in the world: a posture whereby the gospel, Christ, and Culture are always under scrutiny, and the process by which we scrutinize is itself under scrutiny.

---

12. Yoder, "How H. Richard Niebuhr Reasoned," 69.
13. See Kreider, "Christ, Culture, and Truth-Telling."

34

Why I Am (Still) a Christian[1]

The title of this address, "Why I Am (Still) a Christian," is an echo of a question posed to me recently by Derek Elliot, who came in at the beginning of lunch and asked me if I had some time. I actually did not; after all, I had something really important going on—I was on my way to eat lunch. But Derek has an endearing way of getting his question in anyway, and so he fired away, "Why are you still a Christian?" Fair question (I'm glad to learn you think I'm still a Christian), and so in addition to the conversations we've already had, this is an attempt to address the question more formally. I did not say I will *answer* the question definitively, but I intend to *address* it, risking disappointment, because I will not be marshaling any scientific evidence to get at the question.

"Why are you still a Christian?" brings to mind Bertrand Russell's famous piece entitled "Why I Am Not a Christian."[2] Russell, an English philosopher, originally delivered this speech in 1927, and it quickly gained currency when published in essay form. It's a fine essay, understated but firm. He argues that to be a Christian you at least ought to believe in God, immortality, and Jesus Christ (being a Christian used to be a more full-blooded endeavor than that, he says, but in the twentieth century, it's been reduced a bit). But he does not believe, and so he takes on the task of presenting a

---

1. This presentation was given at the farewell dinner for graduating students at Mennonite Brethren Collegiate Institute, a high school in Winnipeg, where I was teaching at the time (2011). The school practices a tradition of having the students nominate the banquet speaker.

2. Russell, "Why I Am Not a Christian," http://www.users.drew.edu/~jlenz/whynot.html.

relatively cogent argument for his unbelief, which I will not rehearse here. He does assert that religion, while partially based on emotion, is almost entirely built on fear. Therefore, he is not a Christian.

This kind of public atheism has gained significant momentum recently, what with the so-called new atheism, represented by folks such as Christopher Hitchens and Richard Dawkins. Dawkins just does not like religion, and is especially keen to point out the dangers of believing in God in his book *The God Delusion*. Here's just a glimpse:

> The God of the Old Testament is arguably the most unpleasant character in all of fiction: jealous and proud of it; a petty, unjust, unforgiving control freak; a vindictive, bloodthirsty ethnic cleanser; a misogynistic, homophobic, racist, infanticidal, genocidal, filicidal, pestilential, megalomaniacal, sadomasochistic, capriciously malevolent bully.[3]

(As someone has recently written, this is an "adjectively promiscuous sentence.")

It would be easy, or better, more predictable for me to launch into an impassioned defense, an enlightened apologetic for the Christian faith, and then end dramatically with a rhetorical flourish. However, I will not do that, because I actually have a different concern: I'm much *less* worried about overt, explicit atheism than I am about Christianity. Let me hasten to explain—I am worried that the kind of Christianity that I claim to embrace and try to pass on is just an illusion. Or, put another way, I worry that the Christianity being passed on to you, that we invite you to, that we hope you might hold on to as you go from here, is in fact *not* Christianity.[4] I fear we have somehow managed to frame a version of the Christian faith in terms that often, upon close inspection and introspection, have precious little to do with authentic Christian faith.

So, while it might be the case that the faith being attacked by the atheists is a false target, wouldn't it be worse if the faith we embrace and pass on is marked by things that bring our very salvation into doubt? Or to say it differently, it seems to me that many of the conventions we have taken to be markers of the faith may not be that at all.

So now what? After all, I'm ostensibly trying to develop a case for why I'm still a Christian, but here I have just raised questions about what it is we think we're doing when we claim to be Christian. If I can't pass on the kinds of conventions we often hold up as litmus tests of the faith, then what? Let

3. Richard Dawkins, *The God Delusion*, 31.
4. Stanley Hauerwas, *Working with Words: On Learning to Speak Christian*, 116, 117.

me be perfectly clear—*I don't know*, exactly. But let me try to put forward my answer, but not by launching a series of truth claims, or propositional statements, or by listing a series of minimal doctrines that must be believed if one is to be considered a Christian. Rather, I want to declare that I am still a Christian because of Jesus, who is right in the middle of things, as Kierkegaard puts it. I know this sounds like a stock Sunday School answer, which incidentally is not the worst kind of answer, but I hope it is not just a cliché.

Bertrand Russell writes a brief conclusion to his famous essay, a section entitled "What We Must Do." He's trying to be constructive, arguing that since we cannot be people of faith, we must find another way.

> We want to stand upon our own two feet and *look fair and square at the world* [italics added]—its good facts, its beauties, and its ugliness; see the world as it is and not be afraid of it. Conquer the world by intelligence and not merely by being slavishly subdued by the terror that comes from it . . . We ought to stand up and look the world frankly in the face. We ought to make the best we can of the world, and if it is not as good as we wish, after all it will still be better than what those others have made of it in all these ages. A good world needs intelligence, kindliness, and courage; it does not need a regretful hankering after the past or a fettering of the free intelligence by the words uttered long ago by ignorant men. It needs a fearless outlook and a free intelligence. It needs hope for the future, not looking back all the time toward a past that is dead, which we trust will be far surpassed by the future that our intelligence can create.[5]

I agree with Russell that we ought to "look fair and square at the world." And one of the main reasons I am still a Christian is that, insofar as I understand it, Jesus forces us to do exactly that, to look "fair and square at the world." Jesus, who Christians believe is the final word on God,[6] became human precisely to do just that, to encounter the world at a radically human level. Whereas Russell sees the Christian faith as something that takes one out of contact with the reality of this world, I see the opposite; followers of Jesus are forced to be the most human of all people, to confront the realities of this world head on, and try to make our way. To do this, to confront the world because of Jesus, does not make life easy—it is not a way of ignoring reality, rather, it is a way of engaging it.

Here we are, thrown into this world like Arnold Schwarzenegger's character at the dramatic beginning of *Terminator 2*. We find ourselves

---

5. Russell, "Why I Am Not a Christian."
6. Peterson, *Practice Resurrection*, 242.

where we are, who we are. I find this condition, this thrown-ness, endlessly fascinating and frustrating at the same time, and perhaps like you, I still mess around with questions such as "Why am I here—right now?" "What difference does it make, if any?" "What kind of a world is this anyway?" . . . and so on, as I lie awake at night staring at the ceiling.

As I try to discuss these matters, let me begin with the belief that the world we live in is one in which a lot of bad stuff happens to a lot of people— as the famous bumper sticker has it, "Shit Happens." And if I may say so, many of those things just make very little sense. There is no equation to be had between the evil, the "natural" disasters, and some notion of good that balances those things out, that old argument that there is a divine plan in which at the end this is the best of all possible worlds. When people try to reconcile the truly nasty dimensions of life in this world within some kind of a utilitarian calculus, and then add to that a Christian veneer that blithely is able to explain *away* even the most horrific of circumstances, I just can't buy it. However, I also believe that the Christian faith does not actually require us or even lead us to frame things in those kinds of terms. Rather, as I see it, Christian faith refuses to ignore or explain away the nasty bits of this world, and it also refuses to draw some bland, facile equation on the other side of things—that is, whenever something pleasant happens, why, that must be the blessing of God. If that's what the faith called me to do, I'm not at all sure I'd be able to continue.

All this is to say that one of the reasons that I'm still a Christian is that I am *not* let off the hook when I face the evils of this world, as though being a Christian would lift me clean from the stream of history and reality. The Christian faith makes me confront those realities, not blow them off to some future time, and not defer them to the distant mists of eschatological utopia. Rather, I believe that embracing the Christian faith calls and invites me to engage this life into which we are thrown. Engage it, not ignore it, not deny it, not defer it, and not count it as less important than the so-called spiritual realm, in some kind of Gnostic, dualistic move that counts the soul as more important than the body, as though it's even possible to separate body and soul without loss. So I am still a Christian in part because of the way the faith pushes me to see what is here—it won't let me *not* do that.

I am also slowly coming to realize that at the same time as we face the nastiness of this world, we are also confronted with nearly unimaginable, and certainly indescribable, assuredly immeasurable, and indubitably inexplicable beauty. Being a Christian also forces me to confront and engage this reality. The beauty of this world is not always self-evident, not immediately obvious, and is easily misunderstood, ignored, warped, or worse. Beauty is also seen in strange, unexpected places, witnessed by people who don't embrace the Christian faith, indeed, who may overtly reject it, but there has to be a way to embrace beauty, to understand it in part, to experience it, even if only to realize just how little we know about the true nature of beauty. Here many of our ways of knowing, our epistemologies simply cannot carry the freight. Real beauty will not bow to scientific experimentation, mathematical formulae; it cannot be encapsulated thus. As Albert Einstein pointed out, "Not everything that can be measured is important, and not everything that is important can be measured."[7]

The 1999 movie *American Beauty*, among other things, serves as a meditation on the nature of beauty in this world. There's a wonderful exchange at one point between two somewhat marginalized teenagers, Ricky and Jane, who are trying to figure out the world. In the middle of a longer conversation, they have the following exchange:

> RICKY: It's like God's looking right at you, just for a second, and if you're careful . . . you can look right back.
>
> JANE: And what do you see?
>
> RICKY: Beauty.[8]

The main character, Lester Bernham, a middle-aged suburbanite with a job in advertising, is, to understate the case considerably, frustrated with the life he has created because he's realized it's not the sort of life he actually wants. Lester is killed near the end of the movie, and as the scene unfolds we hear his voice-over:

> I'd always heard your entire life flashes in front of your eyes the second before you die. First of all, that one second isn't a second at all. It stretches on forever, like an ocean of time. For me, it was lying on my back at Boy Scout Camp, watching falling stars. And yellow leaves from the maple trees that lined our street. Or my grandmother's hands, and the way her skin seemed like paper. And the first time I saw my cousin Tony's brand-new Firebird. And Janie . . . and Janie. And . . . Carolyn. I guess I could be pretty pissed off about what happened to me, but it's hard to stay mad when there's so much beauty in the world. Sometimes I feel like I'm seeing it all at once, and it's too much. My heart fills up like a balloon that's about to burst. And then I remember to relax, and stop trying to hold on to it. And then it flows through me like rain. And I can't feel anything but gratitude for every

---

7. Thanks to Dr. Denny Smith for the reference.

8. Quotations from the *American Beauty* found at http://www.dailyscript.com/scripts/AmericanBeauty_final.html.

single moment of my stupid little life. You have no idea what I'm talking about, I'm sure. But don't worry, you will someday.

I see this search for beauty, this deep-seated desire, wherever it is expressed, as powerful "evidence" for God, and its existence is one of the most compelling reasons why I am still a Christian. But I again want to hasten to add that this is not some vague, oblique, ephemeral notion that is primarily a matter of personal taste. Rather, what the Christian faith provides is a way to be fully human in a world that is both full of *tragedy* and suffused with beauty at the same time.

But what does this notion of being fully human look like? David Bentley Hart, an American Eastern Orthodox theologian, develops a moving discussion of what he calls a "total humanism" which can be found in the Christian faith; the notion that all people have a face—slaves, handicapped, weak, poor, women. "Christians were willing to grant full humanity to persons of every class and condition, of either sex."[9] It is precisely this humanism wrought by the Christian faith that is complained about throughout history—by Julian the Apostate in the fourth century, gazed upon with dismay by Nietzsche in the nineteenth, and now by the "new atheists" of the twenty-first century. However, "the scandal of the pagans . . . was the glory of the church."[10] No doubt this human vision has often itself been compromised by the church, especially when the "church became that most lamentable of things—a pillar of respectable society,"[11] but the Christian faith is an essentially subversive movement; that is, it is subversive precisely because of how human the Christian faith pushes us to be. According to Hart, the glory of God has been revealed in a crucified slave, and thus Christians can see the forsaken of this earth as the very children of heaven. This is

> a vision, that is, of humanity at its widest and deepest scope, one that finds the nobility and mystery and beauty of the human countenance—the human person—in each unique instance of the common nature. Seen thus, Christ's supposed descent from the "form of God" into the "form of a slave" is not so much a paradox as a perfect confirmation of the indwelling of the divine image in each soul. And, once the world has been seen in this way, it can never again be what it formerly was.[12]

---

9. Hart, *Atheist Delusions*, 169.
10. Ibid., 170.
11. Ibid., 171.
12. Ibid., 174.

So, why am I still a Christian? Because if I understand the good news of Jesus Christ, to be a Christian gives me a way to be *in* this world, to be fully human, to face the world fair and square, to face the evil that confronts both the just and the unjust, and to embrace the beauty that finds its way into the vision of those who have eyes to see. Further, what keeps me, at least to this point, is that there is no end to what it means to learn to be a Christian; there is no bottom, no intellectual foundation (other than Jesus himself), there is no arriving. As the great Karl Barth has said, being a Christian can never "be anything but the work of beginners . . . What Christians do becomes a self-contradiction when it takes the form of a trained and mastered routine, of a learned and practiced art. They may and can be masters and even virtuosos in many things, but never in what makes them Christians, God's children."[13]

So here we are—we've spent a year together as beginners, all of us, beginners, trying to understand, trying to come to grips with what we see in front of us, and also to recognize that which is not immediately obvious to empirical observation, to varying degrees of failure and success both on my part and yours. It's unclear just what, if anything, has changed in any or all of us as a result of this process, but one of things that seems to happen to me every year, whether I'm immediately aware of it or not, is that my own faith is challenged, shaken, strengthened, and everything in between, and sometimes, it seems, all of these at once, and for this I am deeply grateful. I cannot mention nearly enough of these moments—Chelsea Claude, who stayed after class to ask me quietly about my brother's grave condition; my conversation with Andrew Brown about the nature of the Incarnation, drawing on Athanasius, and *The Last Temptation of Christ* (both the novel and the movie); listening to Sam Friesen assess the validity (or not) of Charles Darwin's *Origin of the Species*, because he is interested in science and wants to read this stuff for himself; reading part of Dante's *Divine Comedy* with a number of you (I regret we didn't make it out of *Purgatorio*); reading Michael Olfert's wonderful paper on sin; listening to my Advanced Placement class chat on the deck at our house, where, despite our reading of Neil Postman's book *Amusing Ourselves to Death*, some of you cheerfully, without a trace of irony, checked your various communications devices right in front of me and each other. I recall a proud moment when that same class rejected as inappropriate an article I wrote for *The Nexus*, our student paper; I've watched as Erin Segstro quietly pieced together a sky-high average while involved in all manner of things, including mission work in Haiti, as she prepares for medical training in order to be able to serve the poor; I've also seen some of you resist various dimensions and expressions of the Christian

---

13. Quoted in Peterson, *Practice Resurrection*, 191.

faith with sincerity and respect, refusing to accept a Christianity that seems to you to simply be a veneer that covers the pursuit of money and conventional power; I've watched some of you see right through various illusions that we as a school still embrace and perpetuate. For these and many other reasons I am still a Christian.

So, Derek, there's my attempt to address your insightful and completely fair question. I hope that the faith I embrace and seek to pass on is actually Christian—not some pale, perverted, bastardized facsimile of the real thing. I am still a Christian, because I wait in anticipation for God to break through and have his way with me and the world—anticipation, I say, but also wonder and, truth be told, fear.

But Gerard Manley Hopkins's poem also expresses part of why I am still a Christian.

> God's Grandeur
> The world is charged with the grandeur of God.
>   It will flame out, like shining from shook foil;
>   It gathers to a greatness, like the ooze of oil
> Crushed. Why do men then now not reck his rod?
> Generations have trod, have trod, have trod;
>   And all is seared with trade; bleared, smeared with toil;
>   And wears man's smudge and shares man's smell: the soil
> Is bare now, nor can foot feel, being shod.
> And for all this, nature is never spent;
>   There lives the dearest freshness deep down things;
> And though the last lights off the black West went
>   Oh, morning, at the brown brink eastward, springs —
> Because the Holy Ghost over the bent
>   World broods with warm breast and with ah! bright wings.[14]

This fierce and eloquent poem beautifully expresses the profound truth that God's grandeur cannot be depleted, it waits perpetually for us—and that is why I am still a Christian.

---

14. Hopkins, "God's Grandeur," https://en.wikisource.org/wiki/God's_Grandeur.

Bibliography

Abernethy, Bob. "Rev. Lillian Daniel on 'Spiritual but Not Religious.'" *Religion and Ethics Weekly*, January 25, 2013. http://www.pbs.org/wnet/religionandethics/2013/01/25/january-25-2013-rev-lillian-daniel-on-spiritual-but-not-religious/14570/.
Anderson, Gary. "*Necessarium Adae Peccatum*: The Problem of Original Sin." In *Sin, Death, and the Devil*, edited by Carl Braaten and Robert Jenson, 22–44. Grand Rapids: Eerdmans, 2000.
Augustine. *Confessions*. Translated by Henry Chadwick. New York: Oxford University Press, 1991, 2008.
———. Fourth Homily of the First Epistle of John. In *Nicence and Post-Nicene Fathers*. Christian Classics Ethereal Library, edited by Philip Schaff, series 1 vol 7. http://www.ccel.org/ccel/schaff/npnf107.iv.vii.html.
Augustine through the Ages: An Encyclopedia. Edited by Allan Fitzgerald. Grand Rapids: Eerdmans, 2009.
Bader-Saye, Scott. *Following Jesus in a Culture of Fear*. Grand Rapids: Brazos, 2007.
Bailey, Sarah Pulliam. "Interview: Malcolm Gladwell on His Return to Faith While Writing 'David and Goliath.'" *Religion News Service*, October 9, 2013. http://www.religionnews.com/2013/10/09/interview-malcolm-gladwell-return-faith-writing-david-goliath/
Barnes, Julian. *Nothing to Be Frightened Of*. London: Vantage, 2009.
Barth, Karl. *The Word of God and the Word of Man*. New York: Harper and Row, 1957.
Bass, Diana Butler. *Christianity after Religion: The End of Church and the Birth of a New Spiritual Awakening*. New York: HarperOne, 2013.
Bauman, Zygmunt. *Modernity and the Holocaust*. New York: Cornell University Press, 1989.
Bebbington, David W. *Evangelicalism in Modern Britain: A History from the 1730s to the 1980s*. London: Unwin Hyman, 1989.
Bell, Daniel, Jr. *Just War as Christian Discipleship*. Grand Rapids: Brazos, 2009.
Bell, Rob. *Love Wins: A Book about Heaven, Hell, and the Fate of Every Person Who Ever Lived*. New York: HarperOne, 2011.
Bellinger, Charles. Review of *In the Ruins of the Church: Sustaining Faith in an Age of Diminished Christianity*, by R.R. Reno. *Modern Theology* 21 no 1 (2005) 180–83.
Benedict XVI. Homilies, Mass for the Inauguration of the Pontificate, April 24, 2005. https://w2.vatican.va/content/benedict-xvi/en/homilies/2005/documents/hf_ben-xvi_hom_20050424_inizio-pontificato.html.

Bergen, Jeremy. Review of *In the Ruins of the Church: Sustaining Faith in an Age of Diminished Christianity*, by R.R. Reno. *Toronto Journal of Theology* 19 no 2 (2003) 270–71.

Bernard of Clairvaux. "The Three Kisses." In *Readings in Christian Thought*, edited by Hugh Kerr, 96–99. Nashville: Abingdon, 1978.

Berry, Wendell. *Fidelity*. New York: Pantheon, 1992.

———. *Jayber Crow*. Washington: Counterpoint, 2000.

———. *A Place in Time: Twenty Stories of the Port William Membership*. Berkeley: Counterpoint, 2012.

———. *The Unsettling of America*. San Francisco: Sierra Club Books, 1977.

Bethge, Eberhard. *Dietrich Bonhoeffer: Theologian, Christian, Contemporary*. London: Fountain Books, 1977.

Bonhoeffer, Dietrich. *The Cost of Discipleship*. New York: Macmillan, 1963.

———. *Letters and Papers from Prison*. Edited by Eberhard Bethge. London: SCM, 1971.

———. *Life Together*. New York: Harper and Row, 1954.

Bossy, John. *Christianity in the West: 1400–1700*. Oxford: Oxford University Press, 1985.

Bourke, Joanna. *An Intimate History of Killing*. London: Granta, 1999.

Brimlow, Robert. *What about Hitler? Wrestling with Jesus's Call to Nonviolence in an Evil World*. Grand Rapids: Brazos, 2006.

Brown, Peter. *Augustine of Hippo: A Biography*. 2nd ed. Berkeley: University of California Press, 2000.

Brueggemann, Walter. Review of *Between Cross and Resurrection*, by Alan Lewis. *Journal for Preachers* 25 no 2 (Lent 2002) 45–47.

Bunyan, John. *The Pilgrim's Progress*. Westwood, NJ: Barbour, 1990.

Canadian Conference of Mennonite Brethren Churches. The MB Confession of Faith Detailed Edition. http://www.mennonitebrethren.ca/resource/the-mb-confession-of-faith-detailed-edition/#Sinandevil.

Carter, Craig. *Rethinking Christ and Culture: A Post-Christendom Perspective*. Grand Rapids: Brazos, 2006.

Cavadini, John. "Book Two: Augustine's Book of Shadows." In *A Reader's Companion to Augustine's Confessions*, edited by Kim Paffenroth and Peter Kennedy, 25–34. Louisville, KY: Westminster John Knox, 2003.

Cavanaugh, William. "'A Fire Strong Enough to Consume the House:' The Wars of Religion and the Rise of the State." *Modern Theology* 11 no 4 (October 1995) 397–420.

———. *Migrations of the Holy: God, State, and the Political Meaning of the Church*. Grand Rapids: Eerdmans, 2011.

———. *The Myth of Religious Violence: Secular Ideology and the Roots of Modern Conflict*. Oxford: Oxford University Press, 2009.

———. "Stan the Man." In *The Hauerwas Reader*, edited by John Berkman and Michael Cartwright, 17–36. Durham, NC: Duke University Press, 2001.

———. *Theopolitical Imagination: Christian Practices of Space and Time*. London: T + T Clark, 2003.

Chabris, Christopher. "Why Malcolm Gladwell Matters (and Why That's Unfortunate)." *Christopher Chabris: Cognition, Psychology, Science, Games, and More*, October 4, 2013. http://blog.chabris.com/2013/10/why-malcolm-gladwell-matters-and-why.html.

Chesterton, G.K. "The Paradoxes of Christianity." In *Orthodoxy*, chapter 6. New York: Dodd, Mead & Co., 1908.

Childress, Kyle. "Church as Problem and Solution." Review of *Christianity after Religion: The End of the Church and the Birth of a New Spiritual Awakening*, by Diana Butler Bass. *Christian Century*, July 5, 2012, at https://www.christiancentury.org/reviews/2012-06/church-problem-and-solution.

Cone, James. *A Black Theology of Liberation: Twentieth Anniversary Edition*. New York: Orbis Books, 1997.

———. *The Cross and the Lynching Tree*. New York: Orbis Books, 2012.

Cooper, David. "The Anxiety of Eating." *Times Literary Supplement (UK)*, June 28, 2006. http://michaelpollan.com/reviews/the-anxiety-of-eating/.

Crawford, Matthew B. *Shop Class as Soulcraft: An Inquiry into the Value of Work*. New York: Penguin, 2009.

Dann, G. Elijah. *Leaving Fundamentalism: Personal Stories*. Waterloo, ON: Wilfrid Laurier University Press, 2008.

Davis, Ellen. *Scripture, Culture, and Agriculture: An Agrarian Reading of the Bible*. Cambridge: Cambridge University Press, 2009.

DeGruchy, John. "The Development of Bonhoeffer's Theology." Introduction to *Dietrich Bonhoeffer: Witness to Jesus Christ*, edited by John DeGruchy, 1–42. Minneapolis: Fortress, 1991.

———. "The Reception of Bonhoeffer in South Africa." In *Bonhoeffer for a New Day: Theology in a Time of Transition*, edited by John DeGruchy, 353–65. Grand Rapids: Eerdmans, 1997.

Dillard, Annie. *Teaching a Stone to Talk: Expeditions and Encounters*. New York: Harper and Row, 1982.

Dineen, Patrick. "The Whole Hog." *Front Porch Republic*, July 15, 2009. http://www.frontporchrepublic.com/2009/07/the-whole-hog/.

Dintaman, Stephen. "The Spiritual Poverty of the Anabaptist Vision." *Conrad Grebel Review* 10 no 2 (Spring 1992) 205–8.

Dobson, James. *Dare to Discipline*. Wheaton: Tyndale House, 1970.

Doerksen, Paul. "The Air Is Not Quite Fresh: Emerging Church Ecclesiology." In *New Perspectives in Believers Church Ecclesiology*, edited by Abe Dueck, Helmut Harder, and Karl Koop. Winnipeg: Canadian Mennonite University Press, 2010; reprinted by permission in *Direction* 39 no 1 (Spring 2010) 3–18.

———. *Beyond Suspicion: Post-Christendom Protestant Political Theology in the Thought of John Howard Yoder and Oliver O'Donovan*. Eugene, OR: Wipf and Stock, 2010.

———. "Responding but Not Replying: David Bentley Hart and the 'New Atheism.'" *Direction* 40 no 1 (Spring 2011) 80–89.

———. "Simultaneously Satisfying and Insatiable: The Desire for God." Originally published in *Direction* 42 no 1 (Spring 2013) 82–91.

Douthat, Ross. "Is Liberal Christianity Actually the Future?" *New York Times*, July 25, 2012.

Duncan, David James. *The Brothers K*. New York: Bantam, 1992.

———. *God Laughs and Plays: Churchless Sermons in Response to the Preachments of the Fundamentalist Right*. Great Barrington, MA: Triad Institute, 2006.

———. *The River Why*. New York: Bantam, 1983.

Engber, Daniel. "Gladwell Is Goliath." *Slate Book Review*, October 7, 2013. http://www.slate.com/articles/health_and_science/books/2013/10/malcolm_gladwell_s_david_and_goliath_reviewed.html.

Feldman, Matthew. Review of *Atheist Delusions: The Christian Revolution and Its Fashionable Enemies*, by David Bentley Hart. *Implicit Religion* 13 no 3 (15 December 2010) 379–82. http://www.equinoxjournals.com/IR/article/view/10078/7344.

Fields, Leslie Leyland. "The Case for Kids." http://www.leslieleylandfields.com/2009/05/the-case-for-kids-defense-of-large.html.

Flashing, Sarah J. "An Indefensible Faith: Another Review of *Love Wins*." *First Things*, April 5, 2011. http://www.firstthings.com/blogs/firstthoughts/2011/04/an-indefensible-faith-another-review-of-love-wins.

Fulkerson, Geoffrey. "Jonathan Edwards and Reformed Spirituality." Review of *Ravished by Beauty: The Surprising Legacy of Reformed Spirituality*, by Belden C. Lane. *Sweeeney's Booknotes*, August 2011. http://jecteds.org/blog/2011/08/08/sweeneys-booknotes-jonathan-edwards-and-reformed-spirituality/.

Garner, Dwight. "Turning a Dark Place into a Beacon of Discovery." *New York Times*, April 2, 2013. http://www.nytimes.com/2013/04/03/books/my-bright-abyss-a-memoir-by-christian-wiman.html?_r=0.

Girard, René. "The Beheading of Saint John the Baptist." In *The Scapegoat*, 125–48. Baltimore: Johns Hopkins University Press, 1986.

Gladwell, Malcolm. *Blink: The Power of Thinking without Thinking*. New York: Little, Brown, 2005.

———. *David and Goliath: Underdogs, Misfits, and the Art of Battling Giants*. New York: Little, Brown and Company, 2013.

———. *Outliers: The Story of Success*. New York: Little, Brown, 2008.

———. *The Tipping Point: How Little Things Can Make a Big Difference*. New York: Little, Brown, 2002.

———. *What the Dog Saw and Other Adventures*. New York: Little, Brown, 2009.

Gray, John. "Malcolm Gladwell Is America's Best-Paid Fairy-Tale Writer." *New Republic*, November 21, 2013. https://newrepublic.com/article/115467/malcolm-gladwells-david-and-goliath-fairy-tales.

Griffiths, Paul. "The Face of Civilization: Review of *Atheist Delusions*." *First Things* 129 no 7 (Aug/Sept 2009) 54–56.

Haillie, Phillip. *Lest Innocent Blood Be Shed: The Story of the Village of Le Chambon and How Goodness Happened There*. New York: HarperCollins, 1979.

Hart, David Bentley. *Atheist Delusions: The Christian Revolution and Its Fashionable Enemies*. New Haven: Yale University Press, 2009.

———. *The Doors of the Sea: Where Was God in the Tsunami?* Grand Rapids: Eerdmans, 2005.

———. *In the Beauty of the Infinite: The Aesthetics of Christian Truth*. Grand Rapids: Eerdmans, 2003.

Hauerwas, Stanley. "Sinsick." In *Sin, Death, and the Devil*, edited by Carl Braaten and Robert Jenson, 7–21. Grand Rapids: Eerdmans, 2000.

———. *Working with Words: On Learning to Speak Christian*. Eugene, OR: Cascade Books, 2011.

Hauerwas, Stanley, and Jean Vanier. *Living Gently in a Violent World: The Prophetic Witness of Weakness*. Downers Grove, IL: IVP Books, 2008.

Hays, Richard. *The Moral Vision of the New Testament: Community, Cross, New Creation: A Contemporary Introduction to New Testament Ethics*. San Francisco: HarperOne, 1996.

Hedges, Chris. *War Is a Force That Gives Us Meaning*. New York: Random House, 2003.

Hessel-Robinson, Timothy. Review of *Ravished by Beauty: The Surprising Legacy of Reformed Spirituality*, by Belden Lane. *Spiritus: A Journal of Christian Spirituality* 12 no 1 (Spring 2012) 141–43.

Hobbes, Thomas. *Leviathan, with Selected Variants from the Latin Edition of 1668*. Edited by Edwin Curley. Indianapolis: Hackett, 1994.

Huebner, Chris. *A Precarious Peace: Yoderian Explorations on Theology, Knowledge, and Identity*. Scottdale, PA: Herald, 2006.

Huebner, Harry. "Christian Ethics as Art?" In *Church as Parable: Whatever Happened to Ethics?*, edited by Harry Huebner and David Schroeder. Winnipeg: CMBC Publications, 1993.

———. *An Introduction to Christian Ethics*. Waco, TX: Baylor University Press, 2012.

Jacobs, A.J. *The Year of Living Biblically: One Man's Humble Quest to Follow the Bible as Literally as Possible*. New York: Simon and Schuster, 2007.

Jacobs, Alan. *Original Sin: A Cultural History*. New York: Harper, 2008.

John Paul II. Homilies, Mass at the Beginning of the Pontificate, October 22, 1978. https://w2.vatican.va/content/john-paul-ii/en/homilies/1978/documents/hf_jp-ii_hom_19781022_inizio-pontificato.html.

Kaufmann, Bill. "Wendell Berry on War and Peace; or, Port William versus the Empire." In *Wendell Berry: Life and Work*, edited by Jason Peters, 17–33. Lexington: University Press of Kentucky, 2007.

Kierkegaard, Søren. *Works of Love*. Translated by Howard and Edna Kong. New York: Harper Perennial, 1962.

Kreeft, Peter. *Christianity for Modern Pagans: Pascal's Pensées Edited, Outlined, and Explained*. San Francisco: Ignatius, 1993.

Kreider, Alan. "Christ, Culture, and Truth-Telling." *Conrad Grebel Review* 15 no 3 (Fall 1997) 207–33.

Kroeker, P. Travis. "Making Strange: Harry Huebner's Church–World Distinction." In *The Church Made Strange for the Nations: Essays in Ecclesiology and Political Theology*, edited by Paul G. Doerksen and Karl Koop, 92–99. Eugene, OR: Pickwick, 2011.

———. "Sexuality and the Sacramental Imagination: It All Turns on Affection." In *Wendell Berry: Life and Work*, edited by Jason Peters, 119–36. Lexington: University Press of Kentucky, 2007.

Lane, Belden. *Ravished by Beauty: The Surprising Legacy of Reformed Spirituality*. New York: Oxford University Press, 2011.

Leax, John. "Memory and Hope in the World of Port William." In *Wendell Berry: Life and Work*, edited by Jason Peters, 66–75. Lexington: University Press of Kentucky, 2007.

Leclercq, Jean. *The Love of Learning and the Desire for God: A Study of Monastic Culture*. New York: Fordham University Press, 1982.

Lewis, Stephen. *Race against Time: Searching for Hope in AIDS-Ravaged Africa*. Toronto: House of Anansi, 2005.

Lipscomb, Benjamin. Review of *Original Sin*, by Alan Jacobs. *The Cresset* 73 no 1 (2009) 56–59. http://thecresset.org/2009/Michaelmas/Lipscomb_M09.htm.

Longhurst, John. "Spiritual but Not Religious? Path May Still Lead to Church." *Winnipeg Free Press*, October 5, 2013, D15.

Lough, Joseph. "Christianity after Religion: A Review." *Professor Lough's Blog*, January 4, 2013. http://newconsensus.org/wp/2013/01/04/christianity-after-religion-a-review/.

Lynch, Thomas. *The Undertaking: Life Studies from the Dismal Trade*. New York: W.W. Norton, 1997.

Lynch, Thomas, and Thomas Long. *The Good Funeral: Death, Grief, and the Community of Care*. Louisville, KY: Westminster John Knox, 2013.

Manji, Irshad. "How Complex the Culture of Fear." *Globe and Mail*, November 26, 2010.

Margalit, Natan. Review of *The Omnivore's Dilemma: A Natural History of Four Meals*, by Michael Pollan. *Tikkun Magazine* (August 2006). http://hazon.org/the-omnivores-dilemma-a-natural-history-of-four-meals/.

Marsden, George. *Fundamentalism and American Culture*. 2nd ed. New York: Oxford University Press, 2006.

Marty, Martin. *The Mystery of the Child*. Grand Rapids: Eerdmans, 2007.

Matheson, Peter. *The Imaginative World of the Reformation*. Minneapolis: Fortress, 2001.

Mathewes, Charles. "Book One: The Presumptuousness of Autobiography and the Paradoxes of Beginning." In *A Reader's Companion to Augustine's Confessions*, edited by Kim Paffenroth and Peter Kennedy, 7–23. Louisville, KY: Westminster John Knox, 2003.

Miles, Margaret. *The Word Made Flesh*. Oxford: Wiley-Blackwell, 2004.

Mitchell, Mark. "The Tacit Dimension of Shop Class." *Front Porch Republic*, July 16, 2009. http://www.frontporchrepublic.com/2009/07/the-tacit-dimension-of-shop-class/.

Mitford, Jessica. *The American Way of Death Revisited*. New York: Knopf, 1998.

Murdoch, Iris. *The Sovereignty of Good*. Cornwall: Routledge, 1970.

Nelson, F. Burton. "The Life of Dietrich Bonhoeffer." In *The Cambridge Companion to Dietrich Bonhoeffer*, edited by John DeGruchy, 22–49. Cambridge: Cambridge University Press, 1999.

Niebuhr, H. Richard. *Christ and Culture*. New York: Harper Torchbooks, 1951.

———. *The Responsible Self: An Essay in Christian Moral Philosophy*. New York: Harper and Row, 1978.

Nocera, Joe. "Killing Giants." *New York Times*, October 11, 2013.

Norris, Kathleen. *Acedia and Me: A Marriage, Monks, and a Writer's Life*. New York: Riverhead, 2008.

———. *Amazing Grace: A Vocabulary of Faith*. New York: Riverhead, 1996.

———. *The Cloister Walk*. New York: Riverhead, 1996.

———. *Dakota: A Spiritual Geography*. Boston/New York City: Houghton Mifflin, 1993.

———. "Faith Healing." Review of *My Bright Abyss*, by Christian Wiman. *New York Times*, May 24, 2013. http://www.nytimes.com/2013/05/26/books/review/my-bright-abyss-by-christian-wiman.html?_r=0.

———. *The Virgin of Bennington*. New York: Riverhead, 2001.

O'Donovan, Oliver. *The Just War Revisited*. Cambridge: Cambridge University Press, 2003.

———. *Peace and Certainty: A Theological Essay on Deterrence*. Grand Rapids: Eerdmans, 1989.
Oppenheimer, Paul. *Infinite Desire: A Guide to Modern Guilt*. Lanham, MD: Madison, 2001.
Peters, Jason. "Education, Heresy, and the 'Deadly Disease of the World.'" In *Wendell Berry: Life and Work*, edited by Jason Peters, 256–81. Lexington: University Press of Kentucky, 2007.
Peterson, Anna. Review of *Scripture, Culture, and Agriculture: An Agrarian Reading of the Bible*, by Ellen Davis. *Journal for the Study of Religion, Nature and Culture* 13 no 3 (2009) 428–30. https://www.equinoxpub.com/journals/index.php/JSRNC/article/view/6457.
Peterson, Eugene H. *Practice Resurrection: A Conversation on Growing up in Christ*. Grand Rapids: Eerdmans, 2010.
Polanyi, Michael. *Personal Knowledge*. Cornwall: Routledge, 1958.
Pollan, Michael. *The Omnivore's Dilemma: A Natural History of Four Meals*. New York: Penguin Books, 2007.
Poole, Steven. "The Pseudo-Profundity of Malcolm Gladwell." *New Statesman*, October 10, 2013. http://www.newstatesman.com/2013/10/malcolm-gladwell-backlash-pseudo-profundity.
Postman, Neil. *Amusing Ourselves to Death: Public Discourse in the Age of Show Business*. (New York: Penguin Books, 1985.
Rambo, Shelly. *Spirit and Trauma: A Theology of Remaining*. Louisville, KY: Westminster John Knox, 2010.
Rasmussen, Larry. *Dietrich Bonhoeffer: Reality and Resistance*. Nashville: Abingdon, 1972.
Ray, Stephen G., Jr. Review of *The Cross and the Lynching Tree*, by James Cone. *Christian Century* 129 no 3 (Feb 8, 2012) 40.
Reno, Russell R. *In the Ruins of the Church: Sustaining Faith in an Age of Diminished Christianity*. Grand Rapids: Brazos, 2002.
Reno, R.R. [Russell R.]. "Out of the Ruins." *First Things* 150 (February 2005) 11–16.
Richtel, Matt. "Thou Shalt Not Kill, Except in a Popular Video Game at Church." *New York Times*, October 7, 2007.
Rist, John M. *Augustine: Ancient Thought Baptized*. Cambridge: Cambridge University Press, 1996.
Rist, John. *Augustine*. Cambridge: Cambridge University Press, 1994.
Robinson, Marilynne. *Absence of Mind*. New Haven: Yale University Press, 2010.
———. "Bad News for Britain" *Harper's Magazine* (February 1985) 65–72.
———. *The Death of Adam: Essays on Modern Thought*. New York: Picador, 1998.
———. *Gilead*. New York: Farrar, Straus, and Giroux, 2004.
———. *Home*. New York: Picador, 2008.
———. *Housekeeping*. New York: Farrar, Straus, and Giroux, 1980.
———. Interview by Sarah Fay. The Art of Fiction No. 198. *Paris Review* 186 (Fall 2008). http://www.theparisreview.org/interviews/5863/the-art-of-fiction-no-198-marilynne-robinson.
———. *Lila*. Toronto: HarperCollins, 2014.
———. *Mother Country*. New York: Ballantine Books, 1989.
———. *When I Was a Child I Read Books*. New York: Farrar, Straus, and Giroux, 2012.

Roden, Chase. "How Then Shall We Speak?" Review of *Working with Words*, by Stanley Hauerwas. *Englewood Review of Books* 4 no 12 (June 2011). http://englewoodreview.org/featured-working-with-words-stanley-hauerwas-vol-4-12/.

Ruge-Jones, Phil. Review of *Following Jesus in a Culture of Fear*, by Scott Bader-Saye. *Dialog: A Journal of Theology* 49 no 1 (Spring 2010) 82–84.

Runia, Klaas. *The Sermon under Attack*. Exeter, UK: Paternoster, 1983.

Rutledge, Fleming. *The Bible and the New York Times*. Grand Rapids: Eerdmans, 1998.

———. *Help My Unbelief*. Grand Rapids: Eerdmans, 2000.

———. "A New Liberalism of the Word." In *Loving God with Our Minds: The Pastor as Theologian*, edited by Michael Welker and Cynthia A. Jarvis, 248–64. Grand Rapids: Eerdmans, 2004.

———. *Not Ashamed of the Gospel: Sermons from Paul's Letters to the Romans*. Grand Rapids: Eerdmans, 2007.

———. *The Undoing of Death: Sermons For Holy Week and Easter*. Grand Rapids: Eerdmans, 2002.

Sanneh, Kelefa. "Out of the Office." *New Yorker*, June 22, 2009. http://www.newyorker.com/magazine/2009/06/22/out-of-the-office.

Schwöbel, Christoph. "The Preacher's Art: Preaching Theologically." Introduction to *Theology through Preaching*, by Colin Gunton, 1–20. Edinburgh: T&T Clark, 2001.

Scott, James. *Seeing Like a State: How Certain Schemes to Improve the Human Condition Have Failed*. New Haven: Yale University Press, 1998.

Shapiro, Laura. "The Holy Church of Food." *Slate*, December 31, 2007. http://www.slate.com/articles/arts/books/2007/12/the_holy_church_of_food.html.

Shklar, Judith N. "The Liberalism of Fear." In *Political Thought and Political Thinkers*, by Judith N. Shklar, 3–20. Edited by Stanley Hoffman. Chicago: Chicago University Press, 1998.

Sider, Ronald, and Oliver O'Donovan. *Peace and War: A Debate about Pacifism*. Bramcote Notts.: Grove, 1985.

Siggelkow, Ry O. "Just War Is *Not* Christian Discipleship: A Review of Daniel Bell Jr.'s Just War." *The Other Journal*, May 4, 2010. http://theotherjournal.com/article_author/ry-o-siggelkow/.

Skeel, David. "The Edge of All We Know." *Books and Culture: A Christian Review*. http://www.booksandculture.com/articles/2013/marapr/edge-of-all-i-know.html.

Smith, Kimberly. "Wendell Berry's Political Vision." In *Wendell Berry: Life and Work*, edited by Jason Peters, 49–59. Lexington: University Press of Kentucky, 2007.

Solzhenitsyn, Alexander. *The Gulag Archipelago Two*. New York: Harper and Row, 1975.

Song, Robert. "Sharing Communion: Hunger, Food, and GM Foods." In *The Blackwell Companion to Christian Ethics*, edited by Samuel Wells and Stanley Hauerwas, 388–400. Oxford: Wiley-Blackwell, 2006.

Stackhouse, John. *Making the Best of It: Following Christ in the Real World*. New York: Oxford University Press, 2008.

Steiner, George. *Real Presences*. Chicago: University of Chicago Press, 1989.

Stimpson, Catharine. "Review of Christian Wiman's 'My Bright Abyss: Meditation of a Modern Believer.'" *Huffington Post*, May 24, 2014. http://www.huffingtonpost.com/catharine-stimpson/review-of-christian-wiman-my-bright-abyss_b_5024256.html.

Stott, John. *Between Two Worlds: The Art of Preaching in the Twentieth Century*. Grand Rapids: Eerdmans, 1982.
Swinton, John. *Dementia: Living in the Memories of God*. Grand Rapids: Eerdmans, 2012.
Tanner, Kathryn. "Trinity." In *The Blackwell Companion to Political Theology*, edited by Peter Scott and William Cavanaugh, 319–32. Oxford: Blackwell Publishing, 2007.
Walls, Andrew. "The Gospel as Prisoner and Liberator of Culture." In *The Missionary Movement in Christian History: Studies in the Transmission of Faith*, 3–15. Maryknoll, NY: Orbis Books, 1996.
Ward, Graham. *Christ and Culture*. London: Wiley-Blackwell, 2005.
Weedman, Micah. "Practices That Resist the Colonization of the Christian Imagination." Review of *Migrations of the Holy*, by William Cavanaugh. *Englewood Review of Books* 4 no 9 (April 2011). http://erb.kingdomnow.org/featured-migrations-of-the-holy-william-cavanaugh-vol-4–9/.
Weil, Simone. "Reflection on the Right Use of School Studies with a View to the Love of God." In *Waiting for God*, 105–16. New York: Harper, 1973.
White, Mel. "Jesus Was Lynched." Review of *The Cross and the Lynching Tree*, by James Cone. http://melwhite.org/2012/12/jesus-was-lynched/.
Williams, John. "Jolts from Life: Christian Wiman Talks about 'My Bright Abyss." *New York Times*, April 10, 2013. http://artsbeat.blogs.nytimes.com/2013/04/10/jolts-from-life-christian-wiman-talks-about-my-bright-abyss/?_r=0.
Williams, Rowan. *Faith in the Public Square*. London: Bloomsbury, 2012.
———. Review of *When I Was a Child I Read Books*, by Marilynne Robinson. *Dr Rowan Williams 104th Archbishop of Canterbury*, August 10, 2012. http://rowanwilliams.archbishopofcanterbury.org/articles.php/2590/archbishops-review-of-when-i-was-a-child-i-read-books.
———. *The Truce of God*. Grand Rapids: Eerdmans, 2005.
Williams, Stuart Murray. "Interactive Preaching." http://www.anabaptistnetwork.com/book/export/html/322.
Willimon, William. "The Body in Question." *Christian Century* 130 no 22 (October 23, 2013), 36–37.
———. Foreword to *The Bible and the New York Times*, by Fleming Rutledge, xii–xv. Grand Rapids: Eerdmans, 1998.
———. "Making Ministry Difficult: The Goal of Seminary." *Christian Century* 130 no 3 (February 4, 2013) 11–12.
Wilson, Stan. "Of Mules and Mission." Review of *Scripture, Culture, and Agriculture: An Agrarian Reading of the Bible*, by Ellen F. Davis. *Slow Church*, November 13, 2011. http://www.patheos.com/blogs/slowchurch/2011/11/13/sunday-afternoon-book-review-scripture-culture-agriculture-by-ellen-davis/.
Wiman, Christian. "Love Bade Me Welcome." In *Ambition and Survival: Becoming a Poet*, 239–46. Port Townsend, WA: Copper Canyon, 2007.
———. *My Bright Abyss: Meditation of a Modern Believer*. New York: Farrar, Straus, and Giroux, 2013.
Wirzba, Norm. *Living the Sabbath: Discovering the Rhythms of Rest and Delight*. Grand Rapids: Brazos, 2006.
Witherington, Ben. "Do Not Ask for Whom the Bell Tolls . . . A Chapter by Chapter Review of 'Love Wins.'" *The Bible and Culture*, March 23, 2011. http://www.

patheos.com/blogs/bibleandculture/2011/03/23/do-not-ask-for-whom-the-bell-tolls-a-chapter-by-chapter-review-of-love-wins-2/.

Woelfel, James. *Bonhoeffer's Theology: Classical and Revolutionary*. Nashville: Abingdon, 1970.

Wüstenberg, Ralf. "Religionless Christianity: Dietrich Bonhoeffer's Tegel Theology." In *Bonhoeffer for a New Day: Theology in a Time of Transition*, edited by John DeGruchy, 55–71. Grand Rapids: Eerdmans, 1997.

Yancey, Philip. *What's So Amazing about Grace?* Grand Rapids: Zondervan, 1997.

Yoder, John Howard. "Biblical Roots of Liberation Theology." *Grail* 1 no 3 (Sept 1985) 55–74.

———. "Bluff or Revenge: The Watershed in Democratic Awareness." In *Ethics in the Nuclear Age*, edited by Todd Whitmore, 79–94. Dallas: SMU, 1989.

———. "The Challenge of Peace: A Historic Peace Church Perspective." In *Peace in a Nuclear Age: The Bishops' Pastoral Letter in Perspective*, edited by Charles J. Reid Jr., 273–90. Washington, DC: Catholic University of America Press, 1986.

———. "The Credibility of Ecclesiastical Teaching on the Morality of War." In *Celebrating Peace*, edited by Leroy S. Rouner, 33–51. Notre Dame: University of Notre Dame Press, 1990.

———. "The Hermeneutics of Peoplehood: A Protestant Perspective." In *The Priestly Kingdom: Social Ethics as Gospel*, 15–45. Notre Dame: University of Notre Dame Press, 1984.

———. "How H. Richard Niebuhr Reasoned: A Critique of *Christ and Culture*." In *Authentic Transformation: A New Vision of Christ and Culture*, edited by Glen Stassen, Diane Yeager, and John Howard Yoder, 31–89. Nashville: Abingdon, 1996.

———. "How Many Ways Are There to Think Morally about War?" *Journal of Law and Religion* 11 no 1 (1994) 83–107.

———. "Just War and 'Non-violence': Disjunction or Dialogue?" *Proceedings: International Association for Scientific Exchange on Violence and Human Co-Existence*. Montreal: Editions Montmorency, 1995.

———. "The 'Just War' Tradition: Is It Credible?" *Christian Century* 108 no 9 (March 13, 1991) 295–98.

———. "Military Realities and Teaching the Laws of War." In *Theology, Politics, and Peace*, edited by Theodore Runyon, 176–80. Maryknoll, NY: Orbis, 1989.

———. *The Politics of Jesus*. 2nd ed. Grand Rapids: Eerdmans, 1994.

———. Preface to *Theology: Christology and Theological Method*. Grand Rapids: Brazos, 2002.

———. "The Reception of the Just War Tradition by the Magisterial Reformation." *History of European Ideas* 9 (1988) 1–23.

———. "Surrender: A Moral Imperative?" *Review of Politics* 48 no 4 (Fall 1986) 576–95.

———. *When War Is Unjust*. Eugene, OR: Wipf and Stock, 2001.

www.ingramcontent.com/pod-product-compliance
Lightning Source LLC
Chambersburg PA
CBHW050345230426
43663CB00010B/1991